Growing Awareness— How green consciousness can change perceptions and places

Brian Evans & Sue Evans (Editors)

RIAS | The Royal Incorporation of Architects in Scotland

First published 2016 by the
Royal Incorporation of Architects Scotland
15 Rutland Square, Edinburgh EH1 2BE

ISBN-13 978-1-873190-72-2
Editors: Brian Evans and Sue Evans
Jacket and Book Design by Tangent Graphic Ltd

Typeset in Noe Display (designed by foundry Schick Toikka)
and Akzidenz Grotesk (designed by foundry H. Berthold AG)

Printed and bound in Great Britain by The Printing House Ltd

This publication was made possible with the support of:

"I hope that in the twenty first century, the largest accomplishment of art will be to restore the earth."

US presidential citation to Ian McHarg, author of 'Design with Nature' when receiving the National Medal of Art in recognition of his landscape work in 1990.

'Design with Nature' can be interpreted as describing a planning method, deferring to places and peoples or invoking the 'grand design'. It can emphasize the unification of ideas or it can be read as an imperative.

Ian McHarg

Cover image:

Detail (rotated) from: *Melting ice* (triptych) #2, *Loch Moraig, Forest of Atholl, and Lochan Mathair-Eite, Rannoch Moor, Scotland*, 1990, from the continuing series *Change of State*.
Patricia & Angus Macdonald of the Aerographica Partnership
(Cibachrome print in the collection of the National Galleries of Scotland).

Growing Awareness— How green consciousness can change perceptions and places

This is a book about the landscape and physical environment of our cities and regions today and tomorrow. It documents five years of research undertaken by the Central Scotland Green Network Trust through the annual CSGN Forum.

Against a background of climate change, migration, health awareness and ever increasing urban intensification, it is timely to reflect on the role and the benefits of landscapes and ecosystems in our city regions.

The book contains fifteen essays by leading thinkers and practitioners assembled into three sections 'Learning from Thought', 'Learning from Place' and 'Learning from Action' that in some way reflect the manner in which those who work with and intervene in the landscape go about their work.

A short introduction 'Understanding and reasoning the landscape' opens the book and explains the context, and a final section – 'Reflections' – contains two essays: 'Greening Central Scotland – Genesis, vision and delivery'; and 'Towards a new paradigm in landscape and environment' that draws the content together.

Contents

1

Understanding and reasoning the landscape

Professor Brian Mark Evans

This book documents an investigation into the contemporary landscape in city, town and country in the second decade of the twenty-first century: what it means to us, how we use it, why it is important, what action we should take and why. It is a collated series of writings from fifteen leading national and international thinkers and practitioners who each have spent decades concerned with understanding, representing and transforming the contemporary landscape and environment.

Over the last five years, an annual conference has been held in Scotland to investigate 'greening' in its widest sense: to explore what it means, how it is being done, who is doing it and how it can be delivered. The conference is organised by the Central Scotland Green Network Trust (CSGNT) in the form of an annual forum to promote discourse on 'green infrastructure' among institutions, local authorities, agencies and practitioners – in effect, a think tank. The forum seeks to deliver on two objectives: to provide for an exchange of views and practice among those involved in 'greening' in Scotland; and to provide the opportunity of learning from elsewhere from the people and places that have faced similar issues and challenges to those experienced in central Scotland. From the outset, the CSGNT invited leading thinkers and practitioners to address the forum and to bring their experience and success to Scotland.

In the course of five cycles of the forum over the period 2011–2015, it was clear that there was useful learning which could be captured and so, working in collaboration with The Glasgow School of Art, the CSGNT asked fifteen of the speakers to update and document their contributions in order to capture the lessons that were emerging. This book represents a reflective review of these insights together with a commentary on what had been recorded and learned.

A preliminary review of the contributions revealed that some of the participants were concerned primarily with writing about and advocating change; others were concerned with transforming and working with places; and others were concerned with delivering transformational projects. This insight enabled a preliminary classification of the essays into 'learning from thought', 'learning from place' and 'learning from action' – bringing into three groups those who make a contribution to 'thought-leadership' in green infrastructure, those who are working at an extensive scale to bring about transformational change across cities and regions and those who have delivered projects of an inspirational nature that have captured the imagination of professionals and citizens alike.

The division into three sections is, to some extent, a convenience. Self-evidently, all those involved in the transformation of places and the delivery of award-winning projects think about what they are doing and why they are doing it. Equally, the vast majority of those who think about things in order to make sense of the subject do so in order to put convincing arguments before politicians, decision-makers, stakeholders and communities in order to bring about beneficial change.

Whilst all the authors clearly think about what they are doing, they may reason differently. Some seek facts, or at least evidence, and deduce a response; others infer responses from association of circumstances; and yet others make intuitive links between apparently unconnected places and objects in order to define a starting point for the investigation of design – 'thinkers', 'doers' and 'makers' – and they are all present here in this volume and spread throughout its pages.

This is no volume of academic observation from afar, for all of the essayists have been deeply embedded in the process, place or project they describe and in most cases are responsible for it. The texts are, therefore, suffused with first-hand experience. These are the reflections of those who have lived through the creation and delivery of policy initiatives, programmes and projects as well known and diverse internationally as the Emscher Landscape Park, the New York High Line, the Cheonggyecheon River Restoration and Philadelphia's transformational Green City Clean Waters programme. They are joined by ground-breaking British thinking and doing from Jonathon Porritt looking back from the future, Peter Head's innovations in ecological sequestration to the successful and committed programmes and projects in the South Pennines and Scotland's Lowland Canals.

In 'learning from thought', Jonathon Porritt thinks back from the future to identify the points at which decisions can set processes along a beneficial course of action; Sir Harry Burns records the essential relationship between a well-designed environment and both mental and physical health in a paean to 'wellness'; Jonathan Hughes sets out the basis for ecosystem thinking; Peter Head paints the wider context and explores the opportunities for enhanced open access planning through emerging uses of 'big data'; and Tom Armour takes the reader on a tour d'horizon in the practice and lexicography of greening today.

The 'learning from place' section opens with a longitudinal review by Michael Schwarze-Rodrian of the thinking and practice that has characterised the world-renowned Emscher Landscape Park from its genesis in the 1980s until the present day – a remarkable journey and, by any standards, one of the greatest contributions to landscape planning and design in the last 60 years; Howard Neukrug and Tom Leahy explain and demonstrate the fundamental importance of water in the city within the challenges and the opportunities brought about by climate change; and Robin Gray and Richard Millar show how working with the inherited landscape of the Pennines and Scotland's canals, together with a committed vision and determined delivery, can draw people into the future of their environment on the one hand and on the other deliver stunning projects that can help to transform places and communities.

In 'learning from action', the section opens with an essay by Evert Verhagen, who distils his decades of experience with transformational projects into key principles for cities and regions; and Lisa Switkin, Neil Mattinson, Gyeng Chul Kim and Dieter Grau illustrate and describe some of the mould-breaking projects that are inspiring people and transforming the way we think about the design and delivery of landscape.

Nothing of what you will read in this collection has come about by accident. Without exception, the thinking, the transformation of places and the delivery of projects have had to be considered, evolved, tested, refined, reworked and applied again and again. This volume of contributions is made by people who stand for what they believe in. Consider, for example, the vision and dogged determination required to time and again explain why, although a bit more difficult to do, retaining the structure of the High Line in New York would elevate – literally and metaphorically – the appreciation of the city and be so much more than the easier and obvious solution of knocking it down in order to create a park at ground level. In retrospect, of course, it seems inevitable that those who wanted to keep it would prevail. But at the time, and in the face of value-engineering, it took skill, commitment and a degree of faith to keep going.

All of the work that is described in the contributions to this book has in some way been intended to influence the collective consciousness about the possibilities that 'greening' can offer and thereby change people's perceptions of places.

Overall then, the book is about growing an awareness of green consciousness. As a concept, green consciousness has been around for some time. In his lecture to the British Academy in 1990, Chris Smout explored 'The Highlands and the Roots of Green Consciousness.'[1] Smout, like Patrick Geddes and John Muir before, has written about green consciousness emerging in terms of man's relationship with the land, its use and management and how this enters art, culture and poetry. In his lecture, Smout set out the attitudes to landscape and the environment – predominantly in respect of the Highlands of Scotland – as 'traditional': a resource for living (farming and forestry), a resource for sport (huntin', shootin' and fishin') and a resource for industry (mining, smelting and power); and 'post-romantic': for outdoor recreation, spiritual contemplation and a refuge for nature. Significantly, however, Smout was one of the first, on the cusp of the twenty-first century, to observe the transition in green thinking from the romantic views of nature of the eighteenth and nineteenth centuries through the scientific analysis and taxonomy of the nineteenth and twentieth centuries to the political mainstream in the late twentieth and early twenty-first centuries – a journey increasingly seen as essential if we are to address the threats of global population growth and climate change that are returned to in the final chapter of this book.

So this book contends that the green consciousness demonstrated by these thinkers, doers and makers is having an effect on and changing the perceptions of people and the places they work in and the way that we, as a society, are now beginning to think about our landscape and environment.

[1] T C Smout is the Historiographer Royal in Scotland, Professor Emeritus St Andrews University and former Deputy Chair of Scottish Natural Heritage. *See* Chris Smout, *Occasional Paper No 1 – The Highlands and the Roots of Green Consciousness, 1750–1990* (1990). This essay is the text of the Raleigh Lecture on British History, delivered at the University of Glasgow on 24 October 1990 as part of Glasgow's European City of Culture celebrations and again at the British Academy in London on 20 November 1990. http://www.snh.gov.uk/publications-data-and-research/publications

Section 1 —
Learning from thought

Detail (rotated) from: *Order & Chaos* series: *Harrowed fields / dragon currents, near Loch Ness, Scotland, 1990.*
Patricia & Angus Macdonald of the Aerographica Partnership
(Cibachrome print in the collection of the National Galleries of Scotland).

2

Greening the
paradigm

Jonathon Porritt CBE

Sustainability is quite simple: ensuring that we legitimately improve our own lives today without imperilling the lives of people tomorrow.

One of the fundamental challenges that we face today concerns the turning of big visions into practical benefits, whether these be financial, social, cultural or spiritual.

The art of visioning is very important but in the UK and in Scotland we tend to focus on the practicality of the next five-year plan. Other papers in this volume cite European examples of well-conceived and well-executed visions, with the kind of futuristic thinking that is needed to inform our everyday practical deliberations. This paper attempts to address why politicians find longer-term thinking and visioning so difficult. In this context, the Central Scotland Green Network (CSGN) has not only set a vision but also a realistic timescale to bring it about:

"By 2050 Central Scotland has been transformed into a place where the environment adds value to the economy and where people's lives are enriched by its quality." [1]

There are two separate but complementary elements to this visionary statement. The first, "transformed into a place where the environment adds value", goes straight to the heart of the economic imperative, reinforcing an expansive view of the environment, extending well beyond the 'green' – into a clear understanding of the economic context. The second, "where people's lives are enriched by its quality", touches equally emphatically on the human and personal aspects of development that, when done well, can not only look good but also touch people's lives. This combination is critically important.

After more than 40 years trying to make sense of the notion of sustainability, it's surprising that so many people still find it a difficult concept to understand. It is really quite simple: ensuring that we can, and must, seek to legitimately improve our own lives today without imperilling the lives of people tomorrow. That's it – a very big, very simple idea. An idea

Most decisions are still based on short-term thinking and solutions that deny those obligations to the future.

that many seek to complicate or obfuscate but when expressed simply, it is a concept that everyone grasps.

Following this simple tenet, the first question for any developer contemplating sustainability is to ask: "How have you 'baked in' your fundamental obligations to protect the interests of future generations?" More often than not, the answer will be tokenistic and hence pretty depressing. In spite of having the technologies at our disposal that make it possible to deliver remarkable, elegant and genuinely sustainable buildings and infrastructure, most decisions are still based on short-term thinking and solutions that deny or, at best, ignore those obligations to the future."

This worrying reality was what stimulated a two-year enquiry that resulted in the book 'The World We Made'.[2] In earlier books, the narrative invariably started by looking at the status quo and looking forward from that point on. In 1984, in 'Seeing Green', and in 2002, in 'Capitalism as if the World Matters', the books begin with the familiar green premise that our current model of economic growth on a 'business as usual' basis is badly flawed, if not dysfunctional, and the implications for the natural world are, as a consequence, dire.[3]

The narrative then moves forward, as things get worse and worse, until at some point in the not too distant future, when the damage has been done, panic sets in! The narrative then comes back to the present, with the message that sense must eventually prevail and somehow things will get sorted out. Let us hope it is just not too late! Psychologically, this is a difficult narrative for people to deal with. It is not a compelling argument for immediate action and culture change.

'The World We Made' is completely different. It is written from the perspective of 2050 through the eyes of a narrator looking back on how society managed to achieve an amazing feat: to create a genuinely sustainable and just world for 9 billion people by 2050. So how do we make that happen? Through the work of countless millions of heroes and visionaries who act in their own backyard to meet their obligations to people today, without messing things up for the people of tomorrow. That is essentially what all 'big picture' visions are about: act today for life today and life tomorrow. This was a liberating way to think and write because it helped to identify so many insights into how technology can help us create a sustainable world today.

All the amazing technological opportunities that are becoming available now — in renewable energy, transport, water technologies, waste management, manufacturing, smart materials and agriculture — represent an 'innovation pipeline', bursting with great ideas from brilliant entrepreneurs and innovators. This will create the technology platforms that will be needed to build a sustainable world for 2050. It is not the lack of technology that makes us struggle with the notion of a sustainable world, nor is it a lack of money. Sadly, the impediments to bringing this vision into being are lack of political will, leadership, imagination and creativity.

Relatively speaking, this is not such a bad position to be in! Frankly, if the technology was not available to turn this vision of a sustainable world into reality, people would be entitled to despair. Equally, they would be entitled to despair if there was absolutely no money to make it possible. Technology and funding are prerequisites therefore but political will is different; it comes and goes and is essentially based on that moment where politicians decide that a particular cause, movement, big idea or ideological construct is big enough, strong enough and powerful enough for them to follow it. However, we should never expect them to lead it!

This is an important insight. It makes every small step important and just as important as the big ones. The CSGN is a really good example of this thinking. Everything that goes through the CSGN, everything done in its name, gives politicians licence to advocate that this is what the future is all about. The work of the CSGN, the books referred to in this essay and many other initiatives all help to build the platform to make a sustainable future a reality.

So how close is the moment – what Malcolm Gladwell described as 'the tipping point' – when society realises this is the path we have to follow: the moment of critical mass, the threshold?[4] The CSGN is a good place to start answering this question, as the initiative has now reached the point where it is possible to see the massive potential benefits across the whole of central Scotland.

The CSGN's work aptly illustrates the two central tenets as quoted above: "By 2050 Central Scotland has been transformed into a place where the environment adds value to the economy and where people's lives are enriched by its quality."

Many people in the 'Green Movement' are apprehensive about attributing monetary values to aspects of the environment. They wince at the mention of the concept of 'green capital', which seems to imply that all of the astonishing wonders, diversity, productivity and beauty of the natural world – our priceless natural inheritance – can be transformed into a set of 'monetised' economic assets. That is understandable but misplaced. This

— 1
(Previous page)
Le Jardin du Luxembourg, Paris

kind of language helps greatly in decision-making
and it makes it easier for politicians and the business
community to realise that this is something with which
they should engage. For instance, in Richard Millar's
essay, he states that restoration work on the lowland
canals of Scotland has generated over £150 million
in economic impacts.[5] This is a powerful argument to
those involved in the business of building new homes or
converting old buildings.

    Whitehall now has the Natural Capital Commit-
tee.[6] In Scotland, the equivalent is the Forum for Natural
Capital.[7] For good or ill, these committees have teams
of economists that work to find the right way of putting
monetary values on natural systems in such a way that
decision-makers can make better sense of them. This is
very important but not the whole picture. It would be a
dreadful misrepresentation of the challenge if all we had
to do is more effectively monetise our environment to
help planners, decision-makers and developers figure
out what it is they are losing or creating.

    The counterpoint to monetary values is the
enrichment of people's lives. This is the second half of
the argument – non-monetisable improvements in the
quality of people's lives and collective improvements in
community and societal wellbeing. Some well-meaning
economists are keen to establish financial measures
for improving people's individual wellbeing and it is
possible. But is it useful? We should concentrate on
creating an environment that reinforces and underpins
better health and healthier living as practical examples
of what can be done for people today. In this way, the
intangible becomes both tangible and measurable.

    Just think about the work of an organisation called
The Conservation Volunteers (TCV), formerly the British
Trust for Conservation Volunteers (BTCV). From the

> **We should concentrate on creating an environment that reinforces and underpins better health and healthier living as practical examples of what can be done for people today.**

mid-1980s onwards, TCV was the first organisation to assess strategically the contribution that access to the natural world and involvement in conservation schemes can make to people's individual health. Those schemes, sometimes under the title of the 'Green Gym', have evolved over the years.[8]

The programme was monitored and, in two instances, measured for its effectiveness in delivering better health outcomes. It was shown that these green gyms delivered amazing value for money. From the point of view of NHS Health Scotland, it makes it possible to start comparing the relative impacts of GPs choosing to prescribe either medication or involvement in some kind of conservation scheme.[9] The green gym idea is all about a different model of intervention to promote and support individual health, both physical and mental. Mind, one of the most important mental health charities, has produced definitive evidence for the benefits that people suffering from mental ill-health gain from access to, and involvement in, the natural world.[10] Such evidence translates directly into a set of economic benefits, assessing the savings that can be achieved by opting for nature rather than drugs.

In 2005, the Sustainable Development Commission undertook some work for the Department of Health looking at the evidence base available to decision-makers on what favouring access to the natural world over other health interventions (and particularly over repeated drug interventions) would mean.[11] All the evidence points to very significant uplifts in both mental and physical health from enabling people to spend more time in the natural world.

Taken together, these initiatives build a compelling evidence base; and, as is well-recognised, 'evidence-based policy' is meant to underpin all good policymaking. Sadly, the real world has some way to go before we reach the position where evidence truly underpins policymaking and many health professionals in the UK today have yet to fully understand the implications of this evidence base. This will be a critical part of the challenge for the CSGN in embracing this agenda. The CSGN will need to make sure that a key audience for its work should be the amazingly devoted health professionals in the front line of service delivery in the NHS, whose pressures of work sadly leave little time to seek out or examine innovative thought and counter-intuitive research.

To make the most of the evidence, the CSGN will need to investigate and invest in what economists refer to as the 'multiplier effect': seeking out and engaging the individuals and the organisations in the health system that can multiply the work of the initiative. The issue is how to build stronger strategic partnerships capable of amplifying the impact of the CSGN over the next 10–15 years, as the first strategic step towards 2050.

The second 'multiplying constituency' is the business community. Beyond the development industry and the legal and other professional services that serve that development industry, the CSGN may have few business people involved in its work. Although wholly understandable, the CSGN also needs to appeal to, and win over, the 'commercial animal'.

It is necessary to have developers involved in the process, just as it is necessary for the CSGN to engage the business community. If the CSGN relies only on the public sector and non-governmental organisations (NGOs), then achieving the bigger vision will not be deliverable. Wealth creators are needed at the heart of today's sustainability challenges.

The heroes and the visionaries of tomorrow are in our schools today. The more they are involved today, the more likely they are to become the leaders of tomorrow.

The seriously encouraging news from the front line of organisations such as Forum for the Future is that many members of the business community are far more sympathetic to this agenda than the politicians are.[12] Business people know when to embrace a good idea and how to make it work. It matters little that they were absent from the vanguard of the sustainability movement; it matters hugely that they are coming on board today. The backing of the business community multiplies the power of the argument with public sector decision-makers and politicians.

The other significant factor to note about the business community is that they are busy running their businesses. Many are just trying to survive the aftermath of the biggest financial crisis in living memory. This does not mean they are uninterested but they do not have the time to seek out organisations like the CSGN. Instead, the CSGN will need to find ways to reach out to the business community and especially those companies, big and small, that are trying to find effective ways to deliver the concept of social responsibility.

This can in part be achieved through employee programmes, with companies making a small number of days available to employees for volunteering purposes. Companies often demonstrate social responsibility by involving themselves in local charities, making their voice heard through donations, volunteering and other support. Responsible companies like to see their name associated with initiatives that contribute to social wellbeing and social capital. The business community is therefore potentially a resource, a supporter and an advocate for the CSGN.

High-level analysis has identified an astonishing array of companies, from global multinational companies headquartered here and large companies with reach across the whole of the UK to companies specific to Scotland. Numerous small and medium-sized enterprises (SMEs) are part of the supply chains of those bigger companies and deeply embedded in their local communities. The CSGN must take its challenge into the heart of the 'for profit' part of society in Scotland today.

Beyond the health and business sectors, the third multiplier for the CSGN is young people. The heroes and the visionaries of tomorrow are in our schools today. The more that they can be involved in everything that happens today, particularly through initiatives such as the CSGN, the more likely they are to be involved in partnership-based leadership in the future. An outreach programme to schools, colleges and universities in the CSGN area is essential to engaging a huge, young resource in the mission of the CSGN.

One of the biggest challenges in writing 'The World We Made' was how best to address the failure of older generations to recognise young people's entitlements and their rights to a good life in the future.

Today, society only thrives by systematically stealing the entitlements of young people to a reasonable world when they become adults – not least by stealing from young people any prospect of a stable climate for the future. Our collective and continuing inability to address accelerating climate change by radically decarbonising our economies is the biggest challenge – and the biggest threat – to young people today.

It follows, therefore, that opportunities need to be found to work with head teachers of schools, vice chancellors of universities and principals of colleges to involve young people in practical schemes such as the CSGN.

The CSGN has achieved a great deal in a short period of time, making a sustainable future come alive not only in people's minds but in their lives. It had no difficulty demonstrating just how inspirational its vision is but unless it is now able to enlist the powerful support of health practitioners, local businesses and young people, that vision will never achieve its full potential and will never be enough to persuade the Scottish Government to help take the Network to the next level.

Our collective and continuing inability to address accelerating climate change by radically decarbonising our economies is the biggest threat to young people today.

1
Central Scotland Green Network, *The Vision* (Shotts: CSGNT, 2011).

2
Jonathon Porritt, *The World We Made: Alex McKay's Story from 2050* (London: Phaidon, 2013).

3
Jonathon Porritt, *Seeing Green: The Politics of Ecology Explained* (Oxford: Blackwell Pub., 1984) and *Capitalism as if the World Matters* (Sterling, VA: Earthscan, 2005).

4
Malcolm Gladwell, *The Tipping Point: How Little Things Can Make a Big Difference* (New York: Little, Brown & Co., 2000).

5
Richard Millar, "The Lowland Canal Network: creating places and destinations", in the "Learning from Place" section of this volume.

6
The Natural Capital Committee (NCC) advises the government on natural capital, such as forests, rivers, minerals and oceans. https://www.gov.uk/government/groups/natural-capital-committee.

7
The Scottish Forum on Natural Capital aims to protect and rebuild Scotland's natural capital. http://naturalcapitalscotland.com.

8
Green Gym outdoor sessions include practical activities, such as planting trees, sowing meadows and establishing wildlife ponds. http://www.tcv.org.uk/greengym.

9
School of Health and Social Care, Oxford Brookes University, *National Evaluation of TCV's Green Gym*, by Paul Yerrell (Oxford: Oxford Brookes University, 2008). http://www.tcv.org.uk/sites/default/files/green-gym-evaluation-full.pdf.

10
Mind, *Feel better outside, feel better inside: Ecotherapy for mental wellbeing, resilience and recovery* (London: Healeys Print Group, 2013). https://www.mind.org.uk/media/336359/Feel-better-outside-feel-better-inside-report.pdf.

11
Sustainable Development Commission, *The natural environment, health and well-being* (London: SDC, 2007) http://www.sd-commission.org.uk/data/files/publications/HF6-final.pdf.

12
Forum for the Future is an independent non-profit working globally with business, government and other organisations to solve complex sustainability challenges. https://www.forumforthefuture.org.

3

Green infrastructure— Responding to climate change and adapting cities

Tom Armour

"Cities need green in sizes S, M, L and XL otherwise the human ecosystem is incomplete." [1]

Why green infrastructure?

Our cities and urban environments are facing an uncertain future. By 2050, it is predicted that three quarters of the human population will be living in cities.[2] In addition to the pressures on land brought about by this population increase, urban areas are facing a host of critical challenges which include: the effects of climate change (flooding, extreme weather events, urban heat and drought); scarcity of resources; environmental degradation; loss of biodiversity; and pollution of air, soil and water (Figure 2). These effects present clear dangers to human health and wellbeing and they are making urban conditions uncomfortable and, in places, intolerable for people and communities. It is clear that a lack of response to these pressures or 'business as usual' will have dire consequences. The Intergovernmental Panel on Climate Change has reported that 'many global risks of climate change are concentrated in urban areas ... posing risks for people, assets, economies and ecosystems.'[3] Therefore, it is the cities and urban areas where most people will live that will face the biggest challenges.

It is now clear that the natural environment has a critical role to play in supporting healthier urban environments and it can, therefore, contribute to building effective climate change resilience for future generations. There is a large body of global research and scientific evidence that demonstrates how natural systems in the form of urban green and blue infrastructure – the system of city parks, open spaces, city trees, urban woodland and waterways – can perform essential 'ecosystem services' to provide fundamental benefits within cities. These include environmental benefits, such as providing resilience to the impacts of climate change and a wide range of social and economic benefits through creating healthier places and enhancing quality of life for urban residents. 'Green infrastructure' can be integrated into our urban environments at all scales, through new development, refurbishment or through retrofitting (i.e. installing green and blue infrastructure measures and improvements within existing areas and new developments within cities) to deliver significant benefits. This chapter considers the importance and benefits of green (and blue) infrastructure and how it can be delivered in our towns and cities.

— 1

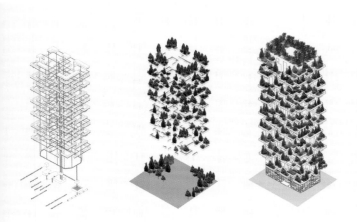

— 1
Bosco Verticale, Milan by
Stefano Boeri – buildings can also
make a valuable contribution to
green infrastructure in cities and
urban areas.
— 2
Issues affecting the city today.

— 2

The importance of ecosystem services

The process of Ecosystem Assessment in the early
2000s looked to understand nature's value to society,
as humankind depends on the benefits provided by the
natural environment in a multitude of ways. Collectively,
these benefits are known as 'ecosystem services' and
can be defined as the processes by which the environment produces resources utilised by human beings, such
as clean air, water, productive soils, food and materials.[4]
The Natural England White Paper from 2011 states
that 'the natural environment underpins our economic
prosperity, health and wellbeing' and supports the importance of 'ecosystem services' in combination with the
promotion of multifunctional land use and connectivity
provided by green infrastructure. In an urban context, the
paper advocates green infrastructure as "one of the most
effective tools available to us in managing environmental
risks such as flooding and heatwaves." [5]

Current European Union policy also acknowledges
the critical role of the natural environment with current
research and the innovation policy agenda promoting
'Nature-based solutions and re-naturing cities' via the
Horizon 2020 Expert Group:

"Nature-based solutions harness the power and
sophistication of nature to turn environmental, social and
economic challenges into innovation opportunities." [6]

The Expert Group further adds that nature-based
solutions "can address a variety of societal challenges
in sustainable ways, with the potential to contribute to
green growth, 'future-proofing' society, fostering citizen
well-being, providing business opportunities and
positioning Europe as a leader in world markets".[7]

The role of green infrastructure

The term 'Green Infrastructure' is defined by
researchers and practitioners in different ways,
although there is general agreement that it is
multifunctional and delivers environmental, social
and economic benefits. Naumann defines green
infrastructure as "natural or semi-natural networks of
green (soil covered or vegetated) and blue (water-
covered) spaces and corridors that maintain and
enhance ecosystem services." [8][9]

There is a burgeoning evidence base that
demonstrates the effectiveness of green infrastructure
at all scales in urban areas in performing essential
ecosystem services. Urban green infrastructure can
play two major roles — first, in contributing to the
quality of life of urban people by enhancing the appeal
of cities and, as a consequence, influencing economic
performance.[10] Green infrastructure provides a range
of benefits including:

— enhanced residential areas and visitor
    destinations that also boost the visitor economy;
— increased access to open space;
— conservation of landscapes and the natural
    environment and increased access to nature;
— the provision of sustainable travel connections,
    including modes of active travel such as cycling
    and walking;
— the encouragement of healthy living by providing
    space for physical activity and areas for
    relaxation; and
— the promotion of sustainable food production.

Green infrastructure can contribute to climate change
resilience as green and blue systems can perform a
range of functions — including protection from extreme
weather conditions, water storage and purification,
urban cooling, improving air and soil quality and
improving biodiversity. The UK National Ecosystem
Assessment states that beneficial effects of climate
change adaptation provided by green infrastructure
can be substantial and these findings are backed up by
other key research sources.[11]

The benefits of green infrastructure

Contemporary research demonstrating the positive
benefits of green infrastructure in urban environments
is gaining wide recognition (Tables 1, 2 and 3).
However, there remains a widespread lack of awareness on how extensive and important the benefits are,
as demonstrated by the frequent failure to plan, design
and manage them appropriately.[12]

    "If every household in England were provided
with equitable access to good green space then
savings of £2.1bn could be achieved every year in
averted health costs."[13]

    The business case for implementing green infra-
structure can be set around its multifunctional qualities
and the wide range of economic, social and environmental benefits that it can deliver. Another important
part of the case for green infrastructure is its economic
effectiveness. The EU Horizon 2020 Expert Group
reported that in many cases "a nature-based approach
is acknowledged to present more efficient and cost-
effective solutions than more traditional approaches".[14]

— Table 1
The benefits of green infrastructure for city stakeholders (Arup, 2014)

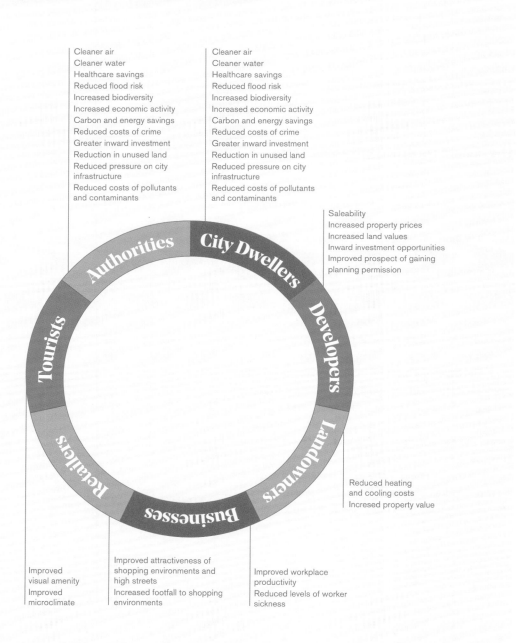

Cleaner air
Cleaner water
Healthcare savings
Reduced flood risk
Increased biodiversity
Increased economic activity
Carbon and energy savings
Reduced costs of crime
Greater inward investment
Reduction in unused land
Reduced pressure on city
infrastructure
Reduced costs of pollutants
and contaminants

Cleaner air
Cleaner water
Healthcare savings
Reduced flood risk
Increased biodiversity
Increased economic activity
Carbon and energy savings
Reduced costs of crime
Greater inward investment
Reduction in unused land
Reduced pressure on city
infrastructure
Reduced costs of pollutants
and contaminants

Saleability
Increased property prices
Increased land values
Inward investment opportunities
Improved prospect of gaining
planning permission

Reduced heating
and cooling costs
Incresed property value

Improved
visual amenity
Improved
microclimate

Improved attractiveness of
shopping environments and
high streets
Increased footfall to shopping
environments

Improved workplace
productivity
Reduced levels of worker
sickness

© Arup

— Table 2   **The benefits of green infrastructure (Arup, 2014)**

Environmental Benefits	Social Benefits	Economic Benefits
Improved Visual Amenity	Encouraging physical activity	Increased Property Prices
Enhanced Urban Microclimate	Improving Childhood Development	Increased Land Values
Improved Air Quality	Improved Mental Health	Faster Property Sales
Reduced Flood Risk	Faster Hospital Recovery Rates	Encouraging Inward Investment
Better Water Quality	Improved Workplace Productivity	Reduced Energy Costs
Improved Biodiversity	Increasing Social Cohesion	Improved Changes of Gaining Planning Permission
Reduced Ambient Noise	Reduction in Crime	Improved Tourism
Reducing Atmospheric CO2	Less Time Taken off in Workplaces	Lower Healthcare costs

© Arup

— Table 3   **Typical benefits of green infrastructure (Arup, 2014)**

Typical Environmental Benefits	
'Existing urban tree cover area can reduce storm water runoff by 4 to 8%, and modest increases in tree cover can further reduce runoff'	Gill et al. 2007
'The creation of 'green walls' in urban areas could cut pollution by up to 30%'	Herrera, 2008
'A pilot study on a hot summer's day in Manchester city centre found surface temperatures in a paved public open space reduced by 13°C under a mature canopy compared to full sunlight'	Thomas et al. 2012

Typical Social Benefits	
'Residents in high greenery environments were 3.3 times more likely to take frequent physical exercise'	Forestry Commission, 2010
'Using data from 5,000 households over 17 years researchers from the University of Exeter found that people reported lower levels of mental distress and higher degrees of life satisfaction when they were living in greener areas'	Kinver, 2013
'Greener neighbourhoods report better social cohesion and fewer crimes'	Kuo et al. 2001

Typical Economic Benefits	
'The Woodland Trust's chief executive has said increasing people's access to urban green spaces could save £2.1bn a year from the National Health Service healthcare bill'	Kinver, 2013
'The New York City's Parks Department used the iTree assessment to determine that the 600,000 street trees provide an annual benefit of $122m – more than five times the cost of maintaining them'	Nowak et al.[2] 2007
'New parks, greenways and street trees have injected an estimated $500m into the city through encouraging inward investment'	Lerner et al. 1999

© Arup

— 4

— 5

Examples of green infrastructure projects

The advantages of green infrastructure are considered below under six headings supported by a selection of case studies that demonstrate inspiring initiatives which promote green infrastructure through multifunctional design approaches.

1. Quality of Life

One of the major benefits of green infrastructure is the deep-rooted psychological benefits of human contact with nature. The first public parks were created to improve the quality of life for urban citizens. Green spaces in cities where people can go to interact socially, exercise and reduce stress levels and where children can play have been shown to significantly benefit physical and mental health. This has consequential economic benefits by reducing health service costs and can add to a city's appeal to attract businesses, workers, tourists and boost economic activity.[15]

Space in denser urban environments with growing urban populations means that land for green space is at a premium due to competition from development space and 'grey' city infrastructure. The city of Madrid took a strategic and bold approach to improving its city environment by digging 43 kilometres of tunnels into which to place the exit routes and a 6-kilometre section of the M30 ring road motorway. This new green urban space has become an integral part of the city, offering Madrileños and visitors attractive, diverse and healthy parkland filled with a wide range of sports, leisure and cultural facilities.

2. Climate Change Resilience

Green space and surfaces can provide significant protection from heavy rainfall and storm events and can provide urban cooling, better air quality and opportunities for people to take physical exercise and relax. In this example, the opportunity to build in climate change resilience was provided by a large scale infrastructure project. For years the site of the 2012 Olympic Park in London was a polluted industrial area and an impediment to urban renewal. A bold decision was made to make the park, containing theprincipal Olympic Games venues, into the centrepiece of this major project.[16] The site in the Lower Lee Valley was radically and rapidly transformed and a multifunctional design approach built in climate change resilience by integrating flood protection into the park, whilst also weaving in and linking wider biodiversity measures. Biodiversity in the park has provided important new ecologically-rich habitats, as well as connections northwards along the Lee Valley Park. Boasting high post-games visitor numbers, the park provides a significant contribution to the economy, health and wellbeing of communities in a deprived area of the city, whilst acting as the centrepiece and key driver for the economic regeneration of the area.

— 3
(Previous page) Green space in cities is increasingly important for city populations but it is under mounting pressure – Central Park, New York.
— 4
Madrid Rio Project: The Salón de Pinos is a key area designed as a linear green space and located almost entirely on top of the new motorway tunnel. Featuring over 8,000 pine trees, it has quickly become an integral part of the city offering an attractive, diverse and healthy environment for citizens and visitors.
— 5
The Queen Elizabeth Olympic Park, London.

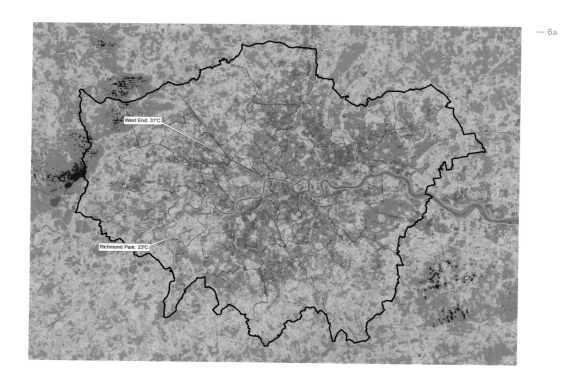

— 6a

West End: 31°C

Richmond Park: 23°C

— 6b

3. Flood Resilience

In terms of retrofitting provision for flood resilience, the Copenhagen Cloudburst Management Plan presents a superb example of positive adaption against future extreme rainfall events that utilises the green and blue spaces in the city.[17] One aspect of the plan is to utilise green areas within the city that can temporarily store flood water - parks, sports grounds and open spaces. These storm protection areas slowly release stormwater back into the city drainage system once it has recovered capacity. It is also noteworthy that green infrastructure solutions can often be cheaper than traditional solutions — as an example, the Cloudburst initiatives are costing 3.8 billion Danish krones (around £399.4 million) but this can set against the cost of single flood event in 2011 that caused damage in the city to the tune of 5-6 billion Danish krones (around £525.5–630.6 million).[18]

4. City Heat

It has been estimated that the heat wave of 2003 led to some 15,000 additional deaths across the UK and France.[19] Urban centres are hotter than their surroundings through a phenomenon known as the 'urban heat island effect'. All types of urban green spaces and water surfaces have the capacity to help cool the urban environment through evaporation. In particular, trees — especially those with large canopy spread — have a significant effect by creating effective shade and cooling.[20] In response to the heatwave of 2003, the Greater London Authority developed the All London Green Grid (ALGG).[21] This is a policy framework intended to promote the design and delivery of green infrastructure across London. It supports the policies on urban greening from the London Plan by encouraging the establishment of a multifunctional network of high-quality open spaces connecting town centres, public transport hubs and major employment and residential areas with parks and open spaces.

— 6a
Visualisation of land surface temperature across Greater London on a summer's day based on satellite data. Note that the West End with little green space is 8 degrees centigrade hotter than Richmond Park.

— 6b
Comparing this vegetation map of London with Figure 6a, it can be seen that there is a direct correlation between cooler areas and vegetation. This suggests that better planned and more comprehensive urban greening along streets, in spaces and on roofs, façades and walls within the central areas of cities would have huge potential to cool and reduce the urban heat island effect.

— 7

Berlin Biotope Area Factor – the
objective of the regulation is to
achieve the BAF target values for
different types of development using
standard tables. The developer can
choose different solutions to achieve
the required BAF target, which
allows creativity and flexibility. The
ease of use of the system has made
it popular with developers, architects
and the public.

— 8

Improving air quality – London's
largest green wall at the Rubens at
the Palace Hotel. In addition to air
quality benefits, water collected by
tanks is channelled slowly through
the wall, nourishing the plant life and
helping to reduce the risk of surface
water flooding by storing up to
10,000 litres at any time.

— 9

Victoria BID: analysis of potential for
25 hectares of green roofs ('roofs
with potential' shown in purple) –
an ambitious green infrastructure
proposal in an inner-city area largely
characterised by hard surfacing.
Natural England reports that this
area of green roofs could amount to
around £12,000 in averted carbon
dioxide emissions and £17,500
in energy savings per annum and
result in a 5-degree centigrade de-
crease in peak surface temperatures
during summer months (Jones et al.
2013 / Natural England 2013).

5. Biodiversity

Cities provide habitats for many types of flora and fauna. The viability
and health of ecological systems can be greatly enhanced through green
infrastructure by better linking and optimising the city's many surfaces –
including the use of roofs, walls and façades – to improve biodiversity. In
the example described here, the opportunity to improve city greening and
biodiversity arose because of political change.

Following the reunification of Germany and in response to the severe
shortage of green space in the east of Berlin, the city developed the
'Biotope Area Factor' (BAF), a regulation implemented through 'Landscape
Plans', that measures the proportion of green space to the entire development to create more green space within densely built-up urban locations.[22]
The BAF was formulated for inner-city districts to retain high densities of
development, whilst also developing the city's green infrastructure. Whilst
the BAF has been introduced principally as a nature conservation measure,
it also improves the quality of life for the city, including its microclimate, air
quality and resilience to climate change.

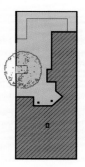

Current situation
BAF = 0.06
Sealed surface = 140m²
Semi-open surface = 59m²
Open soil = 1m²

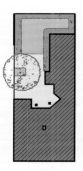

Planning variant
BAF = 0.3
Vegetation = 115m²
Mosaic paving = 25.5m²

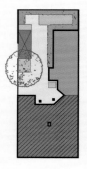

Planning variant B
BAF = 0.3
Concrete surface = 21m²
Vegetation = 79m²
Mosaic paving = 100m²
Green walls = 10m²
Green roofs = 41m²

6. Air Quality

Whilst green areas cannot compensate for all air pollution created by human activity, green infrastructure (in the form of trees and vegetation) can absorb carbon and sulphur dioxide and capture microscopic pollutants known as particulate matter (PM10s) to help deliver local improvements to air quality.

In 2010, the Victoria Business Improvement District (BID) undertook a green infrastructure audit to identify new locations for green space in an area of London largely characterised by hard surfaces. As a result, the Rubens at the Palace Hotel commissioned designs for a green wall, recognising the environmental benefits the wall could deliver to the locality.[23] Covering some 350 square metres and at over 21 metres high, this is London's largest green wall. In terms of reducing air pollution, the wall will be effective in trappingparticulate matter, high levels of which have been shown to cause respiratory illnesses. In addition, the wall will help deaden noise and keep the hotel cooler in the summer and warmer in the winter.

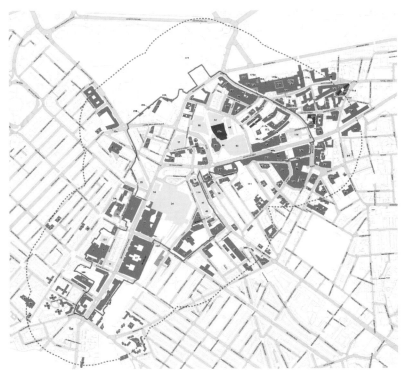

Delivery

There appears to be no consistent global approach or uptake in the provision of green infrastructure, although some cities have embraced green infrastructure as an effective way of delivering wider benefits and environmental protection.

Courageous environmental projects – like the River Park in Madrid or the Olympic Park in London – deliver at a scale that realise substantial city-wide environmental and social benefits. Other cities focus on providing multifunctional spaces that can offer flood risk management along with recreation, amenity and habitat creation. Where urban space is under pressure, projects like the High Line in New York or Promenade Plantée in Paris effectively reuse obsolete city infrastructure to create valuable new community space. In New York, 'road diet' projects are reclaiming space formerly occupied by roads and cars into new city spaces where people can meet and relax.

In some cases, success is down to enlightened individuals, city mayors or city officials. In others, it is driven by large-scale events: the unification of Germany encouraged Berlin to regulate the BAF to address climate change and loss of biodiversity; a series of heatwaves encouraged the Greater London Council to adopt the ALGG.

Though contexts may vary, approaches to implementing new green infrastructure should look to use the resources, delivery mechanisms and policy context available, recognising the potential of green infrastructure in relation to climate change and drawing on research that recognises benefits for economic growth, by creating attractive environments for investment, as well as positive effects on tourism, health, employment and food production. In the future, however, investment in green infrastructure will have to compete with, or be integrated with, other priorities.

Conclusion

Space in our cities is at an increasing premium but planning for 'green' can no longer be an afterthought; it needs to be a fundamental aspect in city planning and design. Green infrastructure can significantly contribute to the quality of life in cities whilst also providing climate change resilience and it can be delivered economically through new design, by retrofitting or refurbishing urban areas and via new technologies.[24]

There are five areas of focus for researchers, policymakers, planners and designers to help achieve this objective. The main focus is to engender a general understanding and cultural consciousness of the potential of green infrastructure, making it more mainstream and influential, whilst understanding how it can be integrated with other urban systems such as energy, transport and resource management. In conclusion:

1. There needs to be a clearer understanding communicated to investors that 'urban green' is far more than an aesthetic consideration, given its multifunctional qualities and the array of benefits it can deliver. Given the need to maintain and enhance the quality of life and build in climate change resilience, green infrastructure and the widespread services it provides should be considered to be as essential and as functional as other city 'grey' infrastructure. Therefore, it should be planned, implemented and managed as such. Green infrastructure should be positioned as a critical infrastructure alongside energy, transport, water and waste and should be planned and designed in unison.

2. Turning policy into practice will require stakeholders to also understand the multifunctional value of green infrastructure. Land in cities is under extreme pressure and green infrastructure can provide for multiple end-uses to positively optimise the use of land.

3. Design creativity is needed to deliver a green city ecosystem at all scales: from city-wide strategic infrastructure and regeneration projects through to smaller interventions that optimise the use of the city's many surfaces (including roofs, walls and facades) to create healthy places for people within the layers of a city.

4. By capitalising on advances in technology, it is possible to measure the value that the natural environment delivers through ecosystems services. Through this, we can better justify green infrastructure design and optimise the planning and design of urban space to meet future demands (Table 4).

5. An integrated approach to delivery is required that better links and connects policy to transgress 'silo-driven' cultures and achieve long-term benefits. Authorities, policymakers, developers, businesses, communities and consultants must work together to realise more effectively the mutual benefits of green infrastructure projects in order to make the best use of urban land as a resource.

— 10
The Garden Bridge, London — connecting people with nature in the heart of the city.

— Table 4
Monitoring and measuring benefits

Using current technologies it is now possible to measure, assess and monitor the benefits to quality of life in urban areas that the natural environment can deliver. The iTree survey provides valuable cost benefit information to establish a baseline from which informed decisions can be taken on the future care and development of a city's green infrastructure resource. This example shows key facts and figures from the City of Chicago iTree assessment (Nowak et al. [1] 2010)

City Of Chicago: iTree Assessment (2010)

Number of trees	33,600,000
Canopy cover	17.2%
Air pollution removal	735 tons/ annum (equates to $6.4m / annum)
Carbon storage	716,000 tons / annum (equates to $14.8m / annum)
Carbon sequestration	Removes 25,200 tons of carbon per annum (equates to $521,000 / annum)
Building energy reduction	$360,000 / annum
Structural value (cost of replacement)	$2.3bn

1

Gil Penalosa quoted in Charles Montgomery, *Happy City* (Penguin Books, 2015). ISBN 978-1-846-14320-5, 2013.

2

United Nations, *Revision of World Urbanization Prospects* (Population Division of the Department of Economic and Social Affairs, United Nations, 2009–2010).

3

C.B. Field, D.J. Barros, D.J. Dokken, K.J. Mach, M.D. Mastrandrea, T.E. Bilir, M. Chatterjee, K.L. Ebi, Y.O. Estrada, R.C. Genova, B. Girma, E.S. Kissel, A.N. Levy, S. MacCracken, P.R. Mastrandrea and L.L. White (eds.), "Intergovernmental Panel on Climate Change (2014) Summary for policy-makers" in *Climate Change 2014: Impacts, Adaptions and Vulnerability. Part A: Global and Sectoral Aspects. Contribution of Working Group II to the Fifth Assessment Report of the Intergovernmental Panel on Climate Change* (Cambridge and New York: Cambridge University Press, 2014), 1–32.

4

MEA – Millennium Ecosystem Assessment, www.maweb.org/en/index.aspx, accessed June 2014.

5

UK Government, *Natural Environment White Paper* (2011), www.gov.uk/government/news/natural-environment-white-paper-discussion-document-record-response.

6

European Commission, *Nature Based Solutions & Re-naturing Cities: Final Report of the Horizon 2020 Expert Group* (Publications Office of the European Union, 2015). ISBN 978-92-79-46051-7.

7

EU, 2015, ibid.

8

S. Naumann, M. Davis, T. Kaphengst, M. Pieterse and M. Rayment, *Design, implementation and cost elements of green infrastructure projects: Final report to the European Commission* (DG Environment: Ecologic Institute and GHK Consulting, 2011). Contract 070307/2010/577182/ETU/F.1.

9

In Scotland, definitions of green networks and green infrastructure are set out in: Scottish Government, *Green Infrastructure: Design and Placemaking* (Edinburgh: Scottish Government, 2011).

10

H. Pötz and P. Bleuzé, *Urban green-blue grids for sustainable and dynamic cities* (Delft: Coop for Life, 2012). ISBN 978-90-818804-0-4.

11

Naumann et. Al, 'UK National Ecosystem Assessment' (2011), 362–3; J. Foster, A. Lowe and S. Winkelman, *The value of green infrastructure for urban climate adaptation* (USA: The Centre for Clean Air Policy, 2011).

12

The Landscape Institute, *Green Infrastructure: An integrated approach to land use* (London: The Landscape Institute, 2013) and The Landscape Institute, *Public Health and Landscape: creating healthy places* (London: The Landscape Institute, 2013).

13

Natural England, 'Green shoots appear for London's economy and environment with support from Natural England' media release 28 February 2013, www.naturalengland.org.uk/ourwork/planningdevelopment/greeningforgrowthfeature.aspx, accessed June 2015.

14

EU, 2015, ibid.

15

M. Kinver, (2013) BBC Science and Environment News, bbc.co.uk/news/science-environment-24806994, accessed June 2015.

16

Neil Mattinson, "London: designing the Olympic green legacy", in the "Learning from Action" section of this volume.

17

Dieter Grau, "Ecological waterscapes: celebrating water in cities", in the "Learning from Action" section of this volume.

18

City of Copenhagen, *Cloudburst Management Plan 2012* (City of Copenhagen Technical and Environmental Administration, 2012).

19

Department of Health, *Heatwave Plan for England - Protecting health and reducing harm from extreme heat and heatwaves* (London: NHS/ Department of Health, 2008).

20

S.E. Gill, J.F. Handley, A.R. Ennos and S. Pauleit, "Adapting cities for climate change: the role of the green infrastructure", *Built Environment* 33 (1), (2007), 115–133.

21

Greater London Authority, *Green infrastructure and open environments: The All London Green Grid – Supplementary Planning Guidance – London Plan 2011. Implementation Framework* (London: Mayor of London/ Greater London Authority, 2011). ISBN 978-1-84781-505-7.

22

A. Kazmierczak and J. Carter, *Adaptation to climate change using green and blue infrastructure: A database of case studies - Berlin: the Biotope Area Factor* (Manchester: University of Manchester, 2010) for the Interreg IVC green and blue space adaptation for urban areas and ecotowns (GRaBS) project.

23

Victoria BID – Victoria Business Improvement Districts, *Green Infrastructure Audit – Best Practice Guide* (London: Victoria BID, Natural England, Arup, Mayor of London, Cross River Partnership, 2014). See also www.victoriabid.co.uk/news-and-press/londons-largest-living-wall-unveiled/, accessed June 2015; BID – British Business Improvement Districts, www.britishbids.info, accessed June 2015.

24

Further reading:
Arup, Cities Alive (2014) – www.arup.com/Homepage_Cities_Alive.aspx.
—
J. Delgado, H. Shaw, J. Weeks, H. Doran and T. Butterworth, *Horizon Scanning: the greening of urban areas to 2060: A report for Natural England* (Cranfield University, Institute for Environment, Health, Risks and Futures and Natural England, 2014).
—
Forestry Commission, *The case for trees in development and the urban environment* (Forest Commission, 2010).
—
Herrera Environmental Consultants Inc., *The effects of trees on stormwater runoff* (Seattle: Seattle Public Utilities, 2008). WA 98124-4018.
—
S. Jones and C. Somper, "The role of green infrastructure in climate change adaption in London", *The Geographical Journal*, 180 (2), (June 2014), 191–196, doi: 10.1111/geoj.12059.
—
T. Juniper, *What Has Nature Ever Done For Us?* (Profile Books, 2013). ISBN 978 1 84668 560 6.
—
F.E. Kuo and W.C. Sullivan, "Effects of Environments via mental fatigue/ Aggression and violence in the inner city – does vegetation reduce crime?", *Environment and Behaviour*, 33 (1 and 3), (2001), (Sage Publications Inc., USA).
—
S. Lerner and W. Poole, *The economic benefits of parks and open space: how conservation helps communities grow smart and protect the bottom line* (San Francisco: The Trust for Public Land, 1999).
—
Natural England, *Our Natural Health Service, A Manifesto for the Natural Environment* (Natural England, 2009). www.naturalengland.org.uk.
—
D.J. Nowak [1], R. Hoehn, D.E. Crane, J.C. Stevens and C.I. Fisher, *Assessing urban forest effects and values: Chicago's urban forest* (Delaware: US Department of Agriculture Forest Services, 2010).
—
D.J. Nowak [2], R. Hoehn, D.E. Crane, J.C. Stevens and J.T. Walton, *Assessing urban forest effects and values: New York's urban forest Resource Bulletin NRS-9*. Newtown Square, Pennsylvania. 24pp (US Department of Agriculture Forest Services, 2007).
—
A.M. Thomas, A. Pugh, R. MacKenzie, J.D. Whyatt and C.N. Hewitt, "Effectiveness of Green Infrastructure for Improvement of Air Quality in Urban Street Canyons", *Environmental Science and Technology*, 46 (14), (2012), 7692–7699 (Lancaster Environment Centre, Lancaster University UK/American Chemical Society).
—
UK Government, *National Planning Policy Framework* (2012), www.gov.uk/government/publications/national-planning-policy-framework--2. ISBN 9781409834137.
—
UK National Ecosystem Assessment, *UK National Ecosystem Assessment technical report* (Cambridge: UNEP-MWMCM, 2011).
—
R. Watson and S. Albon, *UK National Ecosystem Assessment - Synthesis of key findings* (Cambridge: UNEP-WCMC, 2011).

4

Wellness not illness—
Why 'place' matters for health

Professor Sir Harry Burns

The reality is that a 'complete state of physical, mental, social well-being' seldom receives much overt discussion or promotion.

Rarely do briefs for infrastructure require the creation of an environment that supports wellbeing.

As a society, we focus on illness when we should be thinking more about wellness.

This chapter challenges some concepts concerning health and how it is created. It also challenges some preconceived notions about Scotland's health. A good starting point is to define what is meant by health. The World Health Organization was founded in 1948 and its first act was to come up with this definition:

"Health is a state of complete physical, mental and social well-being and not merely the absence of disease or infirmity." [1]

The reality is that health systems spend all of their time and resources addressing the 'absence of disease or infirmity' and health care – in reality, treating sickness – represents the biggest single item in the Scottish Government's budget. Work on promoting health is mainly limited to providing advice: telling people to do things that will stop them getting sick; and, when they don't listen, telling them even more firmly until the hectoring provokes a backlash. The reality is that a 'complete state of physical, mental, social well-being' seldom receives much overt discussion or promotion.

Public money is spent on infrastructure – roads, housing and other built development – and infrastructure delivery is seen as essential, as 'must-do' in the national interest. However, rarely do the briefs for these investments in infrastructure require the creation of an environment that supports wellbeing. It is assumed that, somehow, other elements of our society are there to promote and create wellbeing. As a society, we focus on illness when we should be thinking more about wellness.

A community that cares for itself is powerful in terms of psychological wellbeing. Improvements to the environment help to improve wellbeing. Improved wellbeing helps to improve social cohesion and these all support enhanced economic performance.

Scotland's life expectancy is now the poorest among a group of western European countries. However, this has not always been the case and there is no real reason why it should be so in the foreseeable future. The Glasgow Centre for Population Health assembled over 150 years of life expectancy data for 16 western European countries extending back to 1851. For most of this time, Scottish life expectancy has been

— 1

These images help to illustrate what wellness means in terms of peoples' perception of the built environment and the impact that it has on individual feelings of space, safety and wellbeing.

a

Imagine being transferred to this place – your home for the foreseeable future, seven days a week. Does it provoke a feeling of wellbeing?

b

Somewhere to go or somewhere to drown your sorrows? That's what happens when people live in a place they don't like; they turn to other things to make them feel better.

c

Better? No one completely understands why trees and nature make people feel better but they do and it is also a sign that someone cares for the area.

d

There are people walking and they are relaxed, the area is safe and there are opportunities for social interaction. The area sends out a message of a community that cares about itself and its place.

Scotland's poor health is a reflection of the health of the poorest in our society.

Inequality in life expectancy in our society is primarily driven by the mortality of teenagers and young working-age people.

at the average of western European statistics. It is only in the last few decades that Scotland has fallen behind.

This is a recent phenomenon which has become manifest since 1950 and is related to poverty. When the detail is examined, it becomes apparent that the richest 20% of Scotland's population is doing fine and their life expectancy is increasing. By contrast, for the poorest 20%, life expectancy is not increasing at the same rate. Significantly, if the gap that existed between the richest and the poorest elements of the population of the 1950s had remained the same until today, then Scottish life expectancy would be at or above the western European average. Scotland's poor health is a reflection of the health of the poorest in our society.

The received wisdom is that poor people are dying early or not living so long because they smoke more, eat badly, take little exercise and generally live less healthy lifestyles than their more affluent fellow citizens. The implication is that inequality in mortality is due to different rates of the major killers such as cancer and heart disease. However, the major causes of inequality in mortality are rather different. If you display mortality rates in five-year age bands of a population by deprivation quintile, you can calculate the slope of the line which joins the lowest with the highest. By plotting the slope of inequality for each age group, it allows a graph to be drawn that demonstrates strikingly the age groups in the population most affected by inequality in mortality.

Inequality is not something that primarily affects the elderly. A study of inequality of the male population of Scotland shows that inequality increases dramatically from age 10 to 15, is at its peak at about age 35 and then begins to decline from about age 45. This suggests that inequality in life expectancy in our society is primarily driven by the experience of teenagers and young working-age people. However, these younger people are not dying primarily of heart disease and cancer. It seems that the major causes of mortality in these age groups are drugs, suicide, chronic liver disease and diseases of alcohol, violence and accidents. Drugs, alcohol, suicide or violence are not issues that can be resolved by simple lifestyle changes. These are

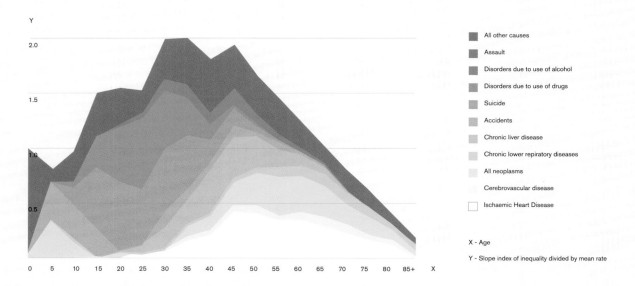

Y

2.0

1.5

1.0

0.5

0   5   10   15   20   25   30   35   40   45   50   55   60   65   70   75   80   85+   X

All other causes

Assault

Disorders due to use of alcohol

Disorders due to use of drugs

Suicide

Accidents

Chronic liver disease

Chronic lower repiratory diseases

All neoplasms

Cerebrovascular disease

Ischaemic Heart Disease

X - Age

Y - Slope index of inequality divided by mean rate

— 2

Relative inequalities in mortality by cause —
men, Scotland 2000–2002.

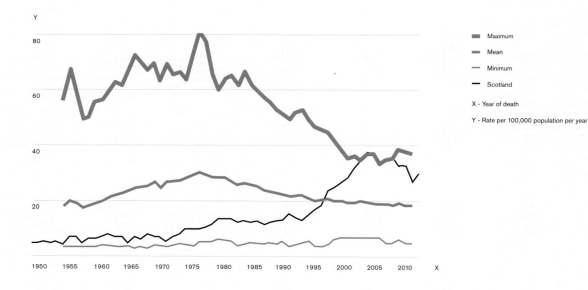

Y

80

60

40

20

1950   1955   1960   1965   1970   1975   1980   1985   1990   1995   2000   2005   2010   X

Maximum

Mean

Minimum

Scotland

X - Year of death

Y - Rate per 100,000 population per year

— 3

Mortality from chronic liver disease, including cirrhosis, age standardised rates among men 15-74 years old.
Scotland in the context of maximum, minimum and mean rates for 16 European Countries.

psychosocially determined causes of disease and if these early deaths are to be avoided, we need a better understanding of the psychological and social drivers behind these problems and why they have emerged now in our society. As Sir Michael Marmot would say, "we need to understand the causes of the causes."

Colleagues in the Glasgow Centre for Population Health have assembled data on deaths from alcohol-related liver disease for 16 western European countries since the 1950s. It is possible to compare the worst-performing countries against the best year on year from 1955 to 2010. From 1950 to 1970, mortality from alcohol-related liver disease in Scotland was just about the lowest in Europe, so the notion of Scots as happy drunks is a myth. In fact, in the early part of this period, France was consistently the country with the most significant liver cirrhosis mortality. From 1970 to 1990, deaths in Scotland increased but were still below the Western European average. It is only since 1995 that Scotland has risen above the mean and, since 2000, that it has exceeded the other countries; so what has changed since the 1970s?

It appears that the culture of alcohol consumption has changed radically in Scotland in the latter half of the 20th century. For most of that time, alcohol was predominantly drunk in pubs by men at the end of a working week and mostly in the form of beer. Since the 1990s, however, the culture has changed with young men and women drinking a range of spirits throughout the week. The change has been dramatic enough to drive alcohol-related mortality for Scottish men and women from one of the lowest in Western Europe to the highest in a twenty-year period.

This societal change in alcohol consumption has been associated with the emergence of the other issues – drugs, suicide and violence – in a society that saw a radical decline in its social and economic wellbeing in the 1950s and 1960s. The local authorities where mortality from these causes is at the highest are those in west central Scotland and Dundee City. These places were the industrial heartland of Scotland, the cities and towns of shipyards, steelworks, engineering, locomotive works and mills.

The new towns of the Clyde Valley Plan caused mass relocation of people in the 1960s and 1970s. We now know this social and economic turmoil has had biological consequences.

There were 130 jute mills in Dundee at one time; all are now gone. Clydeside was, for a century, one of the world's biggest shipbuilding regions. In the 1960s and 1970s, the shipyards of the Clyde virtually disappeared, along with all the jobs that gave purpose and meaning to the lives of men working in them. These jobs, and the skill and status they conferred, have never been adequately replaced.

During these two decades of economic change, people's living conditions were also transformed. Prior to the 1970s and 1980s, working people lived in dense urban areas such as the Gorbals. What is noticeable from early photographs of such places is the number of people in the images: children out playing, adults socialising and showing a real sense of community. There were places at the centre of these concentrated communities such as Bridgeton Cross where people could come together and socialise. At the heart of those communities were the women who would support each other in difficult times, the women who in a tenement close would help a young mother who was struggling with a baby. If there was a problem with domestic violence, people would get together to support the victims. These people helped each other. However, by the 1960s, these houses were thought to be past their useful life and needing to be replaced and Glasgow prepared a plan to raze the city to the ground and to start anew. [2]

The 'Bruce Plan' proposed the demolition of almost every building in central Glasgow – the Art Galleries, the City Chambers, even Mackintosh's masterwork, the Glasgow School of Art – to be replaced with brutal modernist buildings, inspired by the thinking of Le Corbusier. Some of this plan was implemented with the construction of high-rise buildings which have been described as 'filing cabinets for people' with lots of poorly resolved spaces between them. [3] The intent to create these brave new places was no doubt sincere but ultimately misguided and led to a comprehensive loss of wellbeing that people had enjoyed previously through gainful employment and a full community life. The 'Clyde Valley Regional Plan' called for the creation of greenfield new towns and led to further mass relocation of people in the 1960s and 1970s. [4] We now know this social and economic turmoil has had biological consequences.

Early experience as a doctor in the 1980s in Glasgow's Royal Infirmary provided the author with a caseload of patients from the east end of the city with diseases far worse than their smoking history and general lifestyle could explain. This experience provoked an abiding interest, not only in the causes of disease but in the causes of wellness, not just pathogenesis but 'salutogenesis'. Salus was the Roman goddess both of wellbeing and also, interestingly, safety. Predictably, it is the Scandinavians who have spent most time thinking

"Those who have a 'why' to live, can bear almost any 'how'."

about salutogenesis, creating wellness rather than treating illness. The Nordic School of Public Health has mapped some 25 different theories that seem to describe paths to wellbeing. These range from learned resourcefulness, optimism and hopefulness through cultural capital and quality of life to empowerment, coping and attachment.

Viktor Frankl, the Austrian psychotherapist, spent five years in Auschwitz during the war, lived and wrote 'Man's Search for Meaning' to describe how he managed to survive something so horrible. [5] In the introduction to his book, he quotes Nietzsche: "those who have a 'why' to live, can bear almost any 'how'." His conclusion was that if an individual has a sense of purpose and feels his life has meaning, he will do the things he needs to do to survive and fulfil his purpose.

Aaron Antonovsky, the American sociologist, who also looked at concentration camp survivors, found that those who did well and came through that experience psychologically, physically and socially well, had developed in early life what he termed a 'sense of coherence'. He said that a sense of coherence:

"expresses the extent to which one has a feeling of confidence that the stimuli deriving from one's internal and external environments in the course of living are structured, predictable and explicable, that one has the internal resources to meet the demands posed by these stimuli and, finally, that these demands are seen as challenges, worthy of investment and engagement." [6] Antonovsky also believed that if children do not acquire a sense of coherence in their early upbringing, they will interpret all the events that surround them as 'noise', not as information, and, as a result, will be chronically stressed. As a surgeon, this made a lot of sense. A surgeon's job is to create acute stress in people. A surgi-

cal operation activates acute stress responses — cortisol, adrenalin, inflammatory markers and so on flood into the bloodstream to begin to support the healing process. Then, as the patient heals, these responses subside and return to normal. What Antonovsky was saying was that if the individual has not learned to see the event around them as sensible, explainable and coherent, they are simply buffeted by events and the experience leaves them chronically stressed. He has been proved to be right. There are many studies linking adverse social circumstances to chronic elevation of markers of stress. A Canadian study examined cortisol levels in babies raised in orphanages. [7] The longer a child is in an orphanage, the higher are the levels of cortisol in its saliva. The data suggests that it doesn't matter how good the orphanage care is: if a child doesn't have a single significant adult to nurture or teach him, he learns that his world is not structured and predictable and, as a result, becomes chronically stressed.

In the UK, a study of 30,000 civil servants over a 30-year period showed that higher-grade civil servants throughout the day had lower stress levels than lower-grade civil servants, suggesting that the least stressed person in any government department was probably the Permanent Secretary — the boss. [8] Why? The answer is delegation. If the person at the top of a hierarchy has a task he doesn't want to do, he gets someone else to do it and that cascades down any hierarchy to the person at the bottom. The lower down a hierarchy you are, the less control you have of your workload. You just have to do what everyone else dumps on you and you are stressed. The consequences of that stress leads to alterations in a number of other biological systems that lead to increased risk of heart disease, Type 2 diabetes and cancer, as well as mental health problems.

In Eastern Europe, a further study carried out some 10 years after the fall of the Berlin Wall asked residents in post-Soviet countries how much control they had had over their life and related the results to mortality. Russian people reported having the lowest sense of control over their lives and recorded the highest mortality. Polish and Czech citizens reported high levels of control and the lowest mortality. [9]

For someone on the edge of society, how much control over their life will they feel if they have had the bedroom tax imposed; if they have been sanctioned by the Department of Work and Pensions and had benefits taken from them; or if they are worried about their children and drug pushers in their community? These individuals are not in control of their life – they are subject to the will of others, often officials – and this translates into a lack of wellbeing and ultimately an increased chance of illness.

Most tragically for children, chaotic early lives lead to significant changes in brain structure. Neglect or abuse is associated with reduced brain cell density in the prefrontal cortex, an area of the brain involved in decision-making, complex behaviour and personality expression. Prefrontal cortex activity is important in allowing us to suppress inappropriate behaviour and aggression. It allows us to take in new information and to respond appropriately to it. It helps us to make the world seem structured, predictable and explainable.

Another part of the brain, the hippocampus, is the part that deals with short- and long-term memory. In these children, this part of the brain is also under-developed and this in turn reduces their capacity at school. In contrast, the amygdala (the centre of the brain associated with emotional arousal) becomes more active and, as a consequence, individuals are more likely to be anxious, on 'a short fuse', aggressive or fear-ful. The combination of a tendency to aggression and the inability to suppress inappropriate behaviour means that children who are neglected in early life are likely to suffer serious behavioural issues that lead to problems in adulthood.

A large study in the USA looked at children with four or more adverse events in early life including parental mental illness or neglect. [10] These children were more likely to become alcoholics or drug addicts. They were more likely to be involved in violent crime; by the age of 30, about 35% had been arrested for a non-traffic offence. Building on this international research, further research was developed in Glasgow by scanning the brains of a number of Glaswegians.

The research measured hippocampal volume, white cell density and other indices using sophisticated imaging techniques and the findings confirmed what was suspected. The brain structures were affected in the same way as the US studies predicted. Psychometric test of function was carried out. A less well-developed prefrontal cortex means someone takes slightly longer to integrate new data about their surroundings. The tests showed that individuals from difficult backgrounds took 150–200 milliseconds longer to make decisions about new information compared to individuals from more affluent backgrounds. This might not seem much but if two cars are being driven side by side at 80 kilometres per hour (50 miles per hour) and a child walks out in front of them, the car driven by the driver from a difficult background may take one to two car lengths more to stop, with potentially serious consequences for the child. Poor people are or feel constantly under pressure and throughout life are more likely to make poor decisions.

Today's science gives us a clue as to how neglect regulates stress and leads to elevated cortisol level. When a baby is hugged and feels cared for, its brain cells release a chemical called serotonin. The serotonin is transported into the nucleus of cells. Chromosome No. 5 has a gene that binds to serotonin, activating the gene to produce the cortisol receptor. When the cortisol receptor is in the hippocampus and an individual gets high levels of stress hormone, this acts as a signal to the brain to shut off the cortisol response. Neglected children don't develop this key part of the cortisol suppression system. We now know the biology of this in great detail and we know the biology of having a miserable childhood that leads to increased risk of failure at school, mental health problems, offending behaviour, worklessness and other social ills. The hypothesis is that all of this can be directly linked to the disintegration of urban, working class societies that occurred in the 1960s and 1970s. It is of further concern that this epigenetic change is inheritable: the gene is passed on from parents to their children in the 'switched off' state and this effectively is the intergenerational transmission of an inability to be in control of one's life.

Today we now know that prevention is possible but it requires us to reorder our societal priorities. To create wellness we need people to feel that:

— they have an optimistic outlook on their future;
— they are in control of their own lives (they are 'the captain of their own future', not someone else);
— they have a sense of purpose and of meaning in their lives — this often comes from having a fulfilling and useful job;
— they have confidence in their ability to deal with problems;
— they have a supportive network of people around them; and
— they have a nurturing family.

These then are the basic principles for wellness but too often in the most deprived parts of any society people are labelled as helpless and incompetent. They are told where to go and what to do. They are not in control of their lives. This does not promote wellness, so our challenge has to be to find ways of giving people a sense of control over their own lives.

One way of achieving a sense of control is to be involved in decisions that shape the environment in which one lives. One of the key environmental changes needed is to create environments which promote social connectedness. The literature around connectedness shows that high levels of social integration confer an increased likelihood of survival when compared with people with low levels of social integration. [11]

Planning and designing environments that bring people together are a critical factor of what should be happening to support wellness. An early advocate of

We now know that having a miserable childhood leads to increased risk of failure at school, mental health problems, offending behaviour, worklessness and other social ills. This can be directly linked to the disintegration of urban societies.

In the most deprived parts of society people are told where to go and what to do. They are not in control of their lives. This does not promote wellness.

this approach is Jan Gehl from Copenhagen. Jan's wife, a psychologist, introduced him to Maslow's hierarchy of human need. [12] Maslow suggested that we can only achieve the very highest level of being human (morality, creativity, spontaneity and so on) if we have the basics that we need, to keep ourselves alive and feel secure. Feeling secure allows us to develop in ways that give us access to resources. With resources we can support family, develop friendships and increase our capacity for self-esteem and confidence. Thereafter, we can begin to achieve at a higher level of creativity. [13]

In New York, the 'High Line' project demonstrates an innovative and successful way to bring liveability back to the heart of our cities. [14] In its original state, the High Line was literally an elevated railway line in lower Manhattan delivering produce from ships moored along the docks directly into the 'meat-packing district'. It has now been transformed into a park that brings people together.

New York has, with cities across Europe, begun to transform its streets, separating cyclists from cars and reorganising the space much like Copenhagen. In southern Europe, Italian and Spanish villages have a tight urban form where the houses are close together and people are, therefore, close together too. This can be achieved in Scottish cities too. Society needs to do more to design spaces that allow people to come together and socialise.

These ideas are now well known and well understood and in Scotland we have many pioneering examples but we do not yet have universally accepted and

applied methods and techniques for their widespread implementation. We need to change the way we do things in order to define what to do, agree the methods for achieving change and involve people in the testing and implementation of change in order to engage the community in its widest form in shaping the action to be undertaken on their behalf.

Through the 'Early Years' collaborative and related programmes, Scotland is starting to transform childhood, encouraging every local authority and every health board to try the things that we now know will improve childhood. [15] As a result of this pioneering work, the stillbirth rate and infant mortality in Scotland have both fallen significantly; it appears we are one of very few countries in the world achieving this step change at the moment.

An example of good practice is the City of Lakewood Citizens' Planning Academy in Colorado that trains citizens to be involved in planning and taking decisions for their community. They look at the law to establish what changes are possible, consider the policy context of what they are trying to achieve, develop the brief and get involved in the design of places. Scotland could do this too. [16] If we are going to make strides in Scotland in transforming our environment then we need to begin by involving people. This will result in better planning outcomes and the people involved will have a better sense of their own self-worth and feel more in control of their lives. The outcome will be an improved sense of wellbeing in Scotland.

— 4
(Previous page) St. Andrew Square, Edinburgh.

Planning and designing environments that bring people together are a critical factor of what should be happening to support wellness.

Society needs to do more to design spaces that allow people to come together and socialise.

1

Preamble to the *Constitution of the World Health Organization* as adopted by the International Health Conference, New York, 19–22 June 1946; signed on 22 July 1946 by the representatives of 61 States (Official Records of the World Health Organization, no. 2, p. 100) and entered into force on 7 April 1948. The Definition has not been amended since 1948.

2

Glasgow Corporation's First Planning Report from 1945 was known as 'The Bruce Plan' after its author, the City Engineer with a hero's name – Robert Bruce.

3

From Jimmy Reid's address on the occasion of his inauguration as rector of Glasgow University.

4

Sir Patrick Abercromby and R. H. Matthew, *The Clyde Valley Regional Plan* (Edinburgh: His Majesty's Stationery Office, 1946).

5

Victor E Frankl, *Man's Search for Meaning: The Classic Tribute to Hope from the Holocaust* (Beacon Press, 2008).

6

Salutogenesis – an introduction by Bengt Lindström, Professor of Health Promotion, Nordic School of Public Health, Research Director, Health Promotion Research, Folkhälsan Research Center, Helsinki, Finland.

7

Lucy Le Mare and Karyn Audet, *A longitudinal study of the physical growth and health of post-institutionalized Romanian adoptees* (US National Library of Medicine National Institutes of Health, 2006).

8

Steptoe et al., *Psychosomatic Medicine*, 65 (2003), 461–470.

9

M. Bobak, H. Pikhart, R. Rose, C. Hertzman and M. Mamot, "Socio-economic factors, material inequalities and perceived control in self-rated health: Cross-sectional data from seven post-communist countries", *Social Science & Medicine*, 51 (2000), 1343–1350.

10

T. Beauchaine and S. Hinshaw, (eds.), *Child and adolescent psychopathology* (2013).

11

Over 300,000 people recruited into 148 studies show that high levels of social integration confer a 50% higher likelihood of survival at the end of those studies than people with low levels of social integration. Complex patterns suggest a 90% increase. Simple indicators such as living alone versus living with others confer a survival benefit of only 19%. J. Holt-Lunstad, T.B. Smith and J.B. Layton, "Social Relationships and Mortality Risk: A Meta-analytic Review", *PLoS Med* 7 (7) (2010): e1000316. doi:10.1371/journal.pmed.1000316.

12

Maslow's hierarchy of needs is a theory in psychology proposed by Abraham Maslow in "A Theory of Human Motivation" in *Psychological Review* (1943).

13

Life between Buildings and the subsequent books by Jan Gehl and Lars Gemzøe have been enormously influential on design thinking over the past 30 years.

14

Lisa Tziona Switkin, "The New York High Line", in the "Learning from Action" section of this volume.

15

Equally Well - The Report of the Ministerial Task Force on Health Inequalities, http://www.gov.scot/Topics/Health/Healthy-Living/Health-Inequalities/Equally-Well, accessed February 2016.

16

The Scottish Government's Community Charrette Programme is a good start. The scheme was piloted in 2011–2012 and has expanded over the years with support given to over 30 charrettes but it needs to better resourced and rolled out for use by all local authority and institutions' plan-making and development processes. http://www.gov.scot/Topics/Built-Environment/AandP/Projects/SSCI/Mainstreaming - editors, accessed February 2016.

5

The 'nature' of green networks

Jonathan Hughes

This chapter explores three questions: why we need green networks; what nature can do for us; and, in turn, what we can do for nature.

The Central Scotland Green Network (CSGN) vision is that "by 2050 Central Scotland has been transformed into a place where the environment adds value to the economy and where people's lives are enriched by its quality". Deconstructed, the vision has three main components: transformational change; creating synergies (particularly between the environment and the economy); and delivering a good quality of life for people as well as habitat for nature. The vision is, therefore, predicated on both the sustainable use of the natural environment and its enhancement, with both aspects acting in a complementary manner if the vision is to be realised. In the words of the respected social worker and environmentalist, Fred Edwards (1931–2008): "The environment is not one of the three legs of the stool of sustainability, it's the ground on which the stool stands."[1]

Why a green network?

During much of the 20th century, efforts to reverse declines in wildlife tended to focus on species protection and site designation. Whilst much has been achieved through these 'two pillars', the loss of biodiversity has continued at a worrying rate and, as a society, we have come to realise that species- and site-based approaches alone are not credible conservation strategies in the face of rapid climatic change. Instead, conservation organisations, like the Scottish Wildlife Trust, have realised that we need to take action throughout the wider countryside across the ecosystem and on a regional landscape scale. If we fail to take action at this scale, there is a danger that we will maroon nature in 'islands' as more and more land becomes subject to development through infrastructure such as roads, energy and utilities, the expansion of settlements for housing and industry or intensive agriculture that leaves little room for nature.

Frequently, development severs habitats by interrupting the corridors along which nature can move. More mobile species, like larger mammals and birds, can move relatively easily between habitat patches. However, smaller and less mobile species, like plants, invertebrates and smaller mammals, cannot do this unless dedicated corridors reconnect the habitats they rely on to survive. A good example of this principle is traditional hedgerows, which are of value in their own right but also provide an additional service by connecting small woodlands and grasslands.

'Living Landscapes: towards ecosystem-based conservation in Scotland', published by the Scottish Wildlife Trust in 2009, builds on this thinking.[2] The document argues that a new focus of attention should be made on working with ecosystems and wider landscapes. This does not mean abandoning species protection and work on designated sites but rather developing and delivering a coherent package of measures to ensure ecosystem health at multiple scales. This might mean looking after veteran trees or installing green walls or green roofs at the local scale through to better regional spatial planning or developing habitat networks at the larger scale.

Delivery of the CSGN, from local to regional scales and, over time, through the creation of a mosaic of semi-natural areas linked by smaller urban green and blue spaces, meets the imperative of improving the ecosystem across an extensive area of landscape. The challenge now is to realise the concept by influencing policy, landscape planning, developing funding mechanisms, working in partnership and ensuring delivery on the ground.

The term 'Living Landscapes' is in many ways shorthand for a new type of conservation that focuses on restoring the health and functionality of the environment throughout the ecosystem. Analysis of trends from the UK Biodiversity Action Plan, together with other data, suggests that in spite of recent efforts, biodiversity loss and attrition of ecosystem health is continuing globally, across Europe and across the UK.[3] In Scotland, there is a continuing downward trend in the extent and quality of our habitats and in the population range and size of species. Only 11 species (7% of the total) and 5 habitats (13% of the total) were thought to be increasing and a further 49 species (31%) and 8 habitats (20%) were thought to be stable.

The Scottish Wildlife Trust has identified seven systemic threats to our terrestrial environment that are causing declines in wildlife. These are:

— Fragmentation and compartmentalisation
— Unsustainable grazing
— Diffuse pollution
— Poorly located or designed development
— Invasive non-native species
— Climate change
— Unsustainable land management practices

— 1

Fragmentation and compartmentalisation:
Small, isolated fragments of semi-natural habitat that support only small populations of plants and animals are common across lowland Scotland. These populations are particularly vulnerable to changes in climate, land use and development. Here, new infrastructure like roads, communications, housing and industrial development cause further isolation of semi-natural habitats.

— 2

Unsustainable grazing:
Unsustainable grazing by sheep and wild deer has led to modified habitats which bear little resemblance to their natural state or natural functioning. Overgrazing on sensitive habitats, like peatlands, combined with more intense rainfall, can cause erosion leading to loss of peat soils and release of atmospheric carbon dioxide that contributes to climate change. Overgrazing also causes soil compaction and can significantly increase surface water flows, exacerbating flood risk.

— 3

Diffuse pollution:
In Scotland, there are some 488 rivers, 57
lochs and 18 transitional, 59 coastal and
21 groundwater bodies which are affected
by diffuse pollution largely caused by poor
agricultural practices, with some three quarters
of nitrogen input into our surface and ground
waters coming from agricultural sources.[4]
It is estimated that some 384,000 tonnes of
nitrogen fertiliser was applied in 2006 alone.
In lowland Scotland and the in eastern coastal
fringes, this is resulting in eutrophication,
disrupting fresh water ecosystems and encouraging toxic algal blooms which are a hazard to
human health, as well as other species.

— 4

Poorly located and designed development:
Poorly located development can lead to direct
loss of semi-natural habitat and increase
fragmentation. Poor design can be seen in
developments that fail to safeguard existing
natural and semi-natural features or fail to
integrate biodiversity into the fabric of new
built development. This is not just detrimental
for nature: evidence now exists that a green
environment where we live and work is critical
for our mental and physical wellbeing.

— 5

Invasive non-native species:

Non-native species have been introduced over the centuries to provide new crops or materials or to adorn our parks and gardens and others have arrived under their own steam. Many are benign but some non-native species are causing significant damage to our ecosystems. Left unchecked, they can have devastating impacts not just on our native species but also economically.[5]

— 6

Climate change:

Our changing climate is already impacting on human wellbeing and on the natural world. There are changes in phenology such that synchronisation between interdependent species is changing. For example, the breeding periods for some birds and the availability of the caterpillars they feed on are falling out of sync, leading to fewer offspring. Some species are shifting north and to higher latitudes as the climate warms. Alpine species could become extinct and, without networks in place, more southern species might struggle to move northwards over time. Across the world there is evidence of species population explosions and crashes in response to climate change with resultant impacts throughout the food chain.

— 7

Unsustainable land management practices:
There are land use practices that are
impacting on our natural systems. Intensive
farming methods reduce the extent and quality
of wildlife on farmland: inappropriate drainage,
canalisation and damming reduce the quality
of our watercourses; unsustainable forestry
practices through the planting of monocultures
of non-native species and clear-felling rather
than more sympathetic harvesting systems;
and, on some estates, the emphasis on land
management techniques to increase grouse
and deer numbers at the expense of richer,
more natural wildlife habitats.[6]

There are, therefore, significant threats to the biodiversity of ecosystems that need to be tackled at a regional or national scale. Systemic fixes are required, not just small scale, ad hoc or localised responses that deal with only a part of the much bigger problem. Connected, ecologically coherent green networks are one such systemic fix. In this respect, the CSGN can act as a flagship but green networks will be required across the entire country if ecosystem health is to be realised throughout Scotland.

What nature can do for us?

Some ask: 'Why should we care about nature? Because what does nature do for us?' The answer is that natural environments are critical to our wellbeing economically, physically and emotionally and the evidence to support this relationship is growing by the day.

Nature provides us with a range of ecosystem goods. About 50% of our medicines, our food sources and fibre-producing plants, our pets and our garden plants are all derived originally from wild species.[7]

Nature provides us with recreational opportunities and also benefits the economy. From ecotourism to sales of recreational equipment, from provision of travellers' services to licences and park entry fees, eco-recreation is a major player in the economies of many nations today.[8]

Nature provides us with a range of supporting services that are necessary for the production of all other ecosystem services and which underpin the global economy. From soil formation, nutrient cycling, water cycling and primary production, the world stocks of natural capital are the foundation on which society and economy depends.[9]

Nature has profound spiritual and cultural significance. There are places on earth that are sacred to some people and the intense importance of those places to those people ought to override countervailing economic interests.[10] Moreover, 'everyday nature' is a vitally important part of so many people's lives — it enriches us and inspires us.

The Scottish Wildlife Trust contends that, even for those who are not 'into' nature, people should still care because healthy ecosystems dramatically improve human wellbeing and life quality, not just for today but for future generations. This extends to economic benefits. There are studies from across the world and at a range of scales showing the economic value of nature. For example:

—   A study of the 400,000 trees in Canberra has shown benefits of $20–67 million over the period 2008 to 2012 in terms of the value generated or savings realised for the city.[11]
—   A study of the Scottish Wildlife Trust mountain bike trail in Cumbernauld shows a social return on investment ratio (net present value divided by   investment) of 2.53 (£65,382.39 / £25,830.83).[12]

What can we do for nature?

The scale of changes faced by ecosystems, habitats and species is potentially so profound that many of the ecosystem services that humanity benefits from could easily be lost or significantly reduced unless action is taken. Six top priorities have been identified that need to be acted upon in order for nature to flourish in the CSGN area.[13]

1. Ecological Urbanism

We need to create compact, biodiverse, walkable, public transit-oriented, water smart, mixed-use places. Suburban sprawl is a multiple-lose scenario. In 'Architecture: Choice or Fate', Leon Krier considers the suburbs as a parasite, with suburbanisation leading to ever outward expansion of cities through edge development that causes the hollowing out of the centre (the 'doughnut effect').[14] However, it seems that the tide is turning and many out of town malls are now struggling as people seek to move back to vibrant town and city centres.[15] Taking an ecological urbanism approach could create sustainable, vibrant and creative local economies that are the kind of places where people want to live:

"…highly skilled people have become the most critical factor of competitive advantage – economic development has become less about creating and attracting firms, and more about attracting skilled people."[16]

"there is no doubt that for a large part of our sample, access to and quality of the natural environment are major factors in the quality of life that they ('they' being skilled in-migrants) seek in places."[17]

2. Developing a set of Ecosystem Health Indicators

The long-term aim for conservation in ecosystems is to restore or, where this is no longer possible, to improve the natural structure and functioning or 'health' of the system. Measures are needed to assess change in extent and quality over time. Some measures already exist – others need to be developed. Indicators might include ecological condition, habitat connectivity, water quality, soil quality, extent of modification, the presence of non-native species and the presence of functional groups of species. The practice is evolving but many organisations are working up scoring systems that allow report cards to be produced to help with the measurement of change over time. Progress can then be evaluated and reported at agreed intervals.

— 8

Examples of good practice illustrating
the introduction of ecological
values into sensitive development,
ecosystem health through good
agricultural practice and support for
people-focused solutions.

— 8a

— 8b

3. Opportunity mapping

There is a range of ecological network evaluation tools which now exist that can be used to establish best-case scenarios. Organisations like Forestry Commission Scotland and the GCV Green Network Partnership are using such tools to help inform how and where green networks can be developed. Such work can be used to inform development planning and development management decisions. However, developers need to come on board to ensure that new development contributes to the delivery of local green networks and there is more to be done in supporting planners in the use of available tools. Both sides of the development equation need to understand that integrating green infrastructure into schemes can and will make a positive contribution – every green wall, green roof, sustainable urban drainage system, street tree, garden, allotment, square and park make a contribution to an urban ecosystem that, when joined up, can link into regional green and blue networks and the wider countryside beyond.

4. 'Buying' ecosystem health through agricultural support funds

Public funding should be used to secure healthy, functioning habitats and species. There are examples of good practice with forestry grants using ecosystem maps to target resources to improve connectivity of priority woodland habitats. However, in terms of agricultural support, the 'Basic Farm Payment' has no clear nature conservation policy objective. Such public funding needs to do more for the public 'commons'.

Ecosystem health indicator data and opportunity mapping tools should be usedin assessing grant allocations to restore and create small and big connections between isolated habitats.

5. Supporting local 'Living Landscape' programmes

As a wildlife charity, the Scottish Wildlife Trust seeks to encourage the delivery of Living Landscape projects such as those in Cumbernauld and Edinburgh. These projects are about giving nature back to people, securing ecosystem services and thereby adding value, strengthening community pride, raising stakeholder awareness and buy-in, supporting rural development and delivering biological diversity and other policy priorities. They can be a way to ensure value for money and might even reduce societal costs in future.[18]

6. Aiming for multifunctionality

A green network should be a carbon sink, should be a nature reserve, should be a play space, should provide an economic return and should be that 'Ascot hat'. A green network should have heterogeneity and diverse structure. It should be as diverse as possible in habitats and in form and age. This will allow nature to flourish and maximise the potential to deliver the fullest range of ecosystem services possible.

Central Scotland is the perfect place to take an ecological urbanism approach. If we get ecological urbanism right in central Scotland, then the CSGN will achieve an environment that adds value to the economy, where people are happy and healthy and where nature thrives.

1
Fred Edwards (personal communication).

2
Scottish Wildlife Trust, *Living Landscapes: towards ecosystem-based conservation in Scotland*, by J. Hughes and S. Brooks (Edinburgh: SWT, 2009).

3
Scottish Environment LINK, *Call 999: an Emergency for Scotland's Biodiversity. Summary and Assessment for Scotland From The UK Biodiversity Action Plan 2005 Reporting Round* (Scotland: 2007).

4
Scottish Environment Protection Agency, *State of Scotland's Environment* (Scotland: 2006).

5
The net economic value loss to Scotland of the introduction of the salmon parasite Gyrodactylus salaris is believed to be £633 million. Across the UK, Japanese Knotweed affects an area the size of London and would cost £1.56 billion to remove. The estimated cost of removing Rhododendron ponticum from the Loch Lomond and Trossachs National Park is £25 million.

6
The planting of non-native monocultures and clear felling is now much less prevalent in Scotland.

7
J. Harte, "Land use, biodiversity, and ecosystem integrity: the challenge of preserving Earth's life support system", *Ecology Law Quarterly*, (2001), 27, 929–965.

8
Ibid.

9
UK National Ecosystem Assessment, accessed December 2015, http://uknea.unep-wcmc.org/EcosystemAssessmentConcepts/EcosystemServices/tabid/103/Default.aspx.

10
J. Harte, "Land use, biodiversity, and ecosystem integrity: the challenge of preserving Earth's life support system", *Ecology Law Quarterly*, (2001), 27, 929–965.

11
Department of Forestry, Australian National University, Canberra, *Pollution mitigation and carbon sequestration by an urban forest*, C.L. Brack, (Canberra: Australian National University, Canberra, 2002).

12
Independent charity greenspace scotland (http://greenspacescotland.org.uk) has carried out a critical literature review and has identified many more relevant studies.

13
SWT Op.cit.

14
Leon Krier, Architecture: *Choice or Fate* (Windsor: Andreas Papadakis Publisher, 1998).

15
The Economist, March 2011.

16
Demos, 'The Place Race' (2008).

17
Ibid.

18
Royal Society of Wildlife Trusts, *Increasing understanding and defining key aspects of the Living Landscape evidence base*, by John Hambrey, (Strathpeffer: Hambrey Consulting, 2010), 46–47.

6

Ecological
sequestration

Professor Peter Head CBE

Introduction

The Ecological Sequestration Trust was established in 2010. From the outset, it was clear that 2015 would be a critical year, when decisions would be made about new goals for tackling climate change. A key aim for the Trust, therefore, was to be in a position to help city-regions implement the agendas for change agreed by national governments at major United Nations events planned that year. From the perspective of 2010, it was hard to imagine that the Trust would be in a position to help the scale of ambition that would emerge in 2015 from 195 countries on disaster risk reduction in Sendai in February of that year, on finance in Addis Ababa in July, on global sustainable development goals (GSDGs) in New York in September and on climate change in Paris in December.[1]

This chapter describes progress with the development and demonstration of a new open-source digital planning platform 'resilience.io' that will support disaster risk reduction management, delivery of the UN's Global Goals and decarbonisation of city-regions using the Greenhouse Gas Protocol and help connect investment finance with bankable projects.

Growing global instability

The need for the world to agree global goals was a response to growing instability. Jeff Sachs has suggested that the reason for the degree of agreement is that, increasingly, countries are fearful of climate change with effects including increased migration and instability: they realise that global cooperation is the way forward.[2] A key factor causing such global stress has been reliance since the Second World War on the growth of Gross Domestic Product (GDP) as a measure of success. As population has grown, this resource-driven model has led to the accelerated destruction of global ecological systems that support human life but this impact has not been factored into decision-making. Ecological destruction on land and in the oceans, combined with climate change, is creating water stress and conflict that is driving people to migrate from desert areas near the equator towards more temperate regions.

Some hundreds of years ago, the average amount of land available to support each person's life with energy, water, food and materials was 8 hectares (the 'ecological footprint'). As population has grown, the area of land available has reduced to 2 hectares but we are living as if this reduction has not happened and developed countries are consuming at a rate of 6 to 9 hectares per person. Developing countries have the ambition to emulate this lifestyle. China has realised that they cannot complete their urbanisation with this rate of consumption, having reached 3 hectares per person. So they have embarked on a transition to what they refer to as the 'ecological civilisation'.[3] This is also set out in the Global Goals and so, for the first time, the world is aiming for a more resilient future.

Scotland has the opportunity to be a leader in this transition for the benefit of future generations and, in the process, to become an exemplar for countries in how to deliver the transition as well as sharing technology and skills. Scotland has the benefit of a huge area of ocean and wild land to support life and is the envy of many environmentally stressed countries. However, Scotland's ecological footprint remains at 5 hectares per capita and needs to be reduced to meet the objectives of the Global Goals. In parallel, the stresses of increasing storm intensity, flooding and sea level rise also need to be addressed in a cost-effective way by working with and restoring natural systems.

Resource efficiency

A global initiative is being taken forward to move the measure of economic success from measures of GDP to one in which human wellbeing is improved while using resources in a resilient way. This is referred to as the 'circular economy' in which the 'take-make-dispose' model is changed to one in which resource use is circular and regenerative.[4] This transition in economic thinking offers significant opportunities for businesses to take the lead in assisting with the transition. In part, the transition will be to move products from ownership to performance-based services such that materials can be recycled and reused. This will need to be accompanied by cross-sector and supply-chain integration and collaboration. The new business models will also be required to include climate change risk management. The process by which these changes can be

supported is a digital resource flow modelling platform that includes flows from human and ecological system activity operable at the national and regional scale described later in this chapter. In the future, construction industry infrastructure should be designed so that at the end of life, elements can be recycled, reconditioned, reused or refurbished. This should become part of the performance specification for resilience.

The resources critical for life are oxygen, water, energy, food and raw materials. In a changing world, it is the management of these resources that will need to change. It is estimated that by 2030 the world will require 30% more water, 40% more energy and 50% more food. An ambition for Scotland in a resilience economy, including jobs, would be that once it met its own needs, it could aim to export these elements.

When the Trust was set up, the founders wanted to provide open-source tools to enable every country in the world to make this transition quickly and, based on decades of experience in infrastructure and planning, it was concluded that working at the scale of the city-region would be the key to supporting and encouraging this transition. Today, 70% of jobs are created in city-regions. Urbanisation is still increasing and the percentage of jobs in urban areas is likely to increase with it. It will be essential, therefore, to embed integrated planning and decision-making into city-regions that are supported by modelling of urban-rural resource flows from human and ecological activity for food, water, energy and materials including pollution. Modelling should cover the water, carbon, nitrogen and phosphorus cycles that are critical for all life. For this to be useful for decision-making, this modelling needs to include economic, social and environmental aspects, with a common and credible economic and risk management methodology.

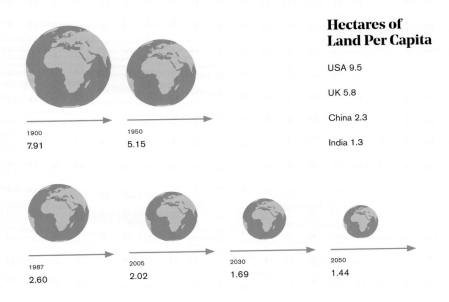

**Hectares of
Land Per Capita**

USA 9.5

UK 5.8

China 2.3

India 1.3

1900
7.91

1950
5.15

1987
2.60

2005
2.02

2030
1.69

2050
1.44

— 1
Our shrinking earth
- population growing
at 80 million per year.

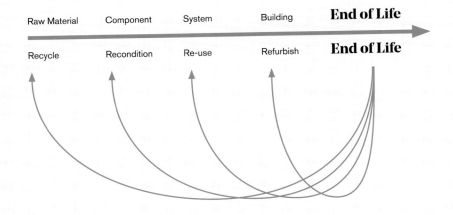

Raw Material   Component   System   Building   **End of Life**

Recycle   Recondition   Re-use   Refurbish   **End of Life**

Resourse Efficient   Flexible & Adaptable Design

— 2
Materials and waste -
a systems approach.

From observatory to 'collaboratory' and global-local systems

In 2010, the Trust concluded that an open-source platform could only be
created and made demonstrable through encouraging thought-leaders in
all disciplines to come together into a collaboration partnership to show
that the proposition was possible. The Trust was created as a UK charity
to occupy the space between private, public and third sectors, including
research and non-governmental organisations (NGOs), in order to create
tools that would enable all these stakeholders to collaborate across
city-regions. It is important to act in an integrated way and to share knowledge internationally about how to establish and improve this approach.
The Trust concluded that ecological practice was a key and powerful
enabler for critical cycles, such as carbon, and so the name was selected
to reflect this belief.

    The vision of the Trust is that any region in the world should be able
to access the 'resilience.io' website, identify a target region and download
a systems modelling platform into which geographic information system
(GIS)-based data could be uploaded for planning and decision-making.[5]
Eventually, the platform would be automatically uploaded with digital
geo-data from earth observation satellites. Before this can happen, the
platform has to be built, demonstrated and enabled for scaling. The
intention is to achieve this within a 5–10 year period enabling end users
to develop apps that can then be used by any city-region to help navigate
the platform. The city-region model is intended to include data on land use,
natural and infrastructure systems built using existing knowledge that can
be changed incrementally over time. The platform needs to include existing
resource flow models, such as water catchment areas, utilities and transport networks, to show change over time to simulate the consequences of
different policy or management regimes.

    It is clear that to be successful a regional platform would require to
exchange data with other national and international database models such
that the global-local interface can be better understood. At the same time
as the Trust was established, the International Centre for Earth Simulation
(ICES) was created to bring together all earth-scale models for climate,
water, oceans, earth plates, earth core, ecology and resource and a partnership was established to facilitate data exchange such that city-regions can
obtain future scenario assessments of climate and other effects to input
into risk assessments and decision-making.[6]

The dialogue between the Trust and ICES revealed an opportunity through the emergence of five new technologies to develop an integrated approach at realistic cost:

— 1   Geo data is being collected in increasing quantities and is available free on a global basis where algorithms can be created to process it. Ground-based sensors are cheap, can be powered by the sun and can be used to supplement this data.

— 2   Communications systems provided through the 'internet of things' is creating networks of smart devices and data that will be accessible to the majority of the population within 10 years. As 4G and then 5G become widely available, access to complex models and visualisations will be possible in real time.

— 3   Systems modelling, including agent-based modelling, is now possible to integrate social and natural sciences as a consequence of developments in mathematics and processing power. Cloud-based server capacity is developing to adequate levels to run and support these models with limited local hardware cost.

— 4   The world is moving quickly to open-source data that is available from private-public-community-NGO sources. Examples include the EU INSPIRE database and the GEOSS programme for data brokering.

— 5   The growth of digital visualisation technology using digital film and drones for data gathering is such that a city-region can be visualised and resource flows and changes assessed more easily in real time.

Current thinking and emerging practice can take advantage of these changes through the concept of a 'data observatory' linked to smart city-regions using the 'internet of things' to create an interconnected system between users and devices. As yet, however, huge amounts of data are being assembled in such 'observatories' without a clear purpose and the means to utilise the data for truly integrated and collaborative planning, investment and decision-making. The Trust, therefore, aims to provide a platform that can place selected data into a systems model that can then process and align the data with current policy and practice. Thereafter, the data can be made freely available for all stakeholders to use in a collaborative way to assist decision-making and to guide, inform and de-risk investment, leading to the emergence of the term 'collaboratory' or collaborative laboratory for the community.[7]

Within its first year, the Trust brought together Imperial College (with expertise in city-region resource flow modelling), the Institute for Integrated Economics Research (IIER) in Zurich (resource economics for human wellbeing) and the European Forestry Institute at Lund University (the PROFILE soils and agriculture model). The intention in bringing the group together was to start the design and prototype the configuration of the model that would underpin 'resilience. io'. A key and unique feature for the model was a world library of human and ecological processes that can be incorporated into regional models to help build a systems approach using human and ecological data including industry, infrastructure, built environment and land use. This configuration should, in theory, enable new technologies to be tested in any region and allow new change models for business to be explored and, in turn, used for performance-based procurement for all aspects of the built environment. In this way, a region could steer itself progressively towards a more resilient future. From this initial feasibility, it became clear that building information modelling (BIM) and infrastructure information modelling (IIM) systems could in turn be linked into regional platforms for data exchange in construction and operational phases.[8] This is planned as a future phase of development.

Governance, user interfaces and collaborative intelligence

At the conclusion of the preliminary development phases, the Trust sought to identify regions of the world that might be interested in piloting this model in order to help develop and prove it in use. Workshops were held in Ulaanbaatar in Mongolia, Accra in Ghana, Surat in India and Dorset in the UK. (see Table 1)

Discussions have been held with professional institutions, such as the Royal Institute of British Architects (RIBA), to establish whether a working interface can be created to enable architects and urban planners to use the platform in their work and interest has been expressed in developing online training to assist in capacity building for professional networks. The most impressive example identified through these discussions was the 3D-enabled Geodan Phoenix platform for urban planning, land management and disaster risk planning linked to the INSPIRE database. This did not include ecology and economics but was nonetheless a powerful trial and the Trust now plans to develop the programme further.

Presentations were made to over 30 countries around the world with positive feedback for using the concept of 'resilience.io' to enable communities to develop 'collaborative intelligence' that would elevate outcomes to a higher level than would be possible through individual actors working alone. This degree of integration has long been an aim of the sustainable development community.

Innovation in integrated natural resource management

At the heart of future proposals for 'resilience.io' models are the links between ecology, resources, human well-being and the economics of the market. Although there is considerable research on these different linkages across the world, they have not yet been incorporated into an holistic, decision-making tool. For example, it is recognised that poor air quality affects human health and that this increases long-term health care costs, which in turn has economic impacts. It is also understood that poor health undermines productivity and that this has further negative effects on the economy. If it is to achieve utility and acceptance, a model such as 'resilience.io' will need to incorporate algorithms that connect these issues to enable better investment decisions to address the wider impacts of pollution.

A further example concerns the beneficial effects of tree planting and peat bogs in slowing water runoff from upland slopes with the probable reduction of flooding in downstream urban areas. Similarly, in cities, the model may assist in assessing the benefits of tree planting and sustainable urban drainage in reducing flood risk. Within urban areas, it is recognised that access to biodiversity and green spaces improves mental health and educational performance and accelerates recovery rates in hospital. In turn, these benefits have economic value within city-regions. The platform may also include land and property values so that the benefits of active travel (walking and cycling) can be better understood in urban planning.

— 3
Collaborative regional intelligence.

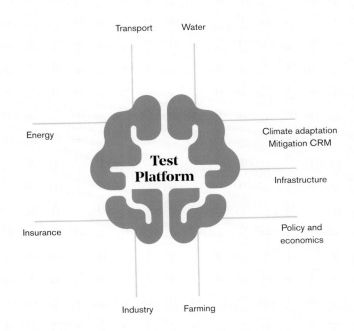

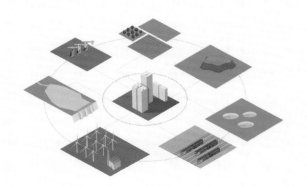

Mobilising effective and efficient long-term finance

An important part of the journey since 2010 has been to engage the international development finance and insurance community to understand how the model can be refined to configure viable projects and thereby attract investment finance with a lower level of risk. An international leadership seminar was convened at the Rockefeller Foundation Bellagio Centre in February 2015 and this meeting came up with 12 clear conclusions:

— 1   The battle to deliver post-2015 GSDGs will be won or lost in cities.

— 2   City-regions need an adequate share of government funds to enable them to attract the necessary private capital; however, the availability of finance is not an issue.

— 3   The principal barriers are the lack of capacity and tools to bring forward 'bankable' projects.

— 4   Transfer of knowledge, best practice and human and ecological resource data is needed at different scales — from local communities through cities and nations up to the global scale. Such practice is being established.

— 5   The best way to connect to funding sources is to set up a dedicated financial vehicle such as an Urban Development Fund (UDF).

— 6   Local data and systems modelling are needed in the platform. Open-source tools that enable the use of local open-data in systems models are now being developed for this purpose.

— 7   Projects are best taken forward using the Public Private Partnership (PPP) model, in which the platform is used to support planning, design, delivery and ongoing maintenance.

— 8   Projects need to integrate human and ecological systems to reduce the cost of mitigation and adaptation to support human wellbeing.

— 9   Local capacity for planning, modelling and project development needs to be developed urgently in city-regions, so that there are the tools and training required to plan, design and implement such projects with appropriate governance arrangements.

— 10   Overseas Development Aid (ODA) funding can be targeted specifically at capacity building and the provision of the necessary tools for city-regions.

— 11   New financial instruments and mechanisms are needed both within and outside the formal banking sector to enable financing and development to be inclusive and to reach down to the needs of the community.

— 12   The reinsurance sector has a key role to play in risk assessment in developing countries and enabling risks to be better accounted for in the wider financial system.

It is estimated that sufficient mobile capital is available globally to drive the world's urban areas forward to a more resilient and sustainable future where the values described above can provide a return on capital as compared with the volatility of investment return at present. The jobs created in this transition will enable quality of life and poverty reduction to move forward and, as a result, equity can be improved through smarter land use.

— 4

(Previous page) Peatbogs are important for carbon sequestration.

— Table 1
Proof Of Concept For Resilience Models:

The regional workshops delivered similar outcomes in respect
of the 'collaboratory' proposal:

— 1

The concept was welcomed as a vehicle to sit outside government and the private sector and to provide tools to enable all
sectors to move forward efficiently and effectively through collaboration with the community. It should be free to use for everyone.

— 2

The organisational mechanism is well suited to the social enterprise model with a representative governing board to ensure
independence and respect community need.

— 3

The body would have to be supported technically by the best
science and technology available both locally and within global
networks. It must be transparent and accountable.

— 4

The user interfaces would need to be accessible to all sectors
for use effectively and to encourage the exchange of information about future proposed programmes and developments.

— 5

A 'gaming' or simulation version of the platform should be
developed for use in education.

— 6

Funding for both set up and running costs should come from
the value created in terms of efficiency and effectiveness of
capital flow within and into the region.

1

An unprecedented level of global cooperation:
— A comprehensive global framework for disaster risk reduction
  (Sendai, February 2015);
— The UN data revolution to support financing of change
  (Addis Ababa, July 2015);
— 17 globally agreed national and city goals for a resilient sustainable
  world (New York, September 2015);
— A target to reduce global warming to well below 2 degree centigrade
  and to aim to 1.5 degree centigrade with a largely renewable and
  nuclear-powered world by 2050–2100 (Paris, December 2015); and
— $100bn per year to help developing poor countries to mitigate and
  adapt.

2

Jeff Sachs, Director of the Earth Institute, Columbia University, New
York, September 2015.

3

See for example: New Scientist, 11 June 2014 (https://www.newsci-
entist.com/article/mg22229733-400-china-battles-to-be-first-ecologi-
cal-civilisation/); The Diplomat, 30 September 2015 (http://thediplomat.
com/2015/09/chinas-new-blueprint-for-an-ecological-civilization/);
and The Climate Group, February 2014 (http://www.theclimategroup.
org/_assets/files/china-ecocivilisation.pdf).

4

For further information, refer to information on the Ellen MacArthur
Foundation website (https://www.ellenmacarthurfoundation.org/circu-
lar-economy); and also The Guardian website (http://www.theguardian.
com/sustainable-business/10-things-need-to-know-circular-economy).

5

For further information, refer to: http://resilience.io. The document
'Resiliece.io: a revolution in planning' can be downloaded from the
Ecological Sequestration Trust's website (http://ecosequestrust.org/
wp-content/uploads/2015/02/resilience.io-platform-report.pdf).

6

For further information on the International Centre for Earth Simulation,
refer to: http://www.icesfoundation.org/Pages/Home.aspx.

7

A 'collaboratory' was defined in 1989 by William Wulf as a 'center
without walls, in which the nation's researchers can perform their
research without regard to physical location, interacting with colleagues,
accessing instrumentation, sharing data and computational resources,
[and] accessing information in digital libraries'; from W. Wulf, *Towards
a national collaboratory*, unpublished report of a National Science
Foundation invitational workshop, (New York: Rockefeller University,
March 1989).

8

For further information, refer to: http://www.bimtaskgroup.org.

9

For information on the seminar and its findings, see: http://ecoseques-
trust.org/financeforsdgs/ and http://ecosequestrust.org/financeforSDGs.pdf.

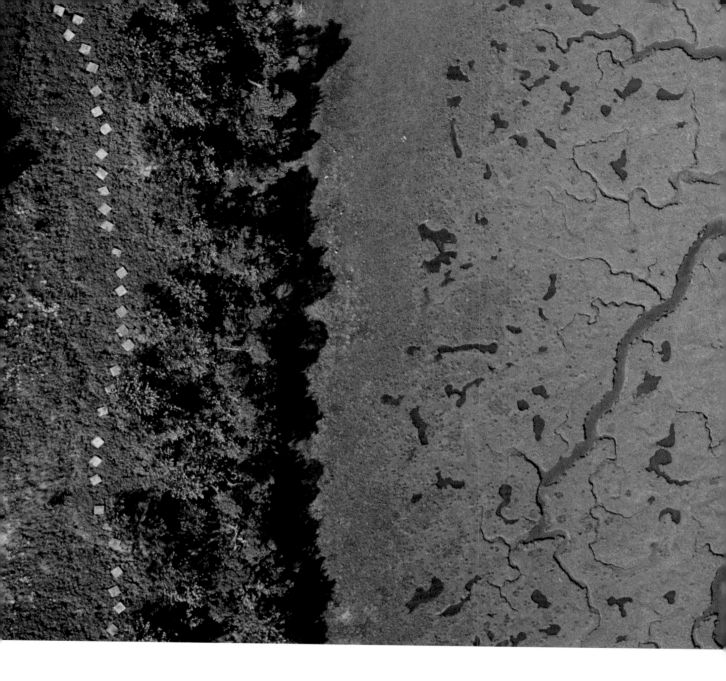

Section 2 —
Learning from place

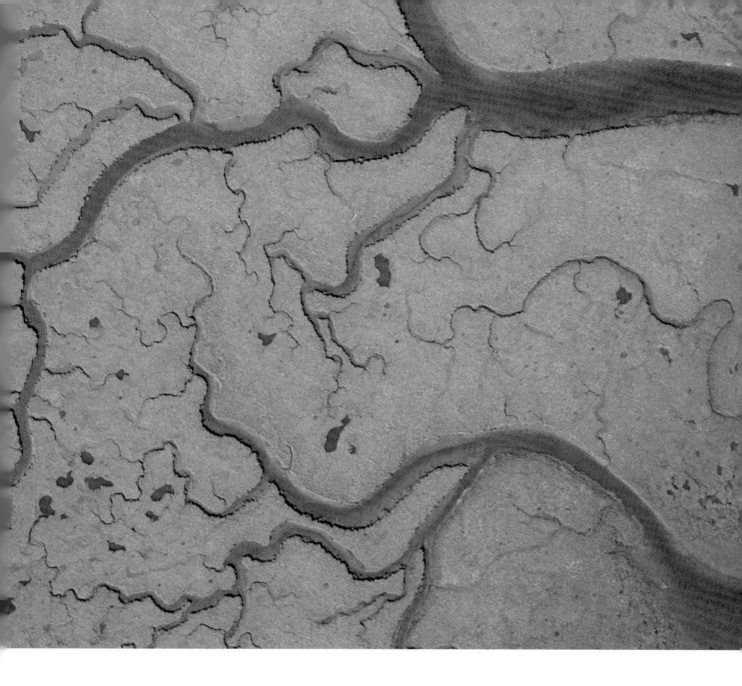

Detail (rotated) from: *Saltmarsh channels and wartime concrete coastal defences, Tyninghame, East Lothian, Scotland*, 1989, from the continuing series *Order & Chaos*.
Patricia & Angus Macdonald of the Aerographica Partnership.

7

The Emscher Landscape Park—A journey of renewal

Michael Schwarze-Rodrian

"The topography of industry is the park's trademark." [1]

The genesis of the Emscher Landscape Park

The Emscher Landscape Park (ELP) in the Ruhr region, Germany's former industrial heartland, is known throughout the world as a case study of long-term, environmentally sound development practice. It is much more than a park in the traditional sense; it is an approach to urban greening supported by a long-term vision of attractive urban landscapes within a regional park system, delivered through a series of public investments underpinned by design and delivery by 20 cities in the densely built-up heart of the Ruhr agglomeration. The approach has been cooperative, pragmatic and based on 'learning by doing' and has resulted in a new green infrastructure and landscape setting for the cities of the Ruhr. The ELP is seen as a central and integrated component of a sustainable, economic regeneration strategy that includes cultural renewal, processes of transformation rather than demolition and the delivery of nature-based landscape solutions in and around cities.[2]

The story of the Ruhr recounts the progress of a cluster of independent cities that have gone through shared, simultaneous and comprehensive transformation to address the structural changes needed to replace old heavy industries based on coal and steel to embrace a diverse service and knowledge-based economy. The Ruhr metropolitan area comprises 53 cities (11 larger cities) and 4 counties distributed along three rivers (the Ruhr, the Emscher and the Lippe) that flow from east to west into the River Rhine. Without a dominant major city, the cities grew together as a polycentric region where cooperation is the basis for economic success. Around 5.1 million people now live in the region, down from a peak of 5.67 million at the height of the area's industrial power in the 1950s.

The remaking of the Ruhr Region has been an important objective for successive regional and federal governments since the 1960s. The transformation of an old industrial region into a modern, knowledge-based metropolitan region followed many strategies and steps. It included significant investments in new universities, new technologies, learning and training together with the complete renewal of sites and neighbourhoods across the cities. Extensive repair and reclamation was necessary and new directions of development had to be discovered.

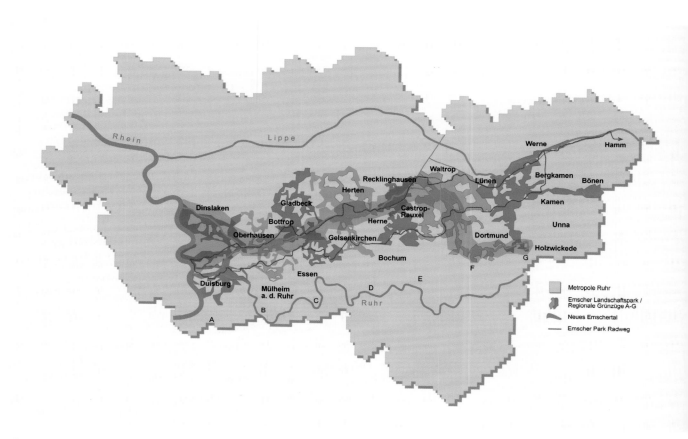

— 1
The Emscher Landscape Park

The transformation of the Ruhr has been continuously supported by subsidies from the State of North Rhine-Westphalia (NRW), the Federal Republic of Germany and the EU. The budgets of the cities individually and collectively were too small for the challenges the region faced. The model for the transformation is based on a remarkable political consensus that has helped to ensure an economic 'soft landing' for the cities and their citizens in place of the 'shock therapy' endured by other regions in both Western and Eastern Europe.

By 1985, the economic decline of old industries had caused the creation of 5,000 hectares (12,400 acres) of brownfield and, in many cases, contaminated land. It became necessary to rethink the approach, the instruments and the standards to find integrated and sustainable solutions to address these extensive areas of post-industrial urban landscape.[3]

In the late 1980s, a new vision emerged to embrace and use the structural change in the economy and society as both a unique opportunity and a challenge to deliver new, sustainable urban development. This approach sounds familiar today but it was completely unknown at the time. It also corresponded with growing concern about the environment and interest in preserving local built heritage, especially in the garden cities built for the miners and steel workers located adjacent to the former industrial sites.

The legacy of 'IBA' Emscher Park

In 1989, the NRW created a unique 'workshop for the future of old industrial regions', the International Building Exhibition Emscher Park Ltd (IBA) in the northern part of the urban agglomeration. Seventeen cities and regional administrations were invited to find and follow new solutions, to stage strategic and design competitions to identify the best solutions and to test and deliver innovative projects on the ground. The IBA programme ran for 10 years until 1999 with a small public office of 30 people under the direction of Prof Dr Karl Ganser. The IBA organisation was state-owned and well networked with all the decision-makers in the cities and the region.

What emerged was a strategy for urban renewal and new development, IBA Emscher Park, that simultaneously retained the industrial legacy and landscape quality of the region at its heart. The aim was to create an attractive, urban landscape providing a new context for economic development that would enable this post-industrial region to compete with other city-regions across the world.

IBA established seven fields of action to deliver innovative and integrated transformation:

—   creating a new park system between the cities, the ELP;
—   ecological regeneration of the Emscher River System;
—   recreational provision around the Rhine-Herne Ship Canal;
—   'Working in the Park' with high-quality recycling of former production sites;
—   'Industrial Heritage Ruhr' as the identity and cultural root of the whole region;
—   housing construction and sustainable urban development on a human scale; and
—   social initiatives, including employment and training programmes to provide people with qualifications and retraining during this period of change.

One of the process innovations adopted during the IBA period was to develop strategies and projects simultaneously in an iterative rather than a linear, hierarchical process. This called for two different approaches and skill sets bringing together individuals who understood the changing conditions and how to develop new ideas and strategies with others who had the operational and technical knowledge to deliver projects on the ground, with both groups playing equal and complementary roles, cooperating and learning from each other as they went along.

—2
Landscape Park Duisburg Nord:
a 200-hectare public park where the remnants
of the coal and steel production act as
significant features within the park.

The five iterations of ELP management – experiences in cooperation and moderation

The author, and others who have worked on the ELP since its beginning, can identify five distinct stages, or versions, of the development of the regional park similar, in some regards, to the different releases of computer software:

ELP 1.0 – Emscher Landscape Park, feasibility (1988–1989): Systematic mapping to explore the spatial, economic and political opportunities to develop a new urban park system using brownfield land and former industrial infrastructures.

ELP 2.0 – Emscher Landscape Park, the IBA planning and delivery system (1990–1999): Inception and delivery of the ELP during IBA with a regional masterplan, 7 inter-municipal development plans and design competitions for 18 major projects (interim report published in1996: 'ELP Parkbericht').

ELP 3.0 – International presentation of the Emscher Landscape Park (part of IBA Finale 1999): Regional concepts and delivered ELP projects showcased through best practice case studies, site visits, presentations at international conferences, information in books, IBA catalogues, journal articles and press items during 1999.

ELP 4.0 – Emscher Landscape Park Masterplan 2010 (2001–2006): Rethinking of the ELP concept after the conclusion of IBA; identifying on-going and new challenges; reshaping the spatial dimension of the park system from 320 square kilometres (123.5 square miles) to 457 square kilo-metres (174 square miles) and growing from 17 to 20 cities; proposing the New Emscher Valley; designing the next suite of projects and the manage-ment of the regional park system; and negotiating and contracting continuity of the ELP with partner cities, the Ruhr Regional Association (RVR) and the NRW. Masterplan ELP 2010 was published in 2006.

ELP 5.0 – Emscher Landscape Park 2020+ (ongoing since 2013): Focusing on further projects and delivery of regional park management and negotiating the next important steps of ELP developments, including priorities and costs.

These five periods of ELP planning and management sought to address the needs of the Ruhr region over a 25-year period. The comparison with computer software makes sense. The concept and operational task of continually evolving an extensive urban landscape needs planning and design instruments that fit to the changing realities. As a consequence, the 'software' – the plans, programmes and priorities for the ELP's development – has to be rewritten from time to time. This also includes new coalitions and new interests that arise with the more developed park. A formal or static plan for ELP dating back from 1990 would not have the content or 'currency' for today's requirements. The development of the regional park, therefore, has to be an iterative process.

Regional moderation and inter-municipal partnership working were, and remain, the unsung secrets of managing the ELP processes. There have always been three spatial and political levels: the regional park itself, extending to 457 square kilometres today with its regional network of bike paths, the 7 inter-municipal

working groups (extending along 7 green belt corridors) and the numerous local projects. Moderation and cooperation are required at all scales from regional to local to maintain the continuity of and to stimulate the future development of the park.

By 1999 and the IBA Finale, more than 100 projects had been completed in the 17 participating cities delivered with an investment of €2.5 billion of public funding (two thirds public and one third private).[5] The exhibition year of 1999 included presentations, exhibitions, conferences and site tours to celebrate what had been achieved. Notable ELP projects included Landscape Park Duisburg Nord, West-Park in Bochum, Nordstern-Park in Gelsenkirchen, Zollverein in Essen, the Gasometer at Oberhausen, a series of 'ELP-Landmarks' and a new regional cycle system.[6]

IBA Emscher Park was successful in demonstrating practice innovation, showing how integrated and quality-driven approaches could address urban, landscape and cultural renewal and raise the profile of the Ruhr region internationally. In his publication 'Liebe

—3
A 230-kilometre cycle-friendly path network provides easy access throughout the ELP. A new cycle super highway is also in development. By 2020, the 101-kilometre 'RadSchnellweg 1' will be the first high-speed cycle way in Germany. It will extend across the ELP from the Rhine in Duisburg, via Essen, to Hamm.[4]

— 4
The Ruhr Museum and the area's main tourism
centre are located at the former Zollverein
Coke Works and Coal Mine, which have been
transformed since 1997.

auf den zweiten Blick' ('Love at second sight'), IBA director Professor
Ganser captured the sense that this post-industrial area was being
transformed and was worth seeing with fresh eyes including its unique
industrial heritage.[7]

Although the IBA had come to an end, there was a network of
people who were now used to working together and there was a strong
desire to continue the cooperation between the cities in the post-IBA
era. The development of a permanent regional park concept after the IBA
concluded built on the skills and insights developed during the ten-year
life of the temporary phase. A new Masterplan Emscher Landschaftspark
2010 was published in 2006, the result of five years of consultations, four
regional conferences and the output of 18 planning offices.[8] Key components of the Masterplan ELP 2010 were:

—   the New Emscher Valley operating as the strategic regional
     cooperation project up to 2020;
—   further development of the ELP with an additional 250 projects;
—   completing the park infrastructure; and
—   developing and putting in place mechanisms to manage the
     regional park.

It was important that the transformation was linked to the cultural
identity of the region and that the cities, towns and local people were
engaged in the process of change. Art installations and creative processes
provided ways of engagement with the planning process and the changing urban landscape. Today, whilst the concept of integrated strategies,
founded on nature-based solutions, to deliver sustainable urban living
still holds true, the masterplan is once again being updated to respond to
current policy imperatives and priorities around climate change mitigation
and adaptation and suitably reframed to suit today's language, including
the use of terms such as green infrastructure and green networks.

The method of a flexible planning system with a focus on a project-
by-project approach holds good in a time of more complex funding
arrangements. There remains the political imperative of meeting today's
needs now, not at a future date. All of this suggested a need to continue
with an integrated approach employing appropriate design and technical
skills, as well as cooperation between the cities and the politicians. The

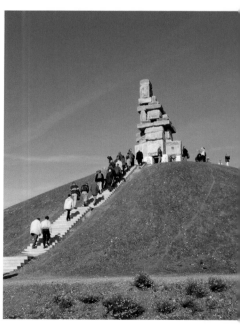

— 5a

Landmark sculptures celebrate the
past and create local identity;
— 5a
Stairs to Heaven by Herman
Prigaan at Halde Rheinelbe reused
locally found concrete waste
materials to create a viewing tower.
— 5b
Tetrahedron by Wolfgang Christ,
a 60-metre–sided, metal-framed,
pyramidal structure set at the top of
a coal mine spoil heap at Bottrop is
accessible by day and lit at night.

latest Emscher Landscape strategy, named ELP 2020+, has been
developed jointly between the 20 participating cities and the NRW
since 2013.

'Green Infrastructure Ruhr' is the current political platform with five
operational layers:

— ELP, furthering the development and management of the classic
'base' layer;
— renewal of the Emscher River, completing the ecological renewal
of the river and its tributaries;
— 'Green Cities' delivering new green urban solutions;
— regional bike networks supporting climate-friendly mobility; and
— climate adaptation and protection, making the cities ready to cope
with a changing climate.

Like the rest of the developed world, the cities of the Ruhr are discussing
climate change mitigation and adaptation, energy efficiency, wise use of
resources and the need for more sustainable modes of transport. The
NRW is organising a Climate Expo NRW (KlimaExpo.NRW) to establish
best practice by 2022.[9]

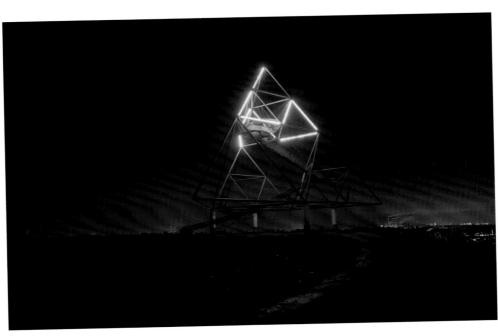

— 5b

Flagship development projects for the new urban park

The reasons for ELP's success and its ongoing political and financial support lie in the track record of delivery of built projects and infrastructure that includes:

— Zollverein in Essen (a converted former coal mine and cookery, which was awarded World Heritage status in 2001);[10]
— NordsternPark in Gelsenkirchen;[11]
— Gasometer in Oberhausen;[12]
— a series of new ELP bridges (crossing streets, canals and other barriers);
— a network of bicycle paths (converted industrial rail tracks – connecting people to the elements of ELP); and
— cultural landmarks (art interventions on former mining spoil heaps).[13]

Figures for the whole ELP development include: 187 individual park projects (extending to 81.64 square kilometres); 116 parkway projects (516 kilometres in length); 37 landmarks; 115 single landscape investments; 72 farmers working in cooperation with the ELP; 17 sites of 'industrial nature' (post-industrial wildlife on 2.44 square kilometres of land); and more than 100 planned projects under the current programme ELP 2020+.

The figures of ELP users are also impressive in terms of annual participation. In 2015, the 'Under the open Sky' annual summer programme had 80,000 visitors, Landscape Park Duisburg-North received 1.1 million visits and World Heritage Zollverein/Zollverein Park 1.5 million visits, whilst the two ELP visitor centres at Ripshorst and Hoheward had 40,000 and 7,500 respectively.

The background for these urban landscape investments is a long-lasting political consensus that economic change has to be integrated with, and supported by, environmental investments. These investments tend not to be funded by the private sector. The NRW has supported the cities and the region by funding up to 80% of the park's investment costs since 1992, an overall public investment of more than £395 million (€500 million). For other infrastructure investments (like railroads, streets, highways or energy), this is a small amount but, compared with other park developments, it represents a unique level of support for the future of the Ruhr region.

— 6
Two of the 14 iconic bridges developed as part of the access network.

Parallel initiatives and projects

The ELP does not stand alone. After the end of the IBA in 1999, several initiatives continued the innovative approach.

Renewal of Emscher River System

The ecological renewal of the Emscher River system started at the same time as the IBA. It is the most significant of the parallel processes and has been a central component of the IBA. One hundred years of coal mining and industry destroyed the natural hydrology of the region's water system. Below-ground extraction of minerals caused changes in ground topography and ground slumps resulting in significant changes in water flow and, as a consequence, the rivers were canalised and used as open sewers.

The project managed by Emschergenossenschaft involves the complete transformation of the river system by 2020, including the 85-kilometre River Emscher together with its 50 tributaries, converting open sewers back to living rivers and accessible banks.[14] The total cost of the restoration works will amount to €4.5 billion. Already €3 billion has been invested in the ecological transformation of 130 kilometres of water courses, in an overall river system of 350 kilometres, and the construction of 290 kilometres of new wastewater canals, out of a planned total of 400 kilometres. All the rivers of the Emscher system are located in the green belts of the ELP and the green infrastructure investments and the blue-water programmes are proceeding in a coordinated programme.

Ruhrtriennale

The Ruhrtriennale was created as an international cultural festival of the highest quality. Planning and preparations began after the completion of IBA Emscher Park in 1999. Since 2002, the Ruhrtriennale has taken place, as its name implies, in three-year cycles. It has featured music, dance, theatre performances and art exhibitions all across the Ruhr. The venues are industrial sites and factories that have been transformed into spectacular settings for cultural events. The main festival hall, the Hall of the Century, is located in the WestPark in Bochum.

The intellectual driver of the Ruhrtriennale is the concept of 'Kreationen' (creation, or invention) that fosters interdisciplinary productions of music, drama and art. Up to eighty performances of thirty productions are performed during each Ruhrtriennale. At the heart of the enterprise are regional, national and international discourses among artists interacting with each other and with the industrial spaces. Each cycle of the Ruhrtriennale is curated by a new art director.

The first festival was held in 2002 and was directed by Gerard Mortier, then director of the Salzburg festival and later director of the Paris Opera. Mortier was fascinated by the challenge of transforming industrial buildings and landscapes into locations for performing arts and exhibitions. Jürgen Flimm was the second art director between 2005 and 2008. The third Ruhrtriennale was directed by Willy Decker between 2009 and 2011. The fourth by composer and stage director Heiner Goebbels between 2012 and 2014 and Ruhrtriennale 2015 to 2017 is being directed by the Dutch theatre director Johan Simons.

— 7

The River Emscher and its tributaries
are being cleaned.

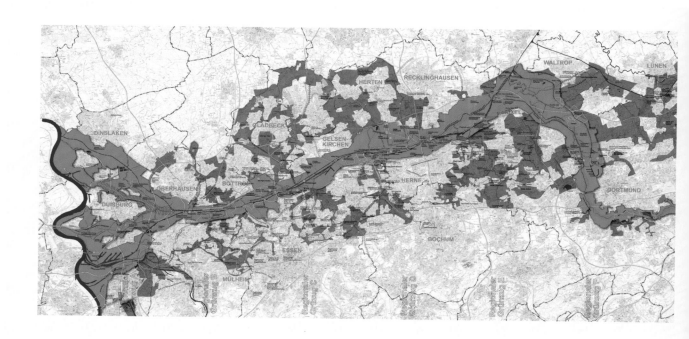

Von der Kloake zum Erholungsraum

Ein Fluss im Wandel der Zeit

Thematic strategies and partnerships

There are a number of these projects including:

Cities Region Ruhr 2030

A voluntary cooperation between the planning directors of the eleven largest cities and the four major districts of the Ruhr since 2003. A steering committee meets every two months to exchange information on current   developments in each municipality.

Wirtschaftsförderung metropoleruhr GmbH (WMR)

Established in 2007, WMR is the regional economic development agency. WMR provides cities with economic data, strategies and projects.

Concept Ruhr

Also dating from 2007, it represents the cooperation of 41 cities (with nearly 400 projects) for insuring sustainable development practices in the coming decades.

Chance of Change

The German government subsidises coal production costs, thus closing the gap between higher German production costs and lower global market prices for coal. In 2007, the Federal government, after intense negotiation with stakeholders in the Ruhr, decided to end the coal subsidies in 2018, reflecting new EU market rules and changes in global energy markets. Since 2008, the coal-mining cities have been cooperating in an inter-municipal working consortium 'Chance of Change' to prepare for the closure of the mines in 2018. A contract was signed in 2014 by the mayors of the cities, the state minister for economic affairs and the chief executive officers (CEOs) of the coal-mining companies to join in a public/private partnership to take on the responsibility of closing the mines and the subsequent clean-up, conversion and development of the sites.

European Capital of Culture 2010 (RUHR.2010)

In 2010, the city of Essen was selected by the European Union to become European Capital of Culture. Essen's successful motto during the competition against other European cities was: 'Change through Culture – Culture through Change'. There had been internal agreement with all the cities of the Ruhr that the bid by Essen would represent the region. If Essen won, the whole region would celebrate the Capital of Culture in 2010. Regional cooperation and trust were again a basis for success in the Ruhr. Essen, and the Ruhr, won the competition because of the recognition by the EU competition jury of the value of industrial heritage as the basis for economic, social and ecological renewal. The Essen bid was not only about creating something new for the year 2010 but was also built on the success of the Ruhrtriennale (1989–1999) and the celebration of the industrial sites that had been converted since the 1980s. Nearly 6,000 events were organised for the 2010 Capital of Culture. Over 10.5 million people visited Essen and the Ruhr in 2010, affirming for the people of the Ruhr that their strategy for redevelopment based on industrial heritage was of international significance.

Innovation City Ruhr

Another success is Innovation City Ruhr. A regional competition was held in 2010 to select one urban neighbourhood of at least 50,000 inhabitants to be converted by 2020 into a low energy consumption, energy-efficient and low climate impact community, including a 50% reduction in gas emissions by 2020. The competition was won by the city of Bottrop and its approach has become the exemplar for climate change in the Ruhr.[15]

Lessons from ELP

Strategic and voluntary cooperation at regional and local level, politically and technically, has been essential to realising the vision and to delivering the new regional park system. Cooperation is based on trust built up over time through careful moderation and inclusive management. Cooperation is unlikely to work without moderation or without the capacity to build on different capabilities and interests in space and time. This requires long-term revenue investment in core teams, not just in capital projects.

Transformation at this scale takes many years. It is necessary and desirable to reassess progress and priorities at regular intervals to refresh proposals and re-engage political support and funding.

Significant public intervention was needed in the first twenty years of the initiative to deliver change such that the private sector felt able to come on board and begin to make significant investments in the area.

Sound investment in quality projects has set a standard that continues to be met irrespective of current issues and imperatives. The Ruhr has a reputation for quality in strategies, programmes and projects; people expect this and the investment is now recouped in economic, cultural and environmental benefits.

1

Regionalverband Ruhr, ed. *Unter freiem Himmel. Emscher Landscaftspark.* (Basel: Birkhäuser, 2010).

2

The idea of working with nature reflects the thinking of landscape architect Ian McHarg. See I. McHarg, ed. *Design with Nature* (Garden City, New York: Natural History Press, 1969).

3

As early as 1979, a revolving fund (Grundstücksfonds Ruhr) was set up to facilitate the purchase and redevelopment of contaminated land. Now operating as NRW.urban, the fund has remediated over one hundred sites since 1979. D.K. Carter, ed. *Remaking Post-Industrial Cities: lessons from North America and Europe* (New York: Routledge, 2016).

4

See Wuppertal Institute: Ruhr Metropolis — European Green Capital. (2012), 78.

5

Rolf Heyer, (NRW.URBAN) *Brownfield Development (Presentation 2011). See: http://www.immo.tu-dortmund.de/EIBURS/Medienpool/ presentations_conf1/Presentation%20Heyer.pdf.*

6

The landmark Landscape Park at Duisburg Nord designed in 1991 by Latz + Partner (Peter Latz), with atmospheric lighting by Jonathan Park (London) established a paradigm shift, turning an abandoned and highly polluted blast furnace site into a remarkable 200-hectare public park where the remnants of coal and steel production were retained and act as significant features within the park. See http://www.ruhr-tourismus.de/en/staedte-im-ruhrgebiet/duisburg/landschaftspark-duisburg-nord.html.

7

K. Ganser, *Liebe auf den zweiten Blick: Internationale Bauausstellung Emscher Park* (Dortmund: Harenberg Verlag, 1999).

8

Projekt Ruhr GmbH. M. Schwarze-Rodrian et al. *Masterplan Emscher Landscaftspark* 2010, (Essen: Klartext Verlag, 2006).

9

See http://www.klimaexpo.nrw/en/join-in/projects-pioneers/themenwelt/.

10

The Zollverein industrial complex consists of the complete infrastructure of an historical coal-mining site, with some 20th-century buildings of outstanding architectural merit. It provides remarkable material evidence of the evolution and decline of an essential industry over the past 150 years. See http://whc.unesco.org/en/list/975.

11

The former Nordstern coal mine was redesigned into a landscape park for the National Garden Show in 1997 and is popular with local people and visitors. The design picks up the routes of the rail lines and former buildings in the layout of features and paths to provide some memory of the former use of the land. The principal Modern Movement buildings have been restored as visitor galleries, offices and conference venues. Most recently, the Grade II listed tower of shaft II was converted into an elevated viewing tower as part of the Capital of Culture programme. See https://www.ruhrgebiet-industriekultur.de/landschaftspark-nord.html.

12

http://www.gasometer.de/en/exhibitions/past-exhibitions/155-ausstellung-christo-bigairpackage.

13

Regionalverband Ruhr, ed. *Unter freiem Himmel. Emscher Landscaftspark.* (Basel: Birkhäuser, 2010).

14

An inter-disciplinary competition delivered a winning Masterplan Emscher Future proposal (Masterplan Emscher-Zukunft Das Neue Emschertal), which set out ideas for open spaces, urban development, ecological and water resource management and access. See http://www.astoc.de/index.php?lan=en&p=p&s=2&id=140&t=.

15

Innovation City Ruhr Region. See: www.icRuhrRegion.de/index.php?id=3&L=1.

8

The South Pennines Watershed— Conservation of a cultural landscape

Robin Gray

The 'Watershed Landscape' is the upland area of the South Pennines where east meets west, North Sea meets Irish Sea and Lancashire unites with Yorkshire. It is a distinctive landscape with high biodiversity interest, rich in archaeological evidence and with a variety of landscape types. These range from remote, expansive moorland summits to deep, secluded wooded cloughs and include the patchwork of upland in-bye pastures enclosed by a network of gritstone walls, as well as rolling farmland and sheltered, settled rural villages. The close proximity of these different landscape types, with industrial valleys dissecting the heart of the high moorland plateau, is one of the most remarkable qualities of the South Pennines.

How the open moorland landscape of the South Pennines came to look the way it does today is a complex story of human exploitation and environmental change. It is a landscape in which countless generations of Mesolithic hunter-gatherers and early farmers of the Neolithic and Bronze Ages lived and is thus one of the best places in the world to study Mesolithic remains. Moving forward to medieval times, the dual economy based on farming and domestic wool weaving provided the foundations for the later mechanised textile industry when the area became a powerhouse of the Industrial Revolution, supplying the world with Lancashire cotton and Yorkshire worsted. The Watershed Landscape is significant in providing the source of power — water and coal — that fuelled the industrial age and for the harsh conditions that prompted welfare reform and the entrepreneurial drive of its people. This industrial legacy is still tangible within the urban and rural landscape.

Culturally, the South Pennines has been described as one of Britain's greatest literary landscapes. The dramatic beauty of the landscape has inspired many writers and the hills provide the backdrop to countless novels. The raw, wild landscape is best associated with the powerful writing of the Brontë sisters of Haworth. Poet Laureate, Ted Hughes, was born locally in Mytholmroyd. The rugged moorlands and harsh, desolate post-industrial landscape provided the inspiration for many of his poems.

Despite it being a unique cultural landscape combining the dramatic wild upland setting with a heritage of national significance, the South Pennines remains one of the few uplands in England which has no statutory landscape designation. As such, it is often called a 'Cinderella landscape' and is sometimes overlooked by policymakers, politicians and tourists as a landscape of significance. The majority of the uplands is, however, designated as a Special Protection Area (covering some 21,000 hectares) and is internationally important for its breeding populations of merlin, peregrine, short-eared owl and golden plover. The moorland also supports a diverse assemblage of breeding migratory birds, especially curlew, lapwing, dunlin, snipe, redshank, skylark and twite.

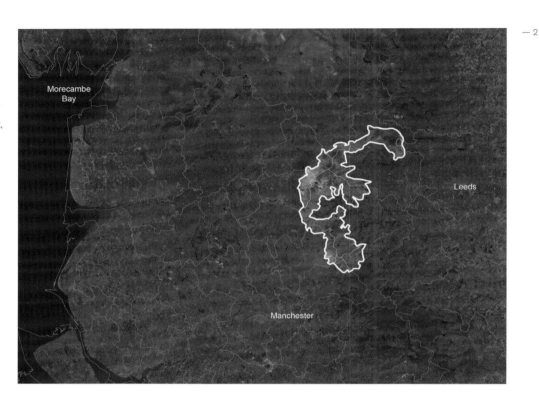

— 2

Morecambe
Bay

Leeds

Manchester

— 1
(Previous page) The Idol stone, Ilkley Moor.
— 2
Watershed project area in context.
— 3
The layers of the landscape.

— 3

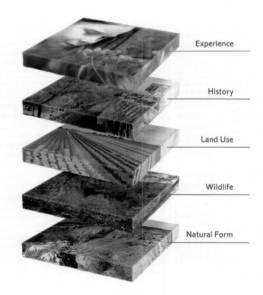

Experience

History

Land Use

Wildlife

Natural Form

"If we try to pick out anything by itself, we find it hitched to everything else in the universe." [1]

Today, the South Pennine uplands provide a range of 'ecosystem services' to the people who live on their fringes. These include vital services such as clean drinking water from upland reservoirs and flood mitigation. Over 70% of the area's water supply comes from the uplands and it has one of the greatest concentrations of reservoirs (at least 35) in the world, the oldest built over 200 years ago. The uplands also provide an essential source of free and healthy recreation for those who are able to access the countryside directly, such as walkers, cyclists and riders. This is an accessible but fragile wilderness with resources that have critical environmental significance, such as the ability of blanket bog to store carbon. Climate change and more extreme events threaten these resources, whether it is through wildfire or loss of bare or eroded peat through runoff.

Peat has been damaged through over-grazing and misguided past efforts to drain the uplands. Nearly 1 million cubic metres of moorland peat was removed in the 1960s to create the nationally important M62 east—west motorway link across the South Pennines, creating both a shop window for the area but also representing an encroachment into a cultural wilderness. The structure of peat bogs continues to be critically harmed through wildfire which, in turn, impacts on water quality and on ground nesting birds. Given the fact that peatlands contain more carbon than any other terrestrial ecosystem on earth, it is these key messages that Pennine Prospects sought to bring to urban audiences through the 'Watershed Landscape Project'.

In 2004, the Heritage Lottery Fund launched its Landscape Partnerships programme. This presented a small rural regeneration company in the South Pennines, Pennine Prospects, with the opportunity to address some of the long standing issues relating to the degradation of the South Pennines upland environment, alongside initiatives to promote the historical and contemporary importance of this landscape both to local residents and, further afield, to our urban hinterland. The South Pennines Watershed Landscape Project, covering 350 square kilometres of the South Pennines uplands, was part of the Heritage Lottery Fund's national Landscape Partnership programme. The project managed by Pennine Prospects received investment from the Fund between April 2010 and December 2013. The bid brought together six local authorities: Bradford, Calderdale, Kirklees, Lancashire, Oldham and Rochdale with Natural England; major landowners, such as United Utilities, Yorkshire Water and the National Trust; and organisations from the private and voluntary sector, such as the RSPB, Groundwork and The Conservation Volunteers. Over the three years of the Watershed Landscape programme, £2.8 million was invested in the South Pennines upland landscape. The project benefited from a grant of £1.87 million from the Heritage Lottery Fund Landscape Partnership programme, £427,000 from South Pennines LEADER and over £700,000 from the 14 project partners. Twenty-eight projects within six themes were delivered to tell the story of the Watershed Landscape, managed by a small team including a project manager, a support officer, a community archaeologist and an interpretation officer. The project was the recipient of the UK Landscape Award in 2012 and a runner-up in the National Lottery Awards: Environment category. There are six themes that underpin the project.

Theme 1: Access to the Water Catchment

This theme focused on selected key visitor points
and addressed the quality of the visitor experience –
creation of, and improvements to, paths, layout of car
parks, signage, habitat improvements and landscape
restoration – alongside interpretation of the features of
the landscape. These 'gateway' projects largely aimed
at creating clear and easily accessed routes on the
moorland edges to encourage a wider range of general
users to explore and enjoy the reservoir landscape but
also included bridleway links and mountain bike trails.
For example, the reservoirs lent themselves to the
provision of easy access trails around the water bodies
through the Reservoir Trails project.

Theme 2: Historic Environment

Improving understanding of the historic development
of the current landscape was key to telling the story.
For example, the underlying geology is essential for our
water supply, explains our landscape and is revealed at
a number of old quarry sites and yet was under-
recorded. Other sites are of international significance
for the many Bronze Age inscribed stones ('cup and
ring' stones). Critical within this theme was the appointment of a community archaeologist for the South
Pennines – the first such appointment for this part of
the world. Through the Watershed Landscape project,
a team of dedicated volunteers recorded almost 500
Neolithic and Bronze Age carved stones, some of them
previously unsurveyed. The team used both new
(including photogrammetry and geo-physical techniques)
and old technology to create records that are publicly
available. The project was recognised by being
awarded a Laureate in the European Union Prize for
Cultural Heritage / Europa Nostra Awards 2013 where
it was the only UK winner in the Education, Training and
Awareness-raising category.

"The jury thought the South Pennines Watershed Landscape a most impressive project for raising
awareness of a rich natural and archaeological heritage.
Impressive in scale and multidisciplinary approach,
it tells fascinating stories, ensuring sustainable
protection of the cultural landscape and enhancing
regional development." [2]

Theme 3: Natural Heritage – the Enhancement of Landscapes

This measure focused on landscape-wide measures
to enhance habitats and species of national importance
under threat, in particular blanket bog, a priority habitat
of international importance, and acid grasslands where
the last remaining breeding pairs of twite in England
breed. Through the Twite Recovery project managed
by the RSPB, and working with 40 landowners and
farmers, 449 hectares of flower-rich hay meadows were
restored. These were adjacent to the moors where twite
can forage – essential to their continued presence.

Theme 4: Engaging Audiences – Inspired by Landscape

This theme focused on the celebration of local culture, using the creative arts as a means of engaging audiences. Over the past centuries, both writers and artists have found the unique sense of place that is generated by the South Pennines moorlands to be a rich source of inspiration from the Brontës to Ted Hughes. Managed by Bradford Museums and Galleries, the 'Inspired by Landscape' theme encouraged people to develop their own understanding and appreciation of the landscape and to use it in their creative activity. Three artists and three writers were appointed to work with communities and groups. Ten exhibitions in museums, galleries, visitor centres and a shop window sought to bring an urban audience to gain a new understanding of the upland environment.

Theme 5: Interpretation and Engagement – Understanding and Enjoying the Landscape

"They've seen it from cars, but not been up there. They might have looked out of the window before and thought there's nothing there, but now they know there is..." [3]

One of the main objectives of the project was to raise awareness of the significance and value of the upland landscape in our towns and cities. Activities included preparation of high quality publications, an interactive website, educational resources and displays at two visitor centres and trails, as well as a travelling display. Community engagement was an integral part of all projects, including schools work, guided walks and events with over 8,000 pupils from 200 colleges and schools taking part in classroom-based activities from poetry writing to geocaching.

Theme 6: Learning – For Now and the Future

Overall, the project worked with over 1,500 volunteers who gave over 15,000 hours of their time. This provided a wide range of training opportunities ranging from field survey techniques through the Twite Recovery project to vocational certificates in drystone walling. Eight full-time equivalent jobs were created, 80 training days with 400 participants were delivered and over 50 vocational qualifications were awarded. Perhaps the greatest investment of the project was the four young apprentices employed through the National Trust and Oldham Council, who all secured both NVQ Level II in Environmental Conservation and full-time jobs through the project.

"It's really helpful, not just for my CV, but also teaches me more about the sector and helps improves my skills." [4]

—4.1

—4.2

—4.3

—4.4

—4.5

—4.6

— 4.1
The Pennine Bridleway.
— 4.2
The Idol Stone with children.
— 4.3
Top Withins, reputedly the inspiration for
Wuthering Heights.
— 4.4
Sculptor Peter Maris at the Stanza Stone,
Scammonden Reservoir.
— 4.5
Interpretive Trail, Worsthorne Moore.
— 4.6
Working with children with hearing difficulties on
the Watershed Landscape.

Reflection and Interpretation –
vision, rationale, critical factors

At the inception of the project there was a belief within Pennine Prospects that informing, changing and shaping the way people think about their surrounding landscape can bring significant environmental, cultural and societal benefits. The Company was inspired by the common purpose between the objectives of the Heritage Lottery Fund's Landscape Partnership programme and the European Landscape Convention 2007:

"Why and how society values landscapes needs to be better captured, translated and fully represented in decision-making. The public should have greater involvement in the management, planning and protection of landscapes, so that as landscapes evolve they can continue to exhibit the characteristics and functions that society values, and reinforce connections between people, place and local identity." [5]

The power of landscape to inspire communities and the individuals that use them is profound. In focus groups individuals related how the landscape had fundamentally supported them through both the best and worst times in their lives.

"When I am sat there nothing can get to me, no one can bother me but anywhere else it can. When I am sat there I hardly get anyone walking past. It is just de-stressing" [6]

Not only will the physical improvements such as the repaired drystone walls and the improved moorland footpaths remain there for many years but the way we now think about the South Pennines will make a difference. For example, in some cases, the programme has resulted in an appetite for volunteers to work independently on a landscape scale across the South Pennines.

The project was designed to improve our understanding of the role that the moorlands have played in providing resources for society in the past and their pivotal future role in addressing climate change issues – flood management, carbon sequestration and renewable energy. This understanding enables us to secure political will and funding to protect and enhance those key features of the landscape that make it not only a unique place but one that continues to be nationally and internationally significant for biodiversity, ecosystems and heritage. The programme also contributes to the current moves to bring payments for 'ecosystem services' to the forefront of both policy and private enterprise. The legacy of our work continues to encourage greater understanding and enjoyment of the special landscape, so that it is further valued and protected, providing a healthy and thriving multifunctional landscape for today's society.

Outcomes – changes, successes, why and how

There were also obvious environmental benefits from many of the projects: nearly 30 hectares of moorland restoration, 449 hectares of haymeadow restoration and 2.5 hectares of woodland creation resulted in rehabilitated habitats.

The biggest barrier in engaging with any heritage asset is an audience not knowing about its existence. Being a 'hidden gem' may be a niche selling point for some heritage features but it does not bring engagement with a diverse range and volume of people. The programme informed people about the heritage on their doorstep so they could appreciate, engage and even become an advocate for it. It has also improved understanding about the role of moorlands in carbon sequestration and flood management. It has changed the way new and returning visitors think about or use the landscape. It has also, in many cases, removed the perceived social, economic or physical barriers to access. Overall, a greater number of people are more deeply engaged in understanding and caring for their local landscape.

"My understanding of the moor and the area that I look at and visit every day is increased 100-fold. I get much more out of walking on there than I ever did before." [7]

Learning – lessons and knowledge transfer

The following lessons can be drawn from the project:

— There is an appetite within local communities to engage wit their upland heritage through activities such as education and volunteering.
— Partnerships can deliver landscape change. Through capital and physical improvements to the landscape, there is delivery of real social and economic benefits.
— There is a pay off between the size of the project area and the impact on local residents, particularly when dealing with such a large urban hinterland, including major cities. Projects should fit together as a coherent whole and present a strong narrative that enables the entire project to benefit from wider recognition.
— Partnerships take time and resources to build capacity and achieve results on the ground. Landscape partnerships should be realistic about the level of project delivery in the early phase of the programme.
— Project planning has to be strong and robust enough to ensure continuity and meet the challenges of changing circumstances.
— Celebrating the success of the project is important and the value of this should not be underestimated. For the South Pennines, national and international awards have helped to reinforce partner and local community engagement.

This award-winning landscape project has not only engaged people but in some cases has had a prolonged and profound impact on people's lives. Perhaps one of the greatest achievements of the Watershed Landscape project has been to shine the spotlight on the amazing heritage of this unique area and to signpost ways to engage with it.

"It's knowing that these plants are going to be planted on the moor and they are going to improve the area. It's not something we have just gone through the process of doing. It is a live project that is happening. I am helping to restore these areas." [8]

Update – how things have moved on

The legacy of the programme can be seen in the physical improvements to the landscape, the scale of engagement, the range of partnership and collaborative working and the cultural shift in collective understanding of the power of landscape change at scale. The Watershed Landscape project for the first time brought about recognition of the South Pennines as a distinct landscape, successfully crossing borders, creating a sense of one landscape across typically divided administrative areas. The project overall has begun to make a strategic difference across the landscape. This has become implicit in all the work done. The recognition of the South Pennines as a Local Nature Partnership by the UK Government in 2012 has formalised this relationship with a continuation of some of the elements of the project such as haymeadow restoration within 'green infrastructure' planning at the city-region scale. In 2015, the Moors for the Future Partnership, hosted by the Peak District National Park, was awarded the largest ever EU LIFE award for the protection of active blanket bog throughout the South Pennines Special Area of Conservation. Over the next five years, there will be investment of €16 million in restoring active blanket bog. The South Pennines Partnership is proud to be an active partner in delivering this critical work.[9]

1
John Muir, Scottish-American naturalist, author, environmental philosopher and early advocate of preservation of wilderness in the United States.

2
The project was recognised as a Laureate in the European Union Prize for Cultural Heritage in the Europa Nostra Awards of 2013 where it was the only UK winner in the Education, Training and Awareness-raising category.

3
A quote from a teacher from Halifax.

4
A quote from an apprentice from Oldham.

5
Natural England, *Position Statement: All Landscapes Matter* (Natural England, 2010) http://webarchive.nationalarchives.gov.uk/20101015025248/http://www.naturaleng-land.org.uk/Images/ALM-ps_tcm6-17120.pdf

6
From workshops facilitated by Pennine Prospects and Natural England, Natural England, 2013, accessed November 2015, http://publications.naturalengland.org.uk/publication/4612053188739072.

7
Project volunteer, Rombalds Moor.

8
Volunteer at Offshoots Permaculture Project.

9
Peak District National Park, Moors for the Future Partnership, accessed November 2015, http://www.moorsforthefuture.org.uk/news/largest-award-eu-life-programme-uk-conservation.

9

Philadelphia—
The 'Green City,
Clean Waters' programme

Howard Neukrug

Overview

Following a massive, capital intensive rebuilding of the US wastewater treatment systems and new laws governing the discharge of industrial waste into the nation's rivers and streams, there has been a sea change in how US cities consider water pollution. Largely, all of the 'point-source' dischargers are well-managed and, as a result, it is now possible to see more clearly the harm caused by too much storm water runoff on water scarcity, flooding, pollution, erosion and fish habitat.

Today, the choice to manage runoff is between grand schemes for large underground storage or tunnel systems and a newer, softer, greener approach of managing water where the rain falls, rather than washing the rainwater down the drain. The US has come once again to value rainfall and to capture it, use it and filter it into the groundwater system. Rain has become a part of a concept of 'One Water' where all sources, reservoirs and discharges of water are a part of one system to be managed in a coordinated and integrated fashion. What is fascinating about this change is that it coincides so well with city leaders' efforts for greener, more liveable cities.

A greener city meets cleaner water

'Green City, Clean Waters' (GCCW) is a City of
Philadelphia programme designed to reduce the
amount of polluted stormwater runoff that enters the
city's rivers and streams. Unlike conventional stormwater management programmes in the US and elsewhere,
this does not rely solely on increasing the capacity of
sewer and treatment plants to manage an increasing
rainwater load. Like many cities globally, Philadelphia is
experiencing unusually heavy intensity, short duration
but more frequent rain events over its highly impervious
ground cover.

     GCCW aims to conserve rainwater, meaning
that rainwater is now valued as an urban asset and not
as a wastewater product. Rather than discarding the
rainwater down a stormwater drain as swiftly as possible, the intent now is to use it to improve the quality of
urban life. Philadelphia wants to use water management techniques to balance nature, development and
people in the urban setting.

Philadelphia, located in the north-eastern United
States, was America's first capital city and, at the turn
of the 20th century, was among the world's greatest
industrial cities. Following a 25% loss of population
over the past 50 years, Philadelphia is transforming
again, this time into a beautiful, vibrant, green city, a
destination for tourists and a great place to live, work
and study.

     However, the storm water system can surcharge
during even small rain events and result in sewage,
trash and flooding in the system of rivers and streams.
Increasing sewer capacity, through the construction
of ever-bigger pipes, tunnels and pumping stations,
can no longer be considered affordable, justifiable
nor sustainable.

     To reduce demand on the sewer system, the
GCCW programme uses a range of 'green stormwater infrastructure' (GSI) soil-water-plant systems to
intercept stormwater, infiltrate a portion of it into the

ground, evaporate and transpire a portion into the air and, in some cases, slowly release a portion back into the sewer system.

Philadelphia Water (PW), like many urban water utilities around the world, is creating a greener, more environmentally sustainable water system that not only improves water quality and the water environment but also the city's resilience to storms, spills and security threats. At the same time, Philadelphia, as a city, is seeking opportunities to use urban redevelopment as a leverage point for coordinating and integrating key system services so as to create a more sustainable, attractive and liveable city.

PW has begun a process to partner, coordinate and integrate its water infrastructure operations and capital improvements into the fabric of the city and, by so doing, has begun a process of leveraging its water capital with parks, schoolyards, businesses, homes, recreation centres, universities and more.

An Introduction to Urban Systems

Cities are in a constant state of change. Today, many cities are seeking a future that is both sustainable and resilient (in terms of social, environmental and economic conditions). The systems that make up a city — its water, energy, telecom and transportation systems; or its schools, parks, libraries and public welfare systems (to name a few) — are most often managed independently of each other. For example, if the public school system wants to upgrade its library system, it is somewhat likely that it would not consult the Public Library System. Each has its own sets of governance, constituents, budgets and missions. Aligning the two may have an obvious set of rewards in leveraging operating funds, book purchases or the joint use of common space but doing so may be extremely complex bureaucratically and politically.

The US water industry is, likewise, highly segmented, meaning that the individual systems of drinking water, wastewater, stormwater, flooding and water resource management, among others, have until recently been governed, engineered and managed independently. Today, the US is moving towards a 'One Water' approach to integrating water management and these silos are beginning to fall. Water conservation is no longer solely about water scarcity; it now includes other concerns such as energy, terrorism, waste treatment capacities and poverty.

The Water Utility–City Nexus

There is one very big area, however, that has remained largely outside the
purview of the water industry – urban land management and its control.
As we learn more about the full impact of urban land use decisions on
water quality and quantity, it is becoming harder and harder to integrate
water sectors without addressing the complexity of the urban systems of
land management.

How is it possible, for example, to integrate and coordinate the
construction and rebuilding of public roads, public spaces and private development to most efficiently and effectively manage water resources, prevent
pollution and create a cohesive, leveraged and sustainable city system?

Opportunities abound! There is urgent need in the US for a new
generation of infrastructure to replace existing but ageing water and sewer
pipe networks. These systems, largely designed and built between the
1880s and the 1940s, are wearing out and becoming obsolete. The grand
problems they solved at the turn of the 20th century (typhoid, sanitation,
delivery of water, etc.) have not kept pace with new, 21st century threats
(emerging pathogens, Cyanotoxins, heavy metals, sewer overflows,
drought, floods, etc.).

The costs to rebuild these systems in the US is estimated at over
$1 trillion and come at a time when the economy can ill afford this outlay,
much less the plethora of other challenges facing 21st century urban
America, such as those attributed to changes in climate, economy, security
and demographics, as well as societal responses to urban issues of
environmental justice and economic inequity.[1]

As we rethink and rebuild our urban centres as sustainable,
attractive and productive places to live and work we are also engineering
them to be more resilient to natural and man-made disturbances. It will
take vision and leadership to overcome the multiple barriers that confront
us in finding local solutions for our global water problems and to do so in
a way that supports a liveable, growing and sustainable city. Given the level
of spending about to take place in urban water systems, it is an ideal time
to integrate environmental protection strategies and responsible land use
and zoning with infrastructure improvements through the use of integrated
urban systems thinking.

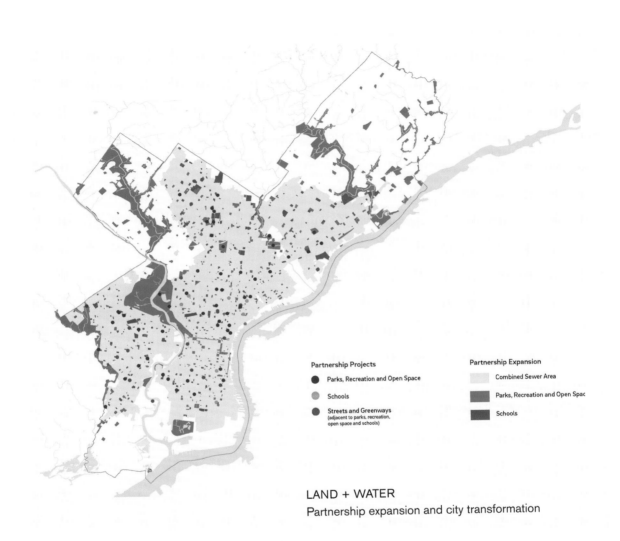

Partnership Projects

● Parks, Recreation and Open Space

● Schools

● Streets and Greenways
(adjacent to parks, recreation,
open space and schools)

Partnership Expansion

Combined Sewer Area

Parks, Recreation and Open Spac

Schools

LAND + WATER
Partnership expansion and city transformation

— 1
Watershed management.

Managing the overflow of raw sewage into rivers and streams

The most significant new programmatic costs to PW are the costs for reducing the overflow of raw sewage into the system of rivers and streams. Up until the 1950s, most of Philadelphia's wastewater was discharged largely untreated directly into rivers. Since that time, the city has invested billions of dollars to build modern and effective water pollution control plants (WPCPs) to treat the wastewater to levels cleaner than the river water itself. Today, PW operates some of the most state-of-the-art, complex and efficient wastewater facilities in the world.

No matter how advanced the facilities are, a problem remains. Nearly every time it rains, the capacity of the sewer network and the pumping and treatment facilities is not sufficiently great to capture and treat all of the polluted surface water that is generated. In fact, only about 67% of the combined sewage/rainfall is 'captured' – the rest continues to pollute the city's rivers and streams. This is unacceptable under the Clean Water Act.[2] Cities across the country are spending many billions of dollars expanding their sewer system to increase capacity. In essence, the cost of managing the rainfall is no longer a hidden fee or tax paid by direct discharge to our streams: it is a new cost to cities and suburbs for years of urbanisation.

A Federal Consent Order signed by Mayor Nutter and the author in September 2012 with the US Environmental Protection Agency (USEPA) and the Pennsylvania Department of Environmental Protection marked a major turning point for Philadelphia and the nation. For the first time ever, it recognised that reduction in demand on the existing sewer system is a positive alternative to increased sewer capacity.

This has enabled partnership working with the City Council, neighbours, Streets Department, City Planning, Parks and Recreation, schools, universities, businesses, parking operators, vacant land, strip malls, hospitals and churches to rethink how rainwater is managed on land and to reuse, recycle, infiltrate and transpire this water rather than simply discharge it into the drainage system.

This approach is not easy to prosecute but for a city of limited financial resources, the $1.2 billion cost over 25 years to evolve the drainage system surely seems to beat the approach of expending $8 billion or more on large, new sewer systems under our homes, parks, streets and rivers.

Working with climate change goals and other city sustainability initiatives

The 2008 mayor's race in Philadelphia unfolded with the election of Mayor Michael Nutter and a very strong mandate for green progressive thinking in the city. Fulfilling a campaign promise, Mayor Nutter formed an Office of Sustainability that spent its first two years developing a policy and benchmarking document for meeting new sustainability goals that addressed issues of energy, green space and water.

This was extremely fortunate for PW, which was, at the time, negotiating with the USEPA on its GCCW programme. This programme called for the conversion of 4,047 hectares (10,000 acres) of impervious land that currently drains to the sewer system into 'Greened Acres' where the first 25 millimetres (1 inch) of rainfall is managed in an environmentally sensitive manner.

These actions helped build consensus and soon many city departments and businesses wished to join the initiative – the City's Streets Department introduced litter control and 'complete streets' as well as bicycle lane projects. The Parks group began a one million tree planting campaign with its non-profit partner, the Pennsylvania Horticultural Society. The Schools District became interested in schemes to 'green' asphalt school-yards and the City Planning Department developed an environmentally friendly 'Plan 2035'.

Most importantly, the citizens of Philadelphia have become involved at all levels and all ages. From pro-grammes for rain barrels and home-situated rain gardens to science, technical, engineering and maths lessons in water management in schools, through to community groups repairing vacant lots and protecting their new neighbourhood parks, everyone is able to be involved.

— 2
Philadelphia Streets Department introduced litter control and 'complete streets' with bicycle lanes and sustainable urban drainage - before and after

— 3a

— 3b

— 3

The 'greening' of school yards programme –
before and after. William Dick Elementary School,
Lower North, Philadelphia.

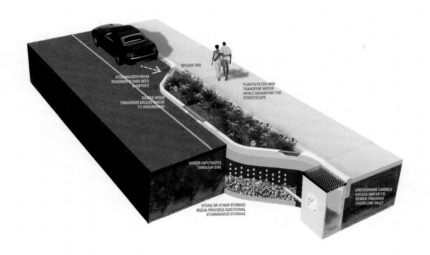

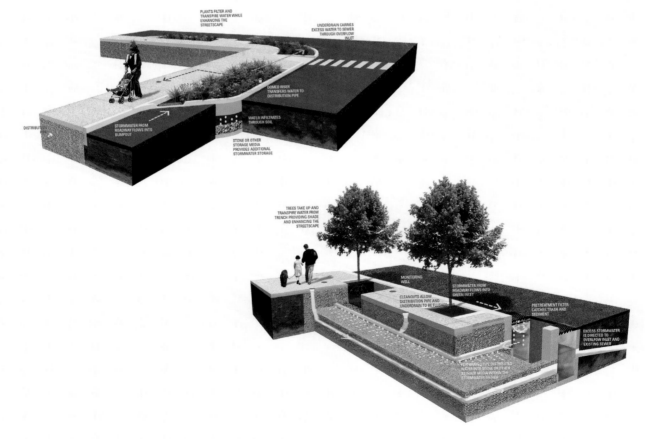

— 4
The design of the 'complete streets'
programme.

— 5a

— 5b

— 5
Examples of sustainable urban
drainage including the use of
porous asphalt.

Using regulations, fees and incentives
and 'inciting the masses' to drive change

During this period of progressive green thinking in Philadelphia, the water
utility was able to embed a number of programmes, regulations and policies
to support its own goals of water quality and the city's goals to improve
liveability, jobs and sustainability.

Perhaps most importantly, the driver for change began with new
stormwater development regulations. In old, industrial cities like Philadelphia,
most development is not on 'green' or undisturbed sites but is through the
redevelopment of land and property. The development community was not
thrilled with the adoption of new regulations that added to the design and
construction costs of a new building. Everyone accepted that plumbing
was needed to run drinking water into the premises and wastewater out but
stormwater was considered 'free' – to be collected by the landowner and
discharged to the sewer. In the old logic of an old city, the sewer capacity
was unlimited, since any overflow just went to the river.

To support the development community, PW quickly learned that time
is money and to compensate for the new costs, it began to issue 'expedited
permits' for green roofs and porous pavement projects. The Authority also
provided engineering expertise and support early on in the conceptual project
design phase. The process took some time to overcome initial misgivings
and build trust between the partners, to find reasonable processes that
allowed for both storm water management and development, but in the end
the process resulted in a city with new modern building designs that led to
Leadership in Energy and Environmental Design (LEED) certifications and
increased market value, as well as a city able to export its architectural and
engineering prowess to other cities across the US.[3] In time, Philadelphia
had plumbers, builders and developers taking pride in a new sense of what
they could accomplish to improve the environment.

— 5c

— 6a

—6
Introduction of
sustainable urban
drainage into
garden areas.

— 6b

— 6c

In 2015, PW worked with the development community in an inclusive process to revise the regulations to provide enhanced management of runoff – from the first 25–37.5 millimetres (1–1.5 inches) of rainfall – together with new incentives for developers to use 'green' alternatives for stormwater management. One stakeholder described working with the development services committee to address changes in the regulations as: "tremendously supportive in helping us understand proposed changes, as well as understand the viewpoints of different members of the development community." This was a very useful dialogue described as: "democracy the way it was intended to be."

In 2006, there was one green roof in Philadelphia. By the end of 2015, there were nearly 150. In the process, an industry was born. Design, construction and maintenance of green roofs became a new business for Philadelphia and green jobs were expanded across the city. Stormwater Development Regulations have helped catalyse a best-in-class GSI industry cluster in Philadelphia, with meaningful consequences for the local economy.[4]

In 2011, perhaps the most important element of a green stormwater programme was put in place based on a billing system for deriving revenues for the proposed $150 million (around £103 million) 'stormwater utility'. For the first time in Philadelphia, rainfall was 'commoditised'. The gross area of every property parcel in Philadelphia was calculated and priced such that every property owner was paying their 'fair share' for managing the rainwater.

This provided the opportunity for private landowners – and government agencies – to reduce their stormwater fees by managing the runoff from their property. In essence, Philadelphia put in place a credit incentives programme for property owners to move off the City's system to decentralised stormwater management. To assist landowners in making the conversion of land into green stormwater management systems, PW also developed a grants program to further incentivise property owners to retrofit their systems.

Perhaps the most rewarding return on investment is watching community groups urge the water utility and the politicians to make changes in their community – whether on a basketball court, a schoolyard or a vacant lot. In many cases, the Water Authority was accused by developers of 'inciting the masses' by encouraging the community to demand green improvement where monies may or may not be available, since water money can support water projects, and when picnic tables or play equipment are involved, other funding sources must be leveraged in support.

At its core, the investment in GCCW has met a triple bottom line goal of improving the environment while making Philadelphia a greener, more viable place to live and work. The city's vision and ability to turn around its water management in ways that add value to urban life have been recognised across the world. As well as other US cities, Philadelphia's experience is providing new ideas and knowledge to cities such as Glasgow, Turin, London and Dublin.

— 7

— 7
The public campaign to
bring people onside.
— 8
Fishfest 2014.

— 8

— 9
Water at the heart
of Philadelphia.

1
http://www.awwa.org/Portals/0/files/legreg/documents/
BuriedNoLonger.pdf.

2
For further information on the Clean Water Act, United States,
see http://www.eoearth.org/view/article/151133/.

3
http://www.usgbc.org/leed.

4
http://gsipartners.sbnphiladelphia.org/wp-content/uploads/
2016/02/SBN_FINAL-REPORT.pdf.

10

The Lowland Canal Network— Creating places and destinations

Richard Millar

Scotland's 250-year-old canals were once the thoroughfares that provided the transportation system to support the Industrial Revolution – arteries that carried goods, passengers and life across the nation and transformed the communities along their banks. Today, these waterways have become a recreation network for many. The days of the coal scows and the Clydesdale horses that pulled them are gone. They have been replaced today with venues for business, leisure and tourism (attracting more than 22 million visits each year) that are helping to drive regeneration and positive transformation through innovative projects on the water, the banks and beyond.

The geography of Scotland's canals is that of Scotland itself, extending over a network of 220 kilometres (137 miles) from coast to coast. From Neptune's Staircase on the Caledonian Canal to the iconic engineering of The Falkirk Wheel and The Kelpies in the Lowlands, Scotland's canals have had a long and sometimes turbulent history since they were first excavated in the eighteenth century and they have witnessed decades of growth followed by many years of decline before their current renaissance. Throughout this long history, the nation's waterways have been a constant feature in our most populous cities, rural villages and open countryside.

Offering sea-to-sea navigation and sustainable, cheap transport, the glory days of the canals were a vital part of industry and innovation. From the creation of the iconic Clyde Puffers and the Charlotte Dundas – the world's first steamship – to the development of the largest sewing machine factory in the world at Clydebank, Scotland's inland waterways were beacons of cutting-edge engineering and industry. From dynamite factories to whisky bonds and ironworks, local employment was plentiful in the industries alongside the canals and the waterways became a defining feature of many local communities.

The glory days of Scotland's canals continued for more than a century before the introduction of rail transformed transportation and signalled the obsolescence of water as an inland transportation system. Trains gradually replaced barges as the chosen mode of transport for both passengers and goods and the sound of industry changed too from the gentle work of heavy horses on the towpaths to the strident urgency of the steam whistle and rhythmic thrum of plant and machinery. By the mid-1960s, the canals had fallen into decline and become unloved backwaters. They were seen as an outmoded form of transport, a barrier to development and a danger to local communities. As a consequence, both the Forth & Clyde Canal and the Union Canal were closed. The Monkland Canal suffered most with sections infilled to make way for the M8 motorway.

— 1
The lowland canals
before regeneration.
— 2
The lowland canals
following volunteer work
and regeneration.

— 1

— 2a

With no life on the water and no one to care for the canals, nature took over. The waterways became overgrown with weeds and filled with rubbish, while the canal-side infrastructure crumbled from lack of maintenance. In spite of these privations, the canals remained much loved by the communities along their banks and many volunteer groups provided support and assistance during a vital period when no official or commercial support was present. Enthusiasts, volunteers, campaigners and local societies worked for decades, running events, celebrating the heritage of the canal network and lobbying to reopen the waterways. The Millennium Link project was the result of that hard work and serves as an enduring legacy for the many volunteers who made the rebirth of the nation's man-made waterways possible.

— 2b

The Millennium Link and the Falkirk Wheel

The Millennium Link is the largest canal project undertaken in Britain and the £84.5 million investment returned Scotland's canals to a navigable state for the first time in almost four decades. The project saw the opening or refurbishment of: 45 canal bridges; 28 road bridges; the construction or refurbishment of 41 locks; and the creation of more than 5 kilometres of new canal, as well as the removal of 300,000 tonnes of silt.

The realisation of the Millennium Link was, in essence, a strategy to bring life back to Scotland's canals and into the heart of the communities nationwide but it was the signature project, The Falkirk Wheel, which captured imagination around the world and served as an enduring symbol of the renaissance of Scotland's historic canal system.

The Falkirk Wheel opened in 2002 after the remediation and transformation of a heavily contaminated former tar works and the replacement of a flight of 11 locks that had formerly stepped the Union Canal down to the level of the Forth & Clyde, in the process dropping the waterway 35 metres over a distance of 1.5 kilometres. Whereas travellers once had a day's heavy work to open and close 44 lock gates to complete the journey between the two canals, The Falkirk Wheel allows vessels to be moved between the two waterways in just a few minutes. The Falkirk Wheel is now Scotland's busiest tourist attraction outside of the principal cities and attracts around 500,000 domestic and international visitors each year to experience the combination of sculpture, engineering and technology employing ancient principles established by Archimedes more than 2,000 years ago.[1]

When one of the structure's gondolas is lowered, the opposite one rises, balancing the 1,800 tonne boats and lifting canal barges 35 metres into the air in a matter of minutes. Each of the gondolas holds 500,000 litres of water — enough to fill an Olympic swimming pool and because of the design and application of balance and weight, it takes only 1.5 kilowatt hours for each rotation — the equivalent power to boil eight domestic kettles. In 2013, the International Federation of Consulting Engineers (FIDIC) — an organisation representing consulting engineers in more than 80 countries — judged the iconic design of the Wheel to rank alongside the achievements and reputation of the Hoover Dam and the Channel Tunnel, as one of the most significant civil engineering projects of the last one hundred years.[2]

The Millennium Link and The Falkirk Wheel are examples of the transformative power of signature projects when backed by an engaged and empowered community. Without this 'buy-in', passion and support, the canals of Scotland may have continued to languish as unloved backwaters and the renaissance they enjoy today may never have started. The experience of the Millennium Link is one which continues to inform the activities of Scottish Canals today (from supporting third sector organisations, such as the Forth & Clyde Canal Society and the Scottish Waterways Trust, to helping social enterprises flourish along the banks and building stronger communities, working with empowered and motivated people) and remains at the core of everything the business does.

North Glasgow

A prime example of the effectiveness of this approach can be seen
at Lambhill on the Forth & Clyde Canal in Glasgow. Here, in an area
once known for long-standing issues with crime, dereliction and lack of
community assets, the Lambhill Stables project has acted as a catalyst
to change perceptions. The Stables have been present in Lambhill since
1812 – originally for the men and horses using the Forth & Clyde Canal
to transport bricks, coal and other raw materials. The decline of industries
after the Second World War and the subsequent closure of the canal led
to the decline of the area. Between the 1960s and 1990s, the Stables
were used as a garage and scrap yard before finally lying derelict. In 2004,
a group of community activists partnered with Scottish Canals and the
Big Lottery Fund to revitalise the area. The Stables were reopened for the
community in the summer of 2011 and now serve as a vital hub for locals,
providing leisure, recreation, training and employment opportunities. The
project has also transformed more than 7,500 square metres of greenspace and created a thriving community garden and allotments.

     This story of regeneration is one that has been replicated throughout
North Glasgow, with partnership working, community engagement and
innovative thinking, building on the unique green and blue assets of the
Forth & Clyde Canal, underpinning the transformation of some of Scotland's most disadvantaged areas. North Glasgow suffers from profound
health and social issues. The area is ranked highest in the country for
almost every major cause of premature death and its young people are
70% more likely to be taken into the social care system than those in the
rest of Scotland. Most shockingly, the numbers of drug and alcohol-related
mortalities in North Glasgow are respectively 223% and 119% above the
national average.[3,4]

     However, innovative use of the green and blue space of the Forth &
Clyde Canal is changing the fortunes of the area. In recent years, Scottish
Canals and its partners in the Glasgow Canal Regeneration Partnership
have undertaken a number of inventive projects designed to improve links
between the area and the city centre – overcoming the formidable barrier
of the M8 motorway – to bring new investment opportunities and increased
activity and amenity to North Glasgow.

     The first phase of the regeneration of North Glasgow – the Garscube
Landscape Link – involved the radical revitalisation of a crucial link to the
city centre which was severed by the construction of the M8 motorway in
the 1960s. The existing route was a hostile environment characterised by
dark, dirty, noisy and intimidating spaces. The new public realm has been
expanded through the motorway crossing and the surface has been unified

by a single, flowing, red resin surface that does not constrain the pedestrian or cyclist to rigid and demarcated routes. Spaces along the route are illuminated by a ribbon of 50 coloured, aluminium 'flowers', whose canopy 'flutters' through the space some 8 metres in the air to draw the visitor through the space in marked contrast with the concrete solidity of the motorway superstructure.[5] The Garscube Landscape Link has been named 'The Phoenix Flowers' in reference to the former Phoenix Park that once occupied the site in a symbolic reference to the rebirth of North Glasgow.

This fusion of art, innovation and regeneration has come to define the ongoing work to revitalise the area. Speirs Wharf, which was once a commercial hub comprising bonded warehouses, distilleries, grain mills and glassworks, is now becoming a hub for culture. A flourishing creative quarter has been established with occupants including the Royal Conservatoire of Scotland, the Glasgow Sculpture Studios, Scottish Opera and the National Theatre of Scotland, together with an extensive range of digital agencies and Turner Prize–nominated artists in the refurbished Whisky Bond. The project has helped to bring new investment, job opportunities and life to a once-neglected area of the city with the green and blue infrastructure of the Forth & Clyde Canal at the heart of a burgeoning creative community.

North Glasgow has received more than £5 million of investment in regeneration projects by Scottish Canals and its partners in recent years, supporting a network of heritage trails to connect the local community and visitors with the rich history of the area, as well as improved paths and new bridges to further improve links to the city centre. Community engagement and involvement remain at the core of the initiative, with the public interacting with an expert team of designers to develop a new masterplan for the area at a special series of public design workshops that saw more than 300 adults and children help shape the future of North Glasgow. A huge number of suggestions were put forward to further improve the public realm and create new recreational facilities and enhanced commercial opportunities, all firmly rooted in the area's proud heritage and diverse ecology.

The future of the community is also at the heart of one of the foremost successes of the North Glasgow Regeneration Partnership. Set in the Pinkston Basin on the Forth & Clyde Canal, Pinkston Watersports is Scotland's first and only competition-standard, purpose-built paddlesports venue and a key driver of the ongoing transformation of the area. Featuring white water and canoe slalom courses, a clean water basin, canoe polo pitches and classrooms, the £3.25 million centre attracts around 25,000 visitors yearly and has transformed the site of a disused power station in a disadvantaged urban area into a catalyst for regeneration and sporting success.[6]

While the centre may train the Olympians of tomorrow, this legacy project from the Commonwealth Games of 2014 is about much more than winning medals. By offering competition-grade facilities and coaching one mile from Glasgow city centre and within an hour's travel for three million of Scotland's people, Pinkston Watersports is bringing jobs and income to North Glasgow and is the latest stage in the transformation of the area.

The establishment of Pinkston has acted as the catalyst for the creation of an urban sports hub, with an inner city wakeboarding park (the only one of its kind in Scotland) opening onto the Forth & Clyde Canal. With plans in place to create an indoor skate park nearby, Pinkston is helping to offer transformational opportunities in the lives of some of Glasgow's most disadvantaged young people that cannot be found elsewhere in Scotland, thereby helping to turn an area once defined by indices of deprivation into a vibrant, active community.

Glasgow Watersports, a charitable body led by a group of volunteer watersports enthusiasts, has played a key role in driving the development of Pinkston and is responsible for the day-to-day running of the centre. Firmly community-focused, the group has trained a number of local youth leaders from the North Glasgow area to take youngsters out on the water for

— 4

The Pinkston Watersports Centre.

— 5

The Phoenix Flowers (the Garscube Landscape Link) involved the
radical revitalisation of a crucial link to the city centre which was
severed by the construction of the M8 motorway in the 1960s.

— 4a

— 4b

exercise, recreation and confidence building. This community engagement, combined with a programme of outreach activities, volunteering opportunities and close working with local authorities and social work services, aims to ensure widespread benefit for many young Scots.

By offering activities, events and training opportunities, the centre is helping to encourage the people of the area to lead more active, social and healthy lives. Young people gain skills and confidence that will improve their life options through participation in paddlesports, while training in coaching offers them the chance to follow a career path in sports and outdoor activities.

The success of the centre has been the impetus for further development in the area, with new public realm works and access improvements, including LED-lighting and new surfaces installed on the towpaths that lead to Pinkston. The centre is used throughout the day and the evening, seven days a week, with paddlers often seen walking on the new routes from the city centre with canoes and kayaks perched on their shoulders. With a busy programme of events and close community working, the centre is a unique force for change in Scotland — an urban sports hub that fosters community involvement and regeneration alongside the development of sporting excellence.

The Helix

From Pinkston to The Falkirk Wheel and beyond, the renaissance of Scotland's canals has had a significant beneficial effect on Scotland, with more
than 170,000 square metres of canal-side development undertaken, generating over £150 million in economic impact over the last decade. As well
as the benefits on the banks, the health benefits attributed to increased
usage of the canals by foot, boat and bike exceed £8 million per annum.[7]

One project, in particular, has placed the nation's inland waterways
firmly in the public eye. The £43 million Helix project has transformed 350
hectares of under-used land on the eastern stretch of the Forth & Clyde
Canal near Grangemouth into a vibrant, new parkland, canal hub and
world-class visitor attraction featuring the largest equine sculptures in the
world – The Kelpies – that form the centrepiece of this major project, which
includes a watersports lagoon, wetland, event space, a significant new
extension to the Forth & Clyde Canal, a visitor centre, several cafes and
over 27 kilometres of paths.[8]

The Helix is focused on creating connections between the many
communities, the extensive parkland and the canal itself. Local people
in the Falkirk area make the most of The Helix's resources by becoming
involved in local community projects including heritage, walking and cycling
groups, whilst the new canal, a complex section of water engineering,
dramatically improves access to the waterway. The one-kilometre extension
reunites the Forth & Clyde Canal with the town of Grangemouth where
work on the canal was begun some 250 years ago; it is the final piece of
the Millennium Link project.

The Kelpies, which tower over the Forth & Clyde Canal in the centre
of The Helix, are the world's largest pair of equine sculptures and an iconic
monument to the horse-powered heritage of the area. The inspiration for
The Kelpies came from the heavy horses which pulled boats and cargo
along the towpaths of the Forth & Clyde and Union Canals. Standing 30
metres tall, they are a striking addition to the skyline of the whole area
and a landmark on the M9 motorway joining Edinburgh with Stirling and
the Highlands. They are a symbol of the history of the waterway and an
ambitious statement for its future.

Around two million people have visited The Helix since it opened in
April 2014, generating an additional annual income of £1.5 million for the
local economy. The popularity of The Helix has also reinforced the success
of the Falkirk Wheel, which recorded its busiest year after the opening of
the Helix with some 500,000 combined visits in 2014–2015. This, in turn,
has provided the incentive to expand the tourism offering of The Falkirk
Wheel and encourage even more people to pay a visit to the area.

The Helix project and the Kelpies have been taken to the heart of the local communities and they have received widespread international recognition for the project, the area and Scotland from New Zealand to America. The three-metre high maquettes of the Kelpies that helped attract the funding to deliver the full-size sculptures have been shown across the UK and spent time in New York's Bryant Park, giving worldwide wexposure both to the project and the local area.

The sculptures were designed by Andy Scott, a Scottish artist, and they celebrate the history of the area and its role in the industrial revolution, particularly metal founding. Originally envisioned to form a moving part of the canal system, the concept evolved during the design process to become monumental symbols

of the industrial past of the canal and its communities. Scott oversaw The Kelpies from concept to reality, as a massive gateway standing abreast the entrance to the canal to welcome sailors and visitors to Scotland.

As well as attracting visitors and income to the area, the project has also been a catalyst for events. The Kelpies and The Helix provide the setting for events including touring Shakespeare troupes, poetry readings and Hogmanay festivals, with many free at point of entry. This continued animation has helped to ensure that the park has become a bustling social and recreational hub and a valuable educational resource for school pupils, college and university students, with the biodiverse wetlands and woodlands offering learning and teaching opportunities for all ages and stages.

— 6

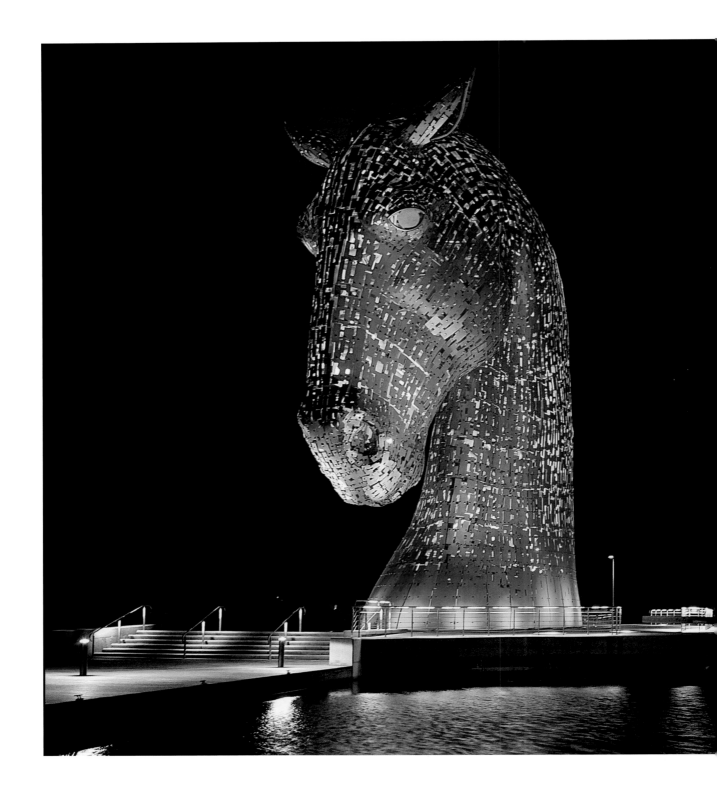

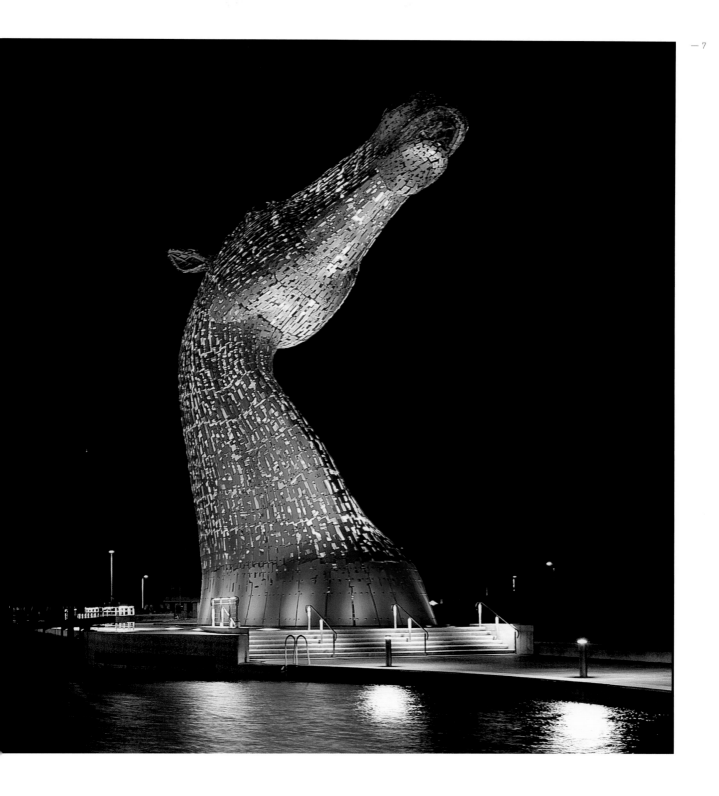

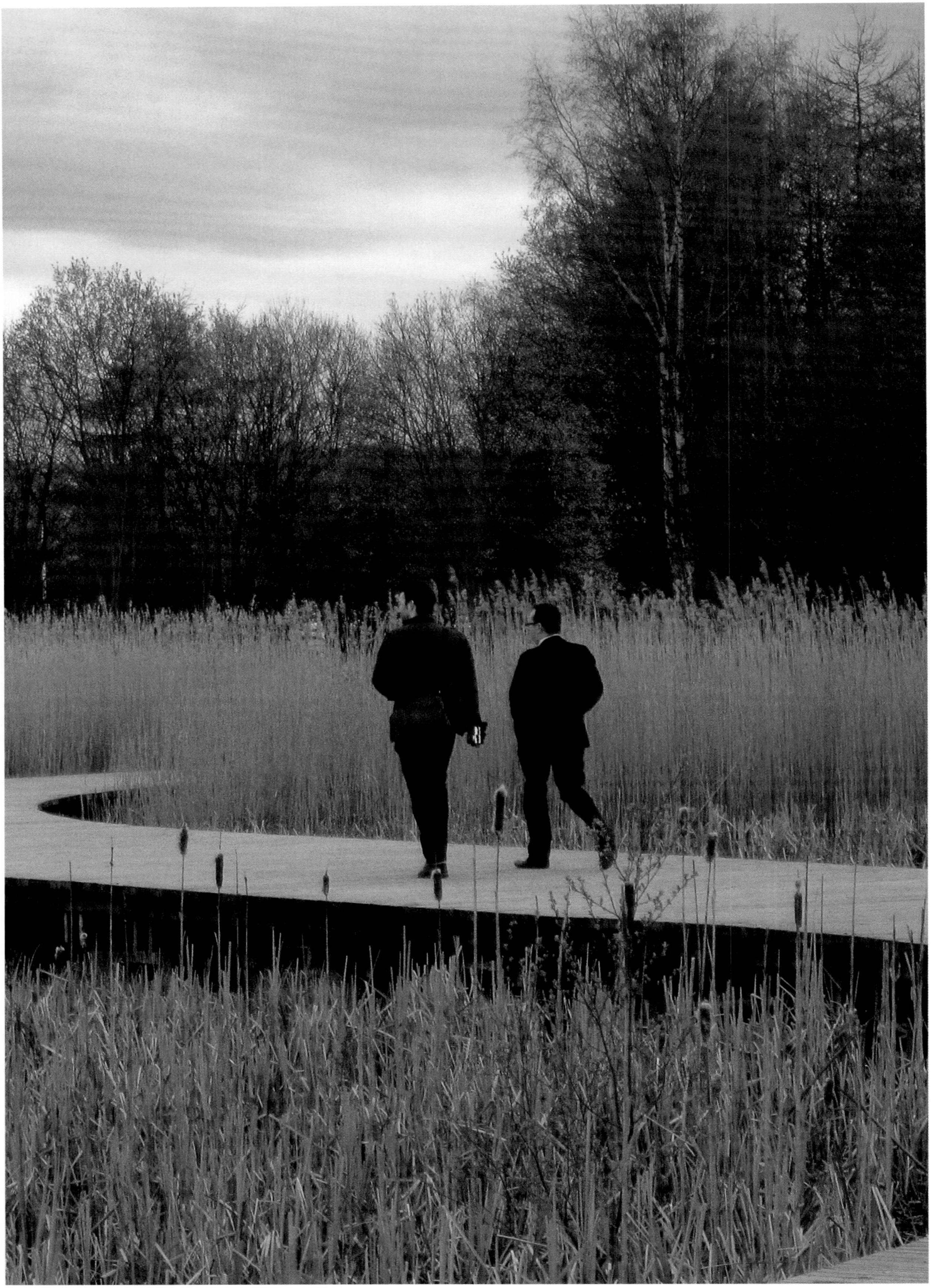

— 8
Wetland area,
Helix Park

Conclusion

The role and character of Scotland's canals have changed greatly since they served as the thorough-fares of the Industrial Revolution. Today, the water-ways play a newly reinforced and equally vital role. By combining innovative thinking, strong partnership working and community engagement, Scotland's canals have been reborn as arteries of regenera-tion, bringing social, economic and environmental benefits to the communities that line their banks and to the nation as a whole.

1
RMJM, Arup, Butterley Engineering and Tony Gee and Partners LLP worked with the British Waterways Board and staff to finalise the design of The Falkirk Wheel.

2
http://fidic.org/node/3200

3
Glasgow Centre for Population Health, *A Community Health and Wellbeing Profile for North Glasgow*, (Glasgow: GCPH, 2008). http://www.gcph.co.uk/assets/0000/0625/NorthGlasgow.pdf

4
Professor Sir Harry Burns, "Wellness not illness— why 'place' matters for health", in the "'Learning from Thought'" section of this volume.

5
7N Architects + RankinFraser Landscape Architecture designed the Garscube Landscape Link. It was awarded 'Best Future Building' at the 2010 Scottish Design Awards. http://www.archdaily.com/69178/garscube-landscae-link-7n-architects-rankinfraser-landscape-architecture

6
Due to a lack of facilities north of the border, when Scots Tim Baillie and David Florence took gold and silver in the Canoe Slalom at the 2012 London Olympics, they did so having trained in England for the majority of their careers. Pinkston is revolutionising watersports in Scotland, provid-ing a home for the nation's paddlers of today and tomorrow.

7
Scottish Canals Corporate Plan https://www.scottishcanals.co.uk/corporate/about-us/our-brand/our-vision/

8
Developed jointly with Falkirk Council and Central Scotland Forest Trust – now Central Scotland Green Network Trust (CSGNT) – the Helix parklands were masterplanned and designed by landscape architects Ironside Farrar Ltd. The park has won numerous awards, including Best Environment Project at the 2014 National Lottery Awards.

Dublin—
A blue system
for a green city

Tom Leahy

Like most European capitals, Dublin experienced a period of economic growth from the late 1990s until the economic downturn of 2008. During the period of growth, business boomed with high-tech companies such as Intel, Hewlett Packard and Google locating in and around Dublin. The city's population rose as Irish citizens returned home and many new workers came to take advantage of the employment opportunities. By 2006, Dublin's population had increased to over 500,000, an increase of 2% over four years. [1] During the same period, the population of the Greater Dublin area rose from 1.23 million to 1.66 million. [2]

Investment in the city has supported the regeneration of the Temple Bar area as a cultural quarter and O'Connell Street as the civic heart, as well as the rejuvenation of the Fatima district through upgraded social housing and new commercial developments. New transport initiatives have seen improvements to the Port Tunnel, upgrades to the public transport system, the introduction of a Light Rail Tram System (Luas) and a very successful public rental and privately sponsored bike scheme. Introduced in 2009, the cycle rental scheme currently provides 100 stations around the city with 1,500 bikes available for general use.

The economic boom of the 1990s and 2000s and the growing population led to intense pressure on land for industrial development and homebuilding. At the same time, severe floods in 1997 and 2002 heralded a growing awareness that Dublin's climate was changing with increasing rainfall becoming a major factor. By 2100, it is anticipated that rainfall will have increased by 20% and that the winters are likely to be 1.5–2 degrees centigrade warmer.

— 1
Dublin from the air.

Planning context and the
Dublin water management initiative

In the early years of the 21st century, it was recognised that there was a need to safeguard the vitality of the city as a destination for business, culture and tourism, whilst ensuring appropriate controls on development and improved management of water. The Dublin Flood Initiative (DFI) was formally established in 2002 and enactment of the Water Framework Directive (WFD) in 2003 provided the context in which this could happen. [3] [4]

The purpose of the DFI is to identify the flooding risks, where they are located and when the risk is high, in order to develop a unified and fully integrated flood risk management strategy to address the five key threats through flooding: drainage, dams, coast, rivers and excess rainfall.

With widespread concern that the existing drainage system was nearing capacity and in the face of real economic and political pressure to allow further development, the first priority for the parallel drainage initiative was to put in place a strategy for water management in the Greater Dublin region up to 2031 and beyond. The Greater Dublin Strategic Drainage Study (GDSDS) of 2005 set out a suite of policies to assist the City of Dublin and the adjacent local authorities in meeting their legal responsibilities, delivering their planning and development objectives and facilitating a consistent approach to urban drainage infrastructure planning, design, construction and operation in line with good practice. The GDSDS also examined the costs of implementing the recommendations that were calculated at €2,585 million over a 25-year period.

The GDSDS included policies that cover overall strategy, new development, environmental management, inflow, infiltration and exfiltration, climate change and basements. Together, these policies addressed a number of key issues, including utilising existing drainage infrastructure assets to their best advantage; minimising the impact of future development on watercourses and the wider environment; tackling the predicted outcomes of climate change (e.g. preparing for higher sea levels and greater rainfall intensities); and protecting basements from sewer flooding.

The New Development Policy requires the implementation of Sustainable Drainage Systems (SuDS) to reduce peak runoff from new development and improve quality of runoff, assisting in achieving the objectives of the WFD and improving biodiversity. To support the implementation of SuDS, a code of practice was developed for all drainage works in the Greater Dublin area. In addition, SuDS thinking was embedded as a policy objective in the development plans of each of the local authorities, requiring a SuDS condition to be included in all planning permissions for new developments in order to comply with the code of practice.

Further studies made recommendations on improvements to safeguard water and electricity supplies, new procedures for defence systems and forecasting to address coastal flooding. Three catchment studies have helped understand how and when Dublin's three main rivers flood. The final element of the DFI has been the work on pluvial flooding from surface water runoff and ponding following intense rainfall using an EU INTERREG–funded project known as 'FloodResilienCity' (FRC) involving Dublin and seven EU partners.[5] The FRC project focuses on raising awareness, avoidance, alleviation and assistance. Spatial planning and water sensitive urban design processes are being used to support avoidance actions and new thinking is emerging on alleviation measures in urban areas, including concepts such as 'Streets as Streams and Roads as Rivers' using SuDS processes.

In tougher economic times, option appraisals are used to ensure multiple wins. Dublin's engineers use the 'FAB-Plus' test to ensure each scheme delivers: (F)lood Risk Mitigation (a 'given'); (A)menity Enhancement; (B)iodiversity Opportunity; and, where possible, carbon reduction or sequestration, waste reuse, potential for regeneration uplift and recreational enhancement.

The island of Ireland is divided into eight river basin districts to help manage implementation of the WFD. The Eastern River Basin District River Basin Management Plan (RBMP) that includes the Dublin area was published in 2009.[6] For each sub-catchment or water body, a comprehensive process assessed the pollution pressures affecting the waters; evaluated their relative importance; identified the measures that will address the specific problems; and assessed the cost and effectiveness of each measure. In this way,

a detailed profile and an action plan for each of the waters were developed.

Through delivery of the RBMP in a series of three 7-year planning cycles, around 55.3% of the waterbodies had, by 2015, achieved 'good status' (improved from 45.5% in 2007). The total cost of delivery of the RBMP is estimated at €2,950 million with the vast majority of waters achieving good status by 2027 (towards the end of the third planning cycle). In line with catchment philosophy, the early focus of the RBMP is to work in the upper catchments to address the pressures in those locations. Without this focus, improvements will not be achieved in the lower reaches of the rivers and estuaries.

The RBMP, and its programme of measures, was adopted in July 2010 and then incorporated into the City Development Plan for 2011–2017. The task of implementing the RBMP rests with the 12 participating local authorities and 33 other public bodies, supported by a coordination team funded by government and set up within Dublin City Council. To support delivery of the plan, an award-winning River Basin Management System (RBMS) was developed by Dublin City and its partners to help facilitate a structured approach to the selection of appropriate measures.[7] A publicly accessible area in the system is available through each local authority offering a map-based facility for users.

In response to the economic downturn and following local elections in 2009, Dublin City Council developed a new Corporate Plan for 2010–2014, prepared following extensive consultation.[8] It set out major work programmes under six themes seen as critical elements of a successful city: Economic Development; Environmental Sustainability; Ease of

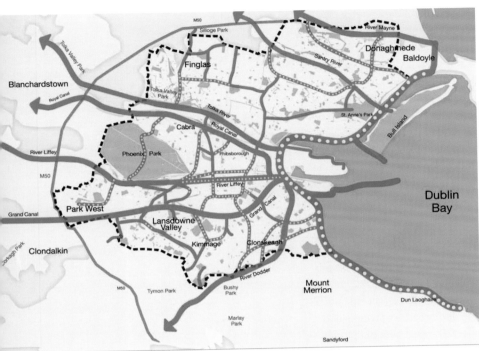

Dublin City Development Plan:
Strategic green network.

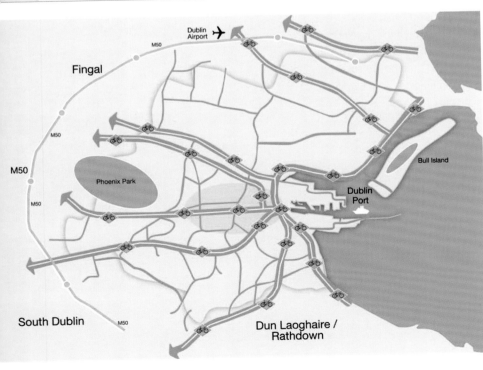

Dublin City Development Plan:
Green city cycle network.

Movement; Culture, Recreation and Amenity; Urban Form; and Social
Cohesion. The plan recognised the value of the Creative Dublin Alliance, a
collaboration between Dublin's local authorities, universities, state agencies, businesses and the not-for-profit sector to help identify, resolve and
implement solutions in response to challenges that Dublin faces as an
international, competitive city region. This led to a focus on further investment in the city's infrastructure to support city living, foster a creative and
smart economy and develop community leisure and recreation facilities. The
city's strong cultural identity was recognised in 2010 when Dublin became
UNESCO's fourth City of Literature. Its reputation of being a friendly and
welcoming city has also seen the city as a destination for tourists travelling
by air and by cruise liners.

Coinciding with the work to address flooding and water quality, Dublin
developed and published a new development plan. The City Development
Plan for 2011–2017 sets out the core strategy for the six years of the
plan and the longer term. [9] Building on the six themes in the corporate
plan and with the concept of creating a sustainable city by 2030, the plan
seeks to deliver a compact, green, clean, connected city with sustainable
neighbourhoods and communities for living and creative networks and
smart innovations to drive economic recovery. The plan sets out proposals
for the public realm, supported by guiding principles to achieve appropriate
built development and, for the first time, includes requirements for strategic
and multifunctional green infrastructure. It also promotes the development
of a green cycle network to create a strategic cycle infrastructure of eight
principal routes along the bay, through the city and out into the suburbs.
The plan is promoted through new forms of communication, including a
website, blogs and a 'My City' interactive display.

— 3
The SuDS Process.

1 Prevention

2 Souce control

3 Site control

4 Regional control

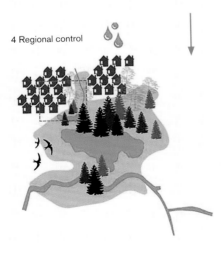

The Art of SuDS

Traditional drainage systems use a collection and disposal approach to managing surface water. They rely on installing pipes of sufficient size to remove surface water as quickly as possible to ensure flooding does not take place. Engineers have come to realise that this approach has practical limitations since it transfers surface water downstream and increases the potential for flooding of other areas. In addition, the pollution in the 'wash-off' from the urban environment is conveyed into the water system and the natural environment.

In contrast, new SuDS offer a total solution to rainwater management. The philosophy behind SuDS is to replicate the natural drainage that would have occurred prior to development. Consequently, SuDS control flooding by reducing the peak flow during a storm event and, in so doing, increase morphology, improve biodiversity and enhance landscape fit. However, there is no standard solution and each situation has to be evaluated on its own merits with suitable SuDS solutions designed for that particular location.

In seeking to manage the hydrological cycle, the city's engineers have adopted the use of SuDS and the CIRIA water 'management train' for planning purposes. [10] This methodology seeks to address water quality, quantity, amenity and biodiversity at a series of levels in the management train or cycle through prevention, source control, site control and regional control into the receiving river. It also adopts the concepts in the Room for the River Project in the Netherlands through the FRC project. [11]

— 4
Portland, Oregon is recognised as a leading
authority in the development of SuDS, which are
having a positive impact on water management,
the quality of streetscapes and urban biodiversity.

Like river basin management planning, the solutions start upstream at the beginning of the water system. Here, the focus is on preventing runoff by reducing impermeable areas through the use of source controls that include:
—   disconnection of downpipes from the below ground infrastructure, allowing rain water to discharge above ground across a lawn or into a rain garden, swale or infiltration bed;
—   use of green roofs where roofing systems are specially designed to grow vegetation, normally consisting of a special waterproof and root repellant membrane, drainage system, filter cloth, lightweight growing medium and plants;
—   porous pavements that allow rain or snowmelt to pass through, including specialised asphalt, concrete, dry-laid interlocking pavers or other materials;
—   rainwater harvesting at various scales, allowing rainwater to be collected and then reused to water garden or houseplants, wash cars and flush toilets;
—   infiltration planters, built above ground, creating a further opportunity to manage stormwater; and
—   below ground dry wells or cisterns, built at a variety of scales to hold water during peak flows.

At the level of site control, many of these elements are scaled up or used in combination. These include, for example:
—   infiltration systems designed to promote stormwater infiltration into groundwater that can include basins, trenches, dry wells and stone beds beneath pervious pavement;
—   open, vegetated swales to replace kerbs, gutters and pipes and provide filtration of storm water runoff, reducing the need for piping and so also reducing infrastructure costs; and
—   shallow topographic depressions using specialised vegetation and soils known as bioretention areas to filter and store stormwater allowing it to be gradually infiltrated into the ground.

Site controls feed into regional control areas known as wet detention ponds. Designed to cope with 100-year storms, these permanent pools have increased capacity so that during heavy rain, excess runoff is detained in the pond for flood and erosion control. In addition, the ponds facilitate algal and vegetative uptake of pollutants and allow solids to settle. Detention ponds should retain water for up to 72 hours.

— 4

These systems can work at the neighbourhood scale. In Augustenborg, an inner-city suburb of Malmö in Sweden, the combined sewer and surface water system failed in 2001, resulting in flooding. The response was to disconnect rainwater runoff from the existing combined sewer and to drain it by means of an open stormwater system. Stormwater is now led through a complex arrangement of integrated green roofs, swales, channels, ponds and small wetlands.

In 2002, tidal flooding caused extensive damage to residential areas along the coast and the tidal regions of the Rivers Tolka, Liffey and Dodder, Dublin's three main rivers. Work was carried out to strengthen the river's flood defences but further heavy flooding occurred again in 2005. In response, major works to deepen and widen the river were carried out on a number of stretches such as Tolka Valley Park, where an integrated constructed wetlands system was developed.

Dublin City is leading the way in SuDS in Ireland and, through its website, provides guidance and information, including site evaluation and other tools for developers and planners. [12] In line with other cities in Europe, Dublin expects developments to include 'living' green roofs and green walls as part of SuDS developments. [13] The industrial city of Linz in Austria was one of the first cities to put in place regulations to require green roofs. [14] Legislation is assisted by a financial support programme introduced in 1989 and developers, investors and residents can ask for free and neutral information through the planning department. [15]

Cities are realising that green roofs and green walls offer a wide range of
benefits that come naturally from living systems, such as water absorption,
decreased carbon dioxide and increased oxygen in the air, carbon
sequestration, better thermal regulation of buildings and reduced urban
heat island effect, as green roofs reflect between 5–10% more light back
than traditional roofs. Consequently, green roofs and walls can reduce
heating demands by up to 10%, leading to a 5–10% reduction in
electricity consumption. [16]

Ethelred Housing Estate in Lambeth provides an example of a
successful green roof retrofit project. The estate had been considered for
demolition in the early 1990s. However, the Tenant Management Organisation (TMO) opposed the demolition and asked for the properties to be
refurbished. As part of a package of improvements, one of Lambeth's
housing officers suggested the use of green roofs that represented good
value in terms of their whole-life cost and that would increase the biodiversity
of the estate. The TMO agreed with the proposal and through a series of
meetings, residents learned how the Sedum green roofs extend the life of
the waterproofing, reduce building maintenance costs and reduce heating
bills. Completed in 2005, at a cost of £716,000, the result is one of the
largest extensive green roof retrofits in Europe at 4,000 square metres.
Lambeth Council has since completed further green roofs in nearby Stock-
well and a biodiverse brown roof in Clapham.

As part of plans by Dublin City Council to make the Dublin Docklands
"one of the great living urban environments of Europe", the area around
the Grand Canal Dock and North Lotts has been designated a Strategic
Development Zone (SDZ), planned to accommodate 2,600 additional
residential units in flatted developments. With SuDS now a requirement for
all new developments with roofs over 300 square metres, the SDZ requires
the creation of green roofs to provide an additional opportunity to address
water management, increase urban biodiversity and provide places for rest
and recreation for residents of these new apartments.

— 5
Dublin's engineers have pioneered the use of
SuDS, including development-led solutions
at City West, Sandyford and at Cherrywood,
where specialist pumping equipment has been
used in a fully integrated SuDS approach.

Learning from Dublin

In January 2014, the Irish Government established a new national utility to take responsibility for, and operation of, the public water and wastewater services from Dublin City Council and Ireland's 30 other local authorities that deliver services under 12-year Service Level Agreements. [17] Irish Water (Uisce Éireann) is responsible for the management of national water and wastewater assets; maintenance of the water and wastewater system; investment and planning; developing and managing capital projects; and customer care and billing. The water policies and actions described here have been adopted by Irish Water, including the use of SuDS, although surface water management and flood risk management remains with Dublin City Council.

Dublin demonstrates how innovative, solution-driven, environmentally sound engineering concepts can inform a city's thinking and forward planning. Dublin, like Philadelphia, also shows how the management and investment of water and wastewater by a single body (first the City and now Irish Water) aids long-term planning and delivery. Solutions need to be holistic, planned and budgeted over a long cycle, at least twenty-five years or more. Cities need to be open to knowledge exchange, sharing thinking and good practice to ensure wise use of resources, in order to bring these improvements to fruition.

— 6
Samuel Beckett Bridge.

1

A population of 506,211 in 2006.

2

This represents 39% of the national population. Despite the downturn, the population is predicted to grow to over two million by 2031.

3

http://www.dublincity.ie/sites/default/files/content//WaterWasteEnvironment/WasteWater/Documents/Dublin%20Flood%20Initiative%20Introduction.pdf, accessed March 2016.

4

The Water Framework Directive (WFD) was introduced by the EU in 2000 to establish systems to manage Europe's water environment, including fresh water rivers and lakes, estuaries and coastal waters. The WFD introduced a system of river basin management planning to prevent further deterioration of, and to protect, enhance and restore the status of, all bodies of water, with the aim of achieving at least 'good ecological status' by 2015. Whilst the WFD is legally binding, countries can ensure that enforceable environmental objectives are supported by flexible approaches and tools to achieve the objectives whilst encouraging innovation. The WFD is supported by The Water Policy Regulations (S.I. No. 722 of 2003), Surface Waters Regulations (S.I. No. 272 of 2009) and Groundwater Regulations (S.I. No. 9 of 2010) to govern the shape of the WFD characterisation – monitoring and status assessment programmes by assigning responsibilities for the monitoring of different water categories, determining the quality elements and undertaking the characterisation and classification assessments. The Surface Waters Regulations institute a wide-ranging set of environmental standards, whilst the Groundwater Regulations establish environmental objectives to be achieved in groundwater bodies. They include quality standards for groundwater to help protect groundwater against pollution or other forms of deterioration in quality. http://www.epa.ie/water/waterleg/#.VtHQUX2LSM8, accessed March 2016.

5

wvhttp://www.dublincity.ie/sites/default/files/content/WaterWasteEnvironment/WasteWater/Documents/Dublin%20Flood%20Initiative%20Introduction.pdf, accessed March 2016.

6

http://www.wfdireland.ie/docs/1_River%20Basin%20Management%20Plans%202009%20-%202015/ERBD%20RBMP%202010/ERBD%20RBMP%206%20July%202010.pdf, accessed March 2016.

7

The RBMS received an International Water Association Award in 2008. An RBMS user guide is available on the ERBD website (www.erbd.ie) and provides an overview of the process and step-by-step guidance for users.

8

http://www.dublincity.ie/sites/default/files/content/Documents/Copy%20of%20DCCPLAN2010-14EN.pdf. The Plan has since been replaced by a new corporate plan for 2015–2019. http://www.dublincity.ie/sites/default/files/content/YourCouncil/CouncilPublications/Documents/DCCCorporatePlan2015_2019.pdf, accessed March 2016.

9

http://www.dublincity.ie/sites/default/files/content/Planning/DublinCityDevelopmentPlan/Documents/DevelopmentPlanWrittenStatementUpdate.pdf, accessed March 2016.

10

http://www.susdrain.org/delivering-suds/using-suds/suds-principles/management-train.html, accessed March 2016.

11

https://www.ruimtevoorderivier.nl/english/, accessed April 2016.

12

www.irishsuds.com,
accessed March 2016.

13

South Dublin County Council, *Green Roofs Over Dublin: A Green Roof Policy Guidance Paper For Dublin*, by Erik van Lennep and Sinéad Finn (Dublin: Tepui, 2008).

14

The 1980s saw a period of rapid industrial and commercial development leading to the loss of green space and concerns about air quality. Linz mapped the loss of green areas and the quality of life in the built environment in a 'Green Space Plan', establishing the need to create green roofs, especially in areas of open space deficit. The research became the basis for legally binding land-use plans in the city with specific greening regulations (including green roofs) introduced in 1985. http://livingroofs.org/linz-green-roof-policy and http://www.igra-world.com/images/city_network/IGRN-Case-Study-Linz-IGRA.pdf, accessed March 2016.

15

The original grant was up to 30% of the eligible green roof costs with no financial limit for any new roof regardless of whether it was stipulated in the land-use plan or not. Support is now capped at 5% of the eligible costs per green roof up to a total value of €7,500.

16

Author's research.

17

Uisce Éireann | Irish Water –
http://www.water.ie

Section 3 —
Learning from action

Detail from: *Coast road and windswept woods, Gosford, East Lothian, Scotland*, 1986, from *Shadow of Heaven* (1989).
Patricia & Angus Macdonald of the Aerographica Partnership.

12

Creative projects and talented people— The power of transformation

Evert Verhagen

This chapter considers projects that can bring about transformational change to the city: what makes them special and what can we learn from them. In the UK and in the Netherlands, as in most of the former industrialised countries in the world, the extent of derelict land, buildings and objects awaiting transformation is growing every day. The tradition of recycling land and buildings began with farm steadings, watermills, churches and castles and soon extended to warehouses, prisons, waterfronts, harbours and factories. Today there are hospitals, offices, railway stations and so much more industrial heritage to reuse: but how? How can we reuse all these artefacts through creative processes to make our cities and neighbourhoods more attractive and more competitive?

The most important questions are never the ones asked at the end of a process: they should be asked at the beginning. Make a good start, with the right people, the right vision and the right attitude, and the chances of making a successful project are greatly enhanced. The challenge is almost never about money but very often about attitude and our collective ability to make things work. In fact, money can sometimes act like a financial avalanche, overwhelming everything in its path. This is what often happens with big top-down projects: it is questionable whether this approach remains valid in today's fast-moving society. It is no longer enough to have clever people thinking about a new future for a regeneration project; to hire an architect and a construction team; to spend a great deal of money; to open the project to great acclaim; and to make a profit. This strategy no longer works – if indeed it ever did. On the other hand, there are now many examples of successful bottom-up projects emerging. Projects that begin with a bottom-up approach usually afford end users a big say and a considerable degree of responsibility in the project. But equally they are often small-scale and take a great deal of time. This can also be problematic.

A new methodology of transformation is needed that combines the best of both these traditional approaches. Transformation projects have been done in many places in the world and, in the Netherlands, we have learned how to deliver this approach. Transformation is not top-down nor is it bottom-up but somewhere in the middle. Transformation needs a vision, a team and a strong future programme that has been developed by the people that matter: the community and the stakeholders. Transformation connects the genius loci of the place with its future use. Transformation is about communication, the added value of branding, co-creation and making a strong statement. Transformation is about inspiration.

With this in mind, it is the future of Central Scotland and its green network that should be discussed first and to be able to do this, it is necessary to consider three major and interconnected trends in today's world: migration, 'creatification' and shrinking cities.

In most of the former industrialised countries in the world, the extent of derelict land, buildings and objects awaiting transformation is growing every day.

Transformation is not
top-down, nor is it bottom-
up. Transformation needs
a vision that has been
developed by the people
that matter: the community
and the stakeholders.

Migration

One of the important societal processes of today, and historically,
is migration. Even more than climate change, the growth of the Chinese
economy or the war in the Middle East, migration defines the world's
future. Democracy is a good thing for the many countries that have it
but frequently the outcome of elections is a response to change, not the
cause of it, and they may have much less influence on the future of a place
compared to the forces of migration. Millions of people vote, not with a
pencil but with their feet. Migration from one country to another is important
and always has been. The Mediterranean Sea is not sufficiently wide to
stop people getting onto boats and trying to cross it. Refugees migrate
to a place where they hope to find a better life but even these movements
pale in comparison to the size of movements within countries that are often
bigger and far more important.

Today, more people than ever before, in absolute as well as in relative
terms, want to live in cities. In 'The Endless City', Burdett and Sudjic
estimate that 25% of the world's population will move from the countryside
to cities in the next 30 years.[1] Not to every city, however: just the successful ones. Migration to cities could be the world's biggest challenge and
liveable cities should be the answer. This is especially the case in shrinking
cities where every regeneration project must first address the question:
why did the people once living in this place leave and now what can be
done to make people come back and stay?

Developments in the world economy have always been the driving
force behind change. Even though migration has always existed and will
never stop existing, the big changes in the world's economy of today give
an extra impulse to disconnection from place.

'Creatification'

There has been a lot of discussion during the last decade about the creative economy and the emergence of a 'creative class'.[2] To use the word 'class' in this context seems incongruous though as a creative economy, that is separate from the rest of the economy, does not really exist. 'Creatives' – in Florida's definition – are those who make up the 'creative class'. Some may be rich but many of them most of the time will have an average or minimal income. What is more important, therefore, is the 'creatification' of the economy as compared with first the industrialisation of the economy, followed decennia later by its automation – or 'computerisation'. During industrialisation, a completely new production economy came into existence. Furthermore, the existing, primary economy of fishing, mining and agriculture was eclipsed and craft industries became industrialised through mechanised production. Years later, the computer brought about automation and an information economy: it also brought about the computerising of the economy itself.

The comparable process today is the 'creatification' of the economy that has been ongoing for some decades now – Daniel Bell foresaw this in 'The Coming of the Post-Industrial Society' in 1976 and later witnessed most of what he predicted come about in the subsequent decades.[3] During these decades, the phenomenon of 'creatification' grew bigger and bigger such that today the added value in products and places that we are prepared to pay for is based more on the brand than on the product. So, in fact, society seeks the 'creatification' of the whole economy rather than an emerging creative economy that is 'owned' by a privileged group of people in a new 'creative class'.

Economic development is about adding value; branding is about adding creative value to a product. This creative added value is no more than a feel-good story projected in a manner that the consumer wants to believe. No company in the world has understood this better then Apple. What people are prepared to pay for in an iPhone is for the large part reflective of the value of the brand. Simply stated, this creative component is the part of the product that you pay for but cannot touch. The total added value of all these creative additions forms an enormous part of the world economy and the greatest part of this creative added value is produced in cities. Since creative added value is not physical, the work to produce it can be undertaken anywhere. However, anywhere is not everywhere: some cities are successful in attracting these economic activities and others are not. The farmer needs the land, the fisherman needs the sea and the miner needs the mine. The production factory needs a transportation system, the energy and the people to work in it. The creative economy needs the attractive city; and they all need a market.

The marketplace of the creative economy can be that successful project around the corner; it is the public space in your favourite city combined with the events and activities that take place there. The attractive space to work combined with the market: that is the thing that can make (mostly young and talented) people stay.

The creative economy needs the attractive city.

Shrinking cities

There are some 4,000 cities in the world with more than 100,000 inhabitants; and increasingly, cities are brands. Every city that counts wants to tell its story: to be different and to be attractive. Density plays a major role in this attraction. Many people think bigger is better but there may be an end in sight to this process. London has become an enclave for the rich and famous; the same can be said about Paris and New York. In Russia, everybody would like to be in Moscow or Saint Petersburg but only 10% of the population can really afford that. In Latin America, the favelas and barrios from Rio de Janeiro to Mexico City are over-crowded. In sharp contrast to the 'world cities' are many medium-sized cities that do not grow at all; in fact, lots of them lose population and economic activity. So how can these not-so-attractive, medium-sized cities become economic magnets once again?

The first and smartest thing to do is to stop cities competing with each other. It would be much better for these places to work together in clusters and regional mega-cities. Even at the level of a small-scale city, it is clear that the neighbourhoods which have higher educational institutions, a well-functioning market, a clean, green and safe environment and a reasonable amount of sports and culture do much better than neighbourhoods in the city that are one-dimensional and lack opportunities for newcomers to connect socially with the local population. Why is it so difficult for many to see that these are exactly the ingredients that every city needs to stand a chance to survive?

The question, therefore, is how to make any city more attractive and to give it a new and extra impetus. That is what projects such as the Central Scotland Green Network (CSGN) can achieve. The transformation of existing land and the reuse of derelict, industrial buildings and land offer the perfect chance for cities to do just that.

In contrast to the 'world cities' many medium-sized cities do not grow at all; in fact, lots of them are losing population and economic activity.

Neighbourhoods which have higher educational institutions, a well-functioning market, a clean, green and safe environment and a reasonable amount of sports and culture do much better than neighbourhoods that are one-dimensional and lack opportunities for people to connect. Why is it so difficult to see that these are exactly the ingredients that every city needs to stand a chance to survive?

From 'detraction' to 'attraction'

To make the CSGN successful, it needs to be thought about in the context of the cities it surrounds. How can the network make cities more attractive, especially for those aged between 15 and 30, to stay or to come back after they have finished their studies elsewhere? When the focus of the project can make the cities more attractive and can encourage investment in their economy, this becomes a compelling argument to achieve the support that it needs. There are three significant elements that have a large impact on making a city attractive.

Education is the first; without education nothing works. Education is the answer to almost everything. Cities that lack higher education are shrinking and declining cities. This is logical since the main reason for migration is very often accessibility to good education. Education (and especially education for girls in Third World countries) stops excessive population growth. It may stop wars. It reduces disease, makes people less vulnerable to disasters and opens the door to the world for the many, not the few. IS, Boko Haram and the Taliban know exactly what they are doing when they destroy girls' schools because educated girls present the biggest existential danger to them.[4]

The time to catch talent is when people are young and when they move in their early career.

The figures illustrating the age at which most people are migrating internally into cities in a country like the Netherlands clearly show the role that education plays. Above the age of 40, only 2% of the Dutch population moves from one place to another in a given year. Below 40, that percentage can be as high as 12%. In some other countries, the percentage can even be higher. Generally, the trend is the same everywhere: above the age of 40, fewer people move. The important point to note is that the time to 'catch' talent is when people are young and when they move in their early career between the ages of 20 and 35. In sharp contrast, many cities think that they should be attractive for people once they are settled and have become tourists.

A key aim should be to provide a city offer that is attractive to young people at the time they are completing their education. This means affordability and availability in the housing market, as well as the possibility of starting a business or working alongside other like-minded people. The quality and the availability of nightlife, as well as festivals and events, are also undoubtedly important. It becomes almost impossible to attract people back to a city after they have settled somewhere else, have a relationship, probably a job and kids, and, in all likelihood, are pushing 40. Transformation projects that address education, that encourage young people to stay and that are magnets for talent are, almost always, the successful projects.

Next to education comes emancipation: the opportunity of personal betterment, achievement and fulfilment. A city that offers many possibilities to start a small business, that offers opportunities for everybody, is far more attractive than a city that doesn't have that quality. In his book 'Arrival City', English journalist Doug Saunders demonstrates this is important for cities everywhere in the world.[5] In a certain way, we are all migrants and, when we arrive in another city, we are always looking for opportunities to connect. The favela, like any other less attractive neighbourhood in a city, can perform an important role in being the first step on the ladder of emancipation.

Talent is the fuel of
the creative economy.
The creative city... is the
city with the greatest
capacity to attract and
connect with talent.

A successful
transformation project
has to be focused on one
thing: attracting talent.

The third important element is the marketplace. Nearly all cities in history began as marketplaces – places for transaction. No one city can function without a market. Today, the food market has for the large part been replaced by financial and retail markets. For talented and creative young people, the market place is the semi-public space. This is the realm where it is possible to meet in safety and with a degree of privacy and anonymity, all essential for a market to flourish. It's in the park or right in front of that building where a lot of people go. It is that coffee corner where they all meet with their laptops open. It's the bar, the theatre, the arena or the restaurant where one can go to meet the other 'by coincidence'. It's the place that feels welcoming. In this space, culture plays an important role. The high culture of museums and theatres is important but, for the creative economy, is overrated. Today, museums are part of city branding. Education, inspiration and accessibility, of course, play a big role but recreation and sport may be more important, for it is simply something that many talented young people practise every day. Culture plays a very important role because, in its widest sense, culture is about creativity, making things different, recognisable and special.

Talent is the fuel of the creative economy. The creative city is not the city that has the biggest number of creative workers, nor is it the city that produces the greatest number of creative products or artists, studios theatres or workshops. It is the city with the greatest capacity to attract and connect with talent. What do we have in mind when we talk about talent? In the Economist special issue of 2006, talent was defined as "brainpower: the ability to solve complex problems or invent new solutions".[6] In all the big companies around the world, the human resources (HR) department knows that without talent the company will die. Every city that wants to become attractive, every project that wants to be successful, should start to think in the terms of the HR department: where to find talented people, how to recruit them and what makes them stay?

The value of a project is much greater than its 'hardware'. The real value is the offer and the way that this is connected to the history of the site, the stories of the people and the genius loci.

Talent is about the best and the brightest and, usually, youth. Talent is young, university-educated people or kids that have learned a trade.Talent is different from the individuals in the creative class; it is also different from knowledge workers. Talent is the most valuable resource of the new economy.

A successful, transformational project has to be focused on one thing: attracting talent to do the job, to run the place, to attract and make the city a better place to live in – for everybody. To attract talent, a city needs to be or become an attractive city with higher education provision, access to enhanced emancipation and with the support to encourage people to develop their own creativity. Urban regeneration projects play an important role in this process. Instead of making big masterplans, it is much more important just to

start. By reusing heritage in a creative way, by inviting talented young people to reuse it, it is possible to create projects with a clear identity that generate both economic spin-off and creative spin-off and act as a magnet for talent.

This brings us to tourists. Why are they important? First and foremost, they are the people who bring their money to a city – and on a voluntary basis. Tourists are an interesting indicator of the attractivness of a city and they are often the parents of the talented people cities need. However, the places where most tourists go are not always the places that the residents of a city prefer. When tourist numbers reach a certain level, they can become a nuisance. However, when the number of tourists is balanced with the city's ability to cope, their effect can be considerable.

Tourists do not visit cities to meet other tourists. They seek an authentic, attractive and living city.

In Europe, most tourists that visit a city spend between €150 and €200 (around £115–160) per day. They help to provide diversity in the services and products available to everyone and they support the diversity of interesting places that everyone can use. The good thing about tourists is that after a short period of time, they leave! Furthermore, if they really like a place and are not ripped off, they may well return and bring their friends with them. However, projects with tourism as the principal focus and with tourism spend as the main source of income will, sooner or later, fail because tourists do not visit cities only to meet other tourists: they seek authenticity and an attractive, real and living city.

A visitor will be happy to visit a restaurant that is favoured by the locals. A visitor is interested in a park that is well used by the locals. A visitor likes to go to a museum that is important for the locals. A visitor is usually happy when there is a natural mix of visitors and residents. This is how tourism can help make projects successful: by welcoming them to facilities that are well-patronised and supported by local people.

The most important questions should be asked at the beginning. Ultimately, defining the vision is the essential element of every project – the 'Factor X'. What is the intent? For whom, why, when and how will it be connected to the known and valued assets of the place?

The value of a project is much greater than its 'hardware'. Value is only partly in the stones, the installations and the location. The real value is in the programme – the offer – and in the way that this programme is connected to the history of the site, the stories of the people and the genius loci.

A vision is essential and should always have a central place in the development process of every project. Visions needs to be clear, short and to the point and should never try to communicate a complex story. Visions need to be embraced in two or three sentences that describe what will be done and why. Visions should be immediately understood by everybody. The vision has to be derived from all the available information: the stories, traditions, history, the building, hardware, location and infrastructure.

The best projects act as catalysts: they create a strong identity and have the capacity to stimulate further beneficial change. The best projects are those that encourage the talented to come and stay. These projects create points of attraction that can make a difference: they are impressive and amazing. Attractiveness creates identity, pride and jobs.

Ultimately, this is why we are all moving, why we are all migrants, travellers or tourists: we need to find out what else is possible.[7]

— 1

— 2

— 3

— 4

— 6

—7

— 1
The masterplan for Cultuurpark Westergasfabriek, Amsterdam. Evert Verhagen played a central role in developing the concept for this transformational project and bringing it to fruition.
— 2
Semi-natural habitats in the park with opportunities for informal recreation.
— 3
Sculpture and artworks are an important feature of the park.
— 4
Reuse of former industrial features to create natural and semi-natural areas for contemplation and wildlife.
— 5, 6, 7, 8
The park is extremely popular for informal recreation, relaxation and social interaction.

1
Ricky Burdett & Deyan Sudjic ed., *The Endless City* (London: Phaidon, 2008).

2
Richard Florida, *The Rise of the Creative Class: And how it's Transforming Work, Leisure, Community and Everday life* (New York: Basic Books, 2002).

3
Daniel Bell, *The Coming of Post-Industrial Society* (New York: Basic Books, 1976).

4
Watch Wolfgang Lutz at You Tube: The Future Population of our Planet: Why Education Makes the Decisive Difference. https://www.youtube.com/watch?v=IlKtMAMX-xA.

5
Doug Saunders, *Arrival City: How the Largest Migration in History is Reshaping our World* (London: Heinemann, 2010).

6
The Economist, October 13, 2006.

7
Thanks to: *Max Frisch, Sketchbook, 1966–1971.*

— 8

The New York
High Line

Lisa Tziona Switkin

The notion of urban liveability is becoming more and more relevant as cities position themselves for growth and compete to attract residents, workers, entrepreneurs and tourists.[1]

A thriving economy, affordability of housing and access to public transportation contribute to urban liveability but many of the top attributes cited by people who describe their cities as 'liveable' are focused on the 'public realm', that includes access to greenspace and nature, 'human scale' walkable streets and a strong sense of community fostered by public spaces. Landscape architects and urban designers are, therefore, well positioned to contribute to and lead this movement due to expertise in the understanding of public space design; sensitivity to natural and social systems; and knowledge of global challenges including water quality management, deforestation, urbanisation and land reclamation.

At a time when meaningful open space in urban areas is becoming a more precious commodity, society is turning to the innovative repair and restoration of land. Decommissioned waterfronts, landfill sites, abandoned infrastructure and other post-industrial detritus can become a new form of urban nature when transformed into open and green spaces that provide environmental, aesthetic and recreational benefits; serve as locations for civic interaction and urban life; and support economic development.

The New York High Line

The High Line project is a visible demonstration of how community activism, quality design, private-public partnership, vision and leadership, and investment in public space led to the transformation of an underperforming neighbourhood of Manhattan into a much loved public park that provides an authentic experience of New York City.

This was not always the case. The first challenge was to convince the city, the surrounding neighbourhoods and the general public that it was worthwhile to save and reuse the structure of the former elevated railway. The conceptual idea of a park in the sky was difficult for many people who didn't believe that anyone would want to 'go up there'. Furthermore, there was a great deal of scepticism that, even if worthwhile, it would simply never happen as a consequence of the complexity and technical challenges of designing and implementing a project of such uniqueness and scale in the middle of the city.

— 1
Concepts for the landscape design

History and context

The High Line is a linear park 9.1 metres (30 feet) in the air and 2.4 kilometres (1.5 miles) long, covering nearly 2.8 hectares (7 acres) of open space on a former elevated railway that runs through twenty-three city blocks on Manhattan's Lower West Side. It crosses three districts of differing character in the city: the Meatpacking District, West Chelsea and the new Hudson Yards development at the Rail Yards. Built in the 1930s as part of the West Side Improvement Project, the High Line was designed to run freight trains above street level in Manhattan's largest industrial area to relieve traffic congestion and reduce fatal accidents caused by the juxtaposition of freight trains and street traffic.

Unused since 1980, the derelict line was considered an eyesore in the neighbourhood and was under threat of demolition. Neglected over 20 years, nature began to colonise this quiet and forgotten space. These qualities of natural regeneration and tranquillity

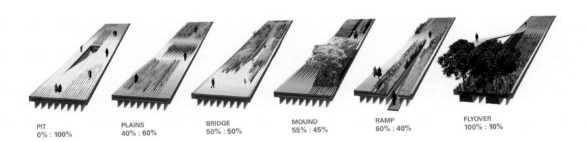

| PIT | PLAINS | BRIDGE | MOUND | RAMP | FLYOVER |
| 0% : 100% | 40% : 60% | 50% : 50% | 55% : 45% | 60% : 40% | 100% : 10% |

captured the imagination of a few intrepid New Yorkers who ventured onto the structure, triggering the idea that these qualities might somehow be conserved and transformed into a park. In 1999, the Friends of the High Line (FHL) was formed with the mission to save the structure and transform it into a public park. The High Line Park is now owned by the City of New York and maintained, operated and programmed by FHL. It was built over 10 years in three phases, each 800 metres (half a mile) in length. The first section from Gansevoort Street to West 20th Street opened in June 2009; the second section from West 20th Street to West 30th Street opened in June 2011; and the third section from West 30th Street to West 34th Street at the Rail Yards opened in September 2014.[2]

A number of strategic steps conceived and organised by FHL were critical to the High Line's early success. In the late 1990s and early 2000s, those aware of the High Line's existence had a primarily negative view of it as a run-down, hulking, dark and foreboding piece of neglected infrastructure. In an effort to counter this negative opinion, FHL commissioned the photographer Joel Sternfeld to capture the unusual beauty and character of the line from above – the topside view – that was generally inaccessible and, therefore, rarely seen. His work was published in 2001[3] and became an invaluable tool for introducing the concept of the High Line as a landscape and as a place to the public. In 2002, an Economic Impact Study requested by the city was able to demonstrate an economic argument for reuse, concluding that the project could generate tax revenue to the City of New York that would be greater than the capital costs associated with its reuse, thus garnering crucial city support for the project.[4]

In 2003, funded in part by a grant from the National Endowment for the Arts, FHL launched an open international ideas competition to generate awareness of the project and act as a catalyst for the creation of visionary ideas. The competition attracted 720 entries and the winning proposal was for a 2.4 kilometre- (a mile and half) long swimming pool – singular, poetic and intriguing, yet impractical. All the entries were displayed in a major exhibition at Grand Central Station, attracting a wide range of locals and visitors. These preliminary steps created an appetite for action and, in 2004, FHL, together with New York City, launched a professional design competition that led to the selection of the team responsible for the design and implementation of the High Line project, led by James Corner Field Operations with Diller Scofidio + Renfro and Piet Oudolf.[5]

Throughout the early stages of the High Line's development (and since), FHL nurtured a strong local volunteer group and hosted numerous edgy and innovative donor and public events and community gatherings. The combination of these grassroots efforts, events and studies created a culture – perhaps a counterculture – around the High Line, invigorating and empowering a large group of New Yorkers to be part of a movement that became referred to as 'my generation's Central Park'.

While these efforts were being led by FHL, a non-profit private organisation, a critical set of design regulations that made the High Line possible was drafted by the City of New York under the leadership of Commissioner Amanda Burden of the Department of City Planning. The 2005 West Chelsea Rezoning Ordnance accomplished two things. First, it provided opportunities for new residential and commercial development within an area zoned for manufacturing; and, secondly, it facilitated the reuse of the High Line as a linear park through the establishment of a 'High Line Transfer Corridor' as a means to protect and permit light and air around the High Line and allow developers to transfer development rights lost through the establishment of these principles to the adjacent area of 10th and 11th Avenues.

In the end, what the High Line represents is a great effort by individuals, community organisations and City Hall, with many players and many narratives but a shared vision. Much of the appeal of the finished project lies in the plurality of meaning for disparate people and groups – politically, ecologically, historically, socially and economically. Politically, the High Line is a testament to community activism, spearheaded by the effort of two neighbourhood residents; ecologically, it is a green roof extending to almost 2.8 hectares (7 acres) in the middle of the city; historically, it is a conservation project, retrofitting and transforming an abandoned rail line into a new public space; socially, it is a neighbourhood and world-class park, where families, tourists and the community meet and socialise; and, economically, it is an entrepreneurial effort that has demonstrated that public spaces can generate revenue, attract businesses and stimulate local economic growth.

— 2, 3
Looking along the High Line –
before & after

Design intent

The Design Team's involvement began in 2004 after winning the high-profile design competition. From the moment the Design Team first stepped onto the magical carpet of the High Line and experienced its 'found condition', it became a fundamental principle to respect the innate character of the High Line itself, to work with what was already there and to 'grow' something new out of something old. The mantra throughout the design process was 'Keep it Simple, Keep it Wild, Keep it Slow and Keep it Quiet'. The intent, therefore, was to guard against overdesign through elaborate interventions but rather work with and amplify the existing context to design the completed work as an immersive experience, an episodic walk and a surreal journey through the city. The aim was to strike a gentle balance between preservation and innovation through the adaptive reuse of the existing structure as a new, compelling and one-of-a-kind recreational amenity and public promenade.

—2

—3

Materiality and layers

— 4
The High Line in summer

The restoration and repair of the existing structure included elaborate site preparation to secure and prepare the structure to receive the landscape design proposal and make it safe for public use. The package included selective demolition; rail track removal, tagging and stockpiling; concrete and steel restoration; lead paint abatement and painting; and drainage and waterproofing. One of the greatest observations made about the finished work is that visitors believe they are seeing the landscape that was found before the project started. Many are surprised to learn that the entire line had to be stripped down to the concrete base in order to remove hazardous materials and repair and waterproof the structure. The finished result is a highly-engineered design and sophisticated construction inspired by the neglected, wild but opportunistic landscape found at the start of the project.

The High Line's past, as a working railroad and an abandoned landscape, is reflected in the design through the use of industrial and robust materials – concrete, weathered steel and reclaimed wood – the selection and arrangement of grasses and perennial plants to further evoke a wild and dynamic landscape, together with the integration of original historical artefacts such as rail tracks and the preservation and exposure of the existing structure at key features, access points and cross streets. When observed in the context of the new park, these features allow for a fresh interpretation of the structure. Designed as an integrated system, the High Line's planting, furnishing, paving, lighting and utilities were conceived and built as one system, working together within the limited width and depth of the structure itself. The signature paving employs an innovative technology to create a walking surface built from individual concrete planks with open joints and specially tapered edges and seams that permit the integration of planting and rail tracks, permit the free flow of water and direct water to planting beds, minimising irrigation requirements. The custom designed 'peel-up' seat grows out of the paving, rising to form an elegant, cantilevered bench oriented towards particular views or arranged for increased sociability.

Truly sustainable

The High Line is an ambitious, urban reclamation project born out of a
desire to preserve and recycle. The project transforms a 2.4 kilometres
(a mile and a half) of neglected infrastructure into parkland that plays a
significant role in reducing the heat island effect of the city, whilst retaining
and creating significant new habitats. Over 300 species were selected to
produce a landscape containing many drought-resistant and native perennials, grasses, shrubs and trees. Green-roof technologies, together with
open-jointed pavements, enhance water retention, drainage and aeration
and minimise irrigation requirements. Recycled materials have been used
including reclaimed wood, recycled steel and local aggregate for precast
concrete and the park is lit with energy-efficient LED lighting. Local and
sustainably grown food is promoted at concession stands and a variety of
free and low-cost educational programmes are offered to the community.

A walk in the park

The High Line's relationship to the city is what makes it so powerful and
unique. It is a consistent line through a varied city landscape. The range of
building types and how they meet the High Line, along with the intimate
choreography of the pathways directed towards views of the Hudson River,
neighbourhood streets and iconic city monuments, create an authentic
New York experience and are a key part of the High Line's appeal. It is a
journey and a place and it has reintroduced the notion of 'promenading'
back into the urban park experience. Elevated some 9.1 metres (30 feet)
above the ground, the High Line provides a unique urban experience,
where one is simultaneously a part of the city and removed from it at the
same time. Rather than an 'escape' from the city, the High Line is in fact a
dialogue with it. The design uses the city for inspiration and exchange, such
that locals and strangers alike ascend onto the High Line to see the city in
new and unexpected ways.

　　The High Line journey is a continuum punctuated by a series of
events. At the top of the Gansevoort Stair, the dense planting and trees
of the 'Gansevoort Woodland' welcome visitors into the thick greenery
of the park. Moving to the north, the 'Washington Grasslands', between
Little West 12th and 13th Streets, showcases dynamic perennial planting
with sweeping views of the historic Meat Packing District beyond. The
'Sundeck', between West 14th and 15th Streets, offers unobstructed sun

—5a

— 5
The High Line is popular
in all seasons. 5a autumn, 5b winter.

—5b

— 6
The High Line is used by
New Yorkers as a local park

— 7
Landscape details:
Examples of the planting palette

and views over the Hudson River. Water on the upper walkway is only a few millimetres deep. People can walk in it and over it while opposite a series of large-scale outdoor 'chaise longue' and 'sofas' ranged along a gentle curve of original rail tracks provide an opportunity for rest and contemplation. The 'Chelsea Market Passage' showcases a variety of local food vendors and is used for public programmes. The 'Tenth Avenue Square' at 17th Street provides amphitheatre seating cut into the existing structure with unexpected views up Tenth Avenue to the north and clusters of seating under the shade of trees oriented towards views of the Statue of Liberty to the south. In the 'Thicket', between 20th and 22nd Streets, densely-planted flowering shrubs and small trees indicate the beginning of a new section of the park, creating an enclosure and a gateway into the residential neighbourhood of West Chelsea. At 22nd Street, the 'Seating Steps' are used for a range of activities, including impromptu performances, family picnics, romantic outdoor dinners, art classes and sunbathing. A lawn 'peels up' over 23rd Street, lifting visitors several feet into the air and offering views from river to river. In the 'Woodland Flyover', between 25th and 26th Streets, a metal walkway rises 2.4 metres (8 feet) above the High Line, allowing plants to grow underneath while carrying visitors into a canopy of trees. Branches off the walkway provide lookout points such as the 26th Street Viewing Spur, whose frame enhances views of the city while recalling the billboards that were once there. The 'Wildflower Field' between 26th and 29th Streets is dominated by hardy, drought-resistant grasses and perennials with variation in bloom throughout the year. At 29th Street, the High Line expresses a long, gentle curve toward the Hudson River paralleled by a long 'Radial Bench' nearly a city block long. At the northern terminus of the central section, the pathway slowly rises above an area where the concrete decking has been removed, showcasing the existing structure. A viewing platform hovers above this 'Cut-Out', creating an arresting moment where visitors can look down through the structure to the traffic on 30th Street below.

Impact and inspiration

— 8
The High Line from
above

The High Line is recognised as a significant contribution to the revitalisation of Manhattan's West Side. It has become a defining feature of its neighbourhood and a powerful catalyst for investment. In 2005, the city rezoned the area around the High Line to encourage development, while protecting the neighbourhood character. The combination of the rezoning and the success of the park has helped to create one of the fastest growing and most vibrant neighbourhoods in the City of New York, with an increase in the local population of more than 60% over the last 10 years. Since 2006, new building permits around the High Line have more than doubled and numerous major development projects have been initiated, accounting for more than $2 billion in private investment.[6] The High Line is now one of New York's top destinations, with nearly 5 million visitors annually, making it one of the world's most popular free attractions.[7] In May of 2015, a new downtown home for the Whitney Museum of American Art opened, serving as a major cultural anchor at the southern end of the High Line. Friends of the High Line create over 400 free public events each year, including many for children and teenagers in otherwise poorly served communities near the park. Friends of the High Line also curate and produce a vibrant annual art programme (including 30 site-specific pieces of art) with exhibitions, performances, video programmes and a series of billboard interventions – all free to the public all year round. The design of the park is recognised internationally as an icon of contemporary design and a design that is specific to its place.[8] The relevance of the High Line to the city and the public has generated a loyal group of supporters and devoted fans and it has inspired others to reimagine their own underutilised spaces, investigating the feasibility of replicating its thinking in their cities.

—8

1

United Nations, "*World Urbanization Prospects 2014*" – According to the United Nations, globally more people live in urban areas than in rural areas and by 2050, 66% of the world's population is expected to be urban.

2

The final section of the HL was opened at the Rail Yards. This final section includes a permanent area built to similar standards as the rest of the HL, as well as a temporary area consisting of a minimal walkway over the exist-ing landscape with a 5–15 year lifespan. This minimal approach included significantly less expensive remediation such as lead paint encapsulation instead of removal, no waterproofing, no lighting, no new landscaping, etc. Prior to funding being released to build it permanently, this approach al-lowed users to walk the entire length of the HL and 'complete it' and also allowed people to experience what the existing landscape was like prior to its redevelopment as a permanent park. Although quite popular, this part of the HL will eventually need to undergo the same rigorous remediation process as the rest of the HL and will be redesigned at that time.

3

Joel Sternfeld, *Walking the High Line* (Gottingen and New York: Steidl & Pace/MacGill Gallery, 2001).

4

HR&A Advisors, "High Line Economic Impact Study" (2002). http://www.hraadvisors.com/featured/the-high-line/#&panel1-3 http://www.nycedc.com/podcast/19-economic-impact-parks

5

After the 2003 Ideas Competition, in 2004, Friends of the High Line and the City of New York partnered to select the High Line's design team. The selection process ran for six months. Fifty-two teams were shortlisted to 7 and then narrowed to 4 finalist teams. Their submissions were exhibited for the public at New York City's Center for Architecture in the summer of 2004. The designs were not intended to be final plans but rather illustra-tions of the direction each team would take the project if selected. Wan Jerina Binti Wan Aikhsan, "High Line Competition", *http://cargocollective. com/Uofanycstudioarch/HIGH-LINE-COMPETITION*

6

Patrick McGeehan, "The High Line isn't just a sight to see; it's also an economic dynamo", *The New York Times*, June 2011.

7

Daniel Geiger and Emily Laermer, "High Line's High Returns", *Crain's New York Business*, September 2014.

8

The project has received numerous awards including: 2009 Engineering Excellence Award, 2010 AIA New York Honor Award for Urban Design, Winner of the 2010 Life-Enhancer of the Year, 2010 Green Roof Lead-ership Award, 2010 Jane Jacobs Medal Award, 2010 ASLA Professional Honor Award – Section 1, 2010 NY Council Design Medallion of Honor Award, 2012 Urban Open Space Award, 2013 Vincent Scully Prize Award and 2013 ASLA Professional Honor Award – Section 2.

14

London—
Designing the Olympic
green legacy

Neil Mattinson

"To have created Britain's largest urban park for over a century out of a contaminated, industrial landscape has taken both determination and clever thinking." [1]

In July 2005, the tension in the room was palpable as the President of the International Olympic Committee (IOC), Jacques Rogge, slowly opened the envelope in front of the hushed General Assembly in Singapore. However, the moment he announced where the Games of the 30th Olympiad would be held, the London 2012 delegation celebrated as did 30,000 people who were packed into Trafalgar Square to hear the announcement. After the announcement, the Mayor of London, Ken Livingstone, promised that the Olympic Games would be staged in a wonderful green and blue landscape setting of restored rivers, waterways and wetlands, lawns and meadows. The site of the Games was to be Europe's most significant new landscape project for a generation and would rekindle the British tradition of integrating public parks, landscape design, city planning and engineering. London determined to follow the example set by Munich in 1972 and Barcelona in 1992, two cities that had successfully exploited the power of the Games to intensify and speed up investment in the infrastructure needed to create new neighbourhoods.

The identification of the location for the London Games was begun in 2001 when four potential sites in the east of London were assessed using the IOC's criteria and evaluated against previous successful Olympic bids. In 2002, Arup was commissioned to undertake an economic analysis for the preferred site in the Lower Lea Valley, an area bordered by the A12 in the north and extending south to Stratford High Street.

The site was dominated by past industrial uses but contained around 110 hectares of open space and the potential to redevelop significant areas of contaminated and derelict land through delivery of the Games. At that time, the area included some of the most deprived communities in England with unemployment rates in Newham at 7.8% compared to 4.5% in London generally.[2]

By July 2003, the deadline for bids to the IOC, nine cities had submitted proposals to host the 2012 Summer Olympics: Havana, Istanbul, Leipzig, London, Madrid, Moscow, New York City, Paris and Rio de Janeiro. Convinced by the vision of the London bid – including the bid masterplan by design practice EDAW (now Aecom) – and the need for social, economic and environmental regeneration in east London, the London bid was successful. The initial plans for the 200-hectare (500-acre) Olympic Park site were approved in September 2004 by the councils of Tower Hamlets, Newham, Hackney and Waltham Forest, opening the way for a major competition to identify the delivery team.

In January 2006, EDAW was selected by the Olympic Development Authority (ODA) to devise an overall masterplan for the Olympic Park. The EDAW team included engineering consultancy Buro Happold, Allies & Morrison, Foreign Office Architects and Populous (formerly HOK Sport). The consortium formed an integrated team supported by two other firms (Arup and Atkins) providing landscape engineering services. The team's remit was to design all the infrastructure elements for the Olympic Park, including utilities, waterways, drainage, landscape (hard and soft), platforms for the venues, roads and bridges.

In 2006, the ODA[3], established to deliver the Games, published two updated Olympic Park Masterplans: for the Games themselves and for the legacy transformation. These built on the plans set out in the bid and finalised details such as venue locations. Agreeing the final masterplan at an early stage of the project gave certainty and provided control on costs during the four years of site redevelopment and construction work. LDA Design and Hargreaves Associates were appointed in March 2008 by John Hopkins (Project Sponsor and Director for the Parklands and Public Realm London 2012) to further develop the masterplan and to prepare the designs and deliverables for the parklands and public realm for the games. LDA Design and Hargreaves Associates were also commissioned to develop the park design for the transformation stage of the project after the Games had finished.

This is important as the overarching brief was to design a permanent park which would deliver a vibrant community green space for the existing and future residents of the newly emerging E20 district in Stratford. The key point is that the park was to be designed with the end use at its heart with the games landscape an interim overlay to be incorporated, without loss, into the final delivery. This design process ensured that the park area in its ultimate form today and now known as the Queen Elizabeth Olympic Park is double the original green space area available for the Olympic Games.

Extending to some 100 hectares in east London, the Olympic Park would be as large as Hyde Park and Kensington Gardens combined. However, the challenge lay less with the scale of the site than with its history. Having seen the genesis of industry in London and the birthplace of petrol and plastic, this part of the Lower Lea Valley had become degraded and was neglected and disconnected from the city. Over 150 years of industrial use, during which the site had housed a gin distillery, tanneries and chemical works, the land had become heavily contaminated with a 'fridge mountain' of thousands of discarded fridges its most well-known landmark. Much of the site lay derelict, with abandoned buildings and railway sidings. It was criss-crossed by overhead power lines and its historic network of waterways was hidden, polluted and forgotten. Even the ways in which nature was reclaiming the site were problematic, with endemic and invasive weeds.

Substantial remediation began in 2006. Over 50 electricity pylons were dismantled and the lines buried underground. Over eight kilometres of waterways were revitalised, with 30,000 tonnes of rubbish dredged out. Over 100 buildings needed to be demolished and 200,000 cubic metres of waste materials were excavated and prepared for reuse on the site. Around 2.5 square kilometres (one square mile) of brownfield land was remediated, requiring 1.5 million cubic metres of soil to be cleaned and decontaminated (the largest ever soil-washing operation in the UK) of petrol, oils, tar and heavy metals, including arsenic and lead in two 'soil hospitals'.

— 1

— 2

— 1
The gardens at night with LED lighting powered by turbines.
—2
Over 8 kilometres of waterways dredged and cleared of rubbish and 52 pylons were diverted underground.
—3
Soil hospital — 1.5 million cubic metres of material were cleaned on site.

— 3

Pushing the environment up the agenda

Sydney 2000 was the first Games to deal explicitly with
the sustainability of the physical environment agenda
as a part of the Games preparation and development.
This concern did not carry through to Athens in 2004
or Beijing in 2008 but London was determined to build
on Sydney's work, updated with 12 years of insight into
how to secure sustainability. The vision for the Olympic
Park was rooted in social and economic sustainability, to
provide east Londoners living in a profoundly deprived
area with a much better quality of life. This included the
provision of high-quality affordable housing, improved
education facilities and improved health facilities.

Environmental sustainability was at the core of
this vision, minimising waste and the consumption of
energy, materials and potable water. The framework
for 'One Planet Living' was used to ensure the Games
and its legacy were sustainable, with the ODA working
with WWF and Bio-Regional to develop 'Towards a
One Planet Olympics', which set out commitments that
would become central to the planning and design of
the facilities and infrastructure for the Games.[4]

A Sustainable Development Strategy became
an essential and practical tool to assist in the measurement of progress with objectives and the delivery
of impacts, thereby ensuring that aspirations became
targets. London was the first Games city to commission
a carbon footprint study to assess both embodied and
created carbon. The ODA established five overarching
policy themes in order to deliver its sustainability vision
for the London 2012 programme and the Olympic Park:
climate change; waste; biodiversity; inclusion; and
healthy living. Twelve objectives were established in
order to measure progress of the strategy:[5]

— 1   Carbon: To minimise the carbon emissions
       associated with the Olympic Park and venues;
— 2   Water: To optimise the opportunities for
       efficient water use, reuse and recycling;
— 3   Waste: To optimise the reduction of waste
       through design and to maximise the reuse and
       recycling of material arising during demolition,
       remediation and construction;
— 4   Materials – To identify, source and use envir-
       onmentally and socially responsible materials;
— 5   Biodiversity and ecology: To protect and
       enhance the biodiversity and ecology of the
       Lower Lea Valley and other venue locations;
— 6   Land, water, noise, air: To optimise positive
       and minimise adverse impacts on land, water,
       noise and air quality;
— 7   Supporting communities: To create new, safe
       mixed-use public space, housing and facilities
       appropriate to the demographics and character of
       the Lower Lea Valley, adaptable to future climates;
— 8   Transport and mobility: To prioritise walking,
       cycling and the use of public transport to and
       within the Olympic Park and venues;
— 9   Access: To create a highly-accessible Olympic
       Park and venues by meeting the principles of
       inclusive design;
— 10   Employment and business – To create new
       employment and business opportunities locally,
       regionally and nationally;
— 11   Health and wellbeing: To provide for healthy life-
       style opportunities during the construction of, and
       in the design of, the Olympic Park and venues; and
— 12   Inclusion: To involve, communicate and consult
       effectively with stakeholders and the diverse com-
       munities surrounding the Olympic Park and venues.

These targets were recorded and monitored at every stage of the design and delivery process from brief to completion of construction and business closeout. This explicit process required designers, contractors and suppliers to actively manage their responses to the sustainability indices and to challenge conventional practice. In this way, the ODA ensured that the process of design and delivery became an exemplar of best practice in terms of the comprehensive and pragmatic delivery of sustainable practice.

Designers and constructors were required to use the Building Research Establishment's (BRE) Green Guide to Specification of Materials.[6] In an innovative approach, the ODA worked with the BRE to develop a bespoke version of its Building Research Establishment Environmental Assessment Method (BREEAM) standard for use on permanent sports venues.[7] All the venues in the Park achieved an 'excellent' rating. The ODA's approach to integrated water management was inclusive of river water quality, flood risk and water habitats, as well as potable and non-potable water supply and demand. The ODA set a target of a 40% reduction in demand for potable water for the permanent venues compared to current industry practice. In practice, an overall reduction of 57% was achieved, in part due to the creation of a 'black water treatment plant' developed in partnership with Thames Water, which delivered site-wide irrigation through a non-potable water network.[8]

— 5

— 6

— 5
Wet woodland and flood plain
mitigation.
— 6
Recycled site material was used in
the bridge abutments.
— 7
(Overleaf) Wildflower meadows,
London 2012 parklands – South Park.

Sustainable materials and biodiversity

Over 400,000 tonnes of concrete was used in the park's construction, with around 170,000 tonnes being comprised of aggregates recycled from the site clean-up. This was used in a number of innovative ways including bridge abutments. This process saved the use of new materials that would have released some 30,000 tonnes of embedded carbon. The process also eliminated the need for more than 70,000 vehicle movements with further carbon savings.

Almost half of the new parklands (approximately 45 hectares) were designed and designated as wildlife habitat. The first half of this provision was delivered for the Games and the remainder through the transformation of the park after the Games. Every opportunity was taken to incorporate wildlife habitats into the construction of the Olympic and Paralympic Village; the Aquatics Centre; Eton Manor and the main press centre. Some 10,000 square metres of living roofs were used on the athlete's village.

The biodiversity-driven landscape designs for the parklands succeeded in providing multiple benefits. An early decision to reduce the areas of paving required for the Games allowed the designers to open up the river corridor of the River Lea, creating spaces for a floodable landscape of wet woodlands and water meadows to absorb and store water.

A hydrological model was developed to predict how construction at the site would change the pattern of water movement in the region, allowing engineering solutions to be developed. These included the creation of an area of wetland marsh on the riverbanks upstream of the stadium that is able to cope with a rise in water level of up to 6.5 metres before spilling into surrounding land. A large culvert was installed to drain water from an area at risk of flooding in order to discharge it further downstream, thereby reducing the flood risk to 4,000 properties in nearby Canning Town.[9]

Biodiversity-driven design has maximised the opportunities for a rich ecology, as well as providing atmospheric cooling, through the introduction of extensive green spaces and tree planting to reduce the effects of the urban heat island post Games.[10]

The planning and design of the park

The challenge of creating a new park on any post-industrial and polluted site is that the starting point is a dead site or barren site (or both), where everything has to be reformed and made anew. After LDA Design and Hargreaves Associates were appointed in 2008 to lead the masterplanning and detailed design of the Olympic Park, the team realised quickly that the design process brought challenges of reconciling the four-year construction programme and technical requirements far beyond the normal level of complexity experienced in landscape design.

More than 30 new buildings and bridges were constructed for London 2012 and the ODA's deep commitment to design led to some internationally recognised and iconoclastic examples of high quality modern design, such as the Velodrome and the Aquatic Centre. However, the parklands and public realm captured the imagination of the media and the public alike and provided a superb setting for the new buildings, structures and venues. The character of the park feels palpable and beautiful, referencing the heritage of the picturesque while developing a strongly muscular approach moving beyond land art to weave in ecology and sustainability.

The parklands were conceived by the ODA in two parts reflecting the hour-glass shape of the site. The North Park responded to a brief for a largely passive, ecologically-rich greenspace environment around the timber bowl of the Velodrome. By contrast, the South Park, with concourses and paving around the Main Stadium and the Aquatics Centre, was conceived as the hub for an urban entertainment complex with a largely hard landscape able to deliver

a cultural offer in the east of the capital of equivalent quality to central London's Southbank. As design and delivery developed, the two parks became one entity retaining the key objectives set out in the original brief and linked by a major spine path (the London Way) and a connected mosaic of new riverbanks, wetland and meadow habitats.

The design had to satisfy very stringent performance specifications. Up to 250,000 spectators per day had to be safely and comfortably accommodated. To achieve the extremely high, short-term numbers for the Games compared with the much smaller permanent visitor numbers, a temporary 'overlay' of the whole site was required for the entire event campus. The temporary interventions had to be delivered without prejudice to the final park design and had to satisfy the ODA's high accessibility standards. No gradients could be greater than 1 in 21, preferably 1 in 60; all seating had to be provided with back rests to accommodate the comfort of everyone, particularly the elderly. A resting place had to be provided every 50 metres across the site, even where the average variation in height between the concourse and the waterways was in excess of 10m.

The design also had to be capable of a cost-effective transition from Games mode to Transformation mode, or holding landscape, that was envisaged until the final site condition and Legacy projects could be been secured. Transformation mode was envisaged to last for 5 to 10 years, although such has been the speed of post-Games development, it was largely redundant after three years. The Legacy Plan is now expected to be delivered in 10 years instead of the projected 20 to 25.

— 8
London 2012 games mode parklands (South Park).
— 9
Queen Elizabeth Olympic Park (South Park).

— 8

— 9

One of the key sustainability objectives was to
minimise the carbon footprint of the Games. Retaining
recycled material on-site as part of the park delivery
made a significant contribution to this target by
reducing vehicle movements. The implementation of
this principle, however, carried a design impact in that
the topography of the park and particularly the level
changes were exaggerated somewhat and there was a
significant design challenge to deliver such landforms
in an integrated and visually harmonious manner.
The resulting landforms, although clearly imposed by
human intent, nonetheless delivered a landscape in
scale with the Games infrastructure, architecture and
spectator experience.

A budget of £9.3 billion for the project was
agreed in 2007 but a year later, in 2008, the UK
economy, together with the global economy, entered
economic recession as a consequence of the financial
crash. The Games were not immune to the consequences of this world event and with property prices
falling a number of private developers, who had been
expected to fund key elements of the Olympic Village
and the Media Centre, withdrew their support. This
led to pressure on all projects to make savings and a
request in 2009 to utilise the Games' contingency fund
set up by the government.[11] This crisis occurred at the
height of the parklands design project between 2008
and 2010, requiring some 20 specialist sub-consultan-
cies, together with a team of 30 designers from LDA
Design and Hargreaves Associates, working collabo-
ratively to design, refine and deliver a product under
severe budgetary constraints.

The layering and sophistication of the landscape
and the ecological support it provides – including large
reed beds, fish refuges, kingfisher walls, swift 'hotels'
and otter holts – have helped the park to be recognised
as an important benchmark for the design of new
landscapes.[12] This is a further exemplar of ecologically
structured landscapes delivering popular ecology
parks and exciting contemporary urban spaces across
the city (such as Gunpowder Park, Northala Fields and
Burgess Park). All these developments demonstrate
common and sound ecological objectives, such as a
minimal approach to the use of resources, the overlaying
of sustainability systems on physical systems and
working with nature as a landscape system.

— 10
London 2012 parklands landform
in October 2011, 12 months after
construction.
— 11
London 2012 parklands, north park
during Super Saturday with the
velodrome in background.
—12
Fish refuges in construction on the
River Lea.

— 10

A permanent park

Post Games, the key aim for the landscape design was to embed the park as a local facility for the enjoyment of the broadest range of users in the communities nearby and 2013–2014 saw the 'Remove-Connect-Complete' phase of the park development begin. The objective of creating a much-loved local park had been established and embedded in the original submission of the London Olympic bid. The opportunity for such extraordinary parklands to perform a core function of newly emerging communities remains very exciting and it is hoped that in time this will make a notable contribution to the UK's reputation for the development and delivery of great, garden cities.

 Since 2013, an investment of approximately £300 million per year, together with two years of construction, has transformed the Olympic Park. Temporary venues, concourses and bridge decks have been dismantled, Games service roads have been connected to local street networks and approximately 5 kilometres of cycle paths and footpaths have been completed. New community cafes and family play parks have been built and approximately 1 hectare of new allotments has been established. Numerous 'stitches', or new green pedestrian connections, have been inserted to encourage visits to the park by providing easy and direct access from surrounding neighbourhoods. All of these measures are intended to facilitate a network where residents, workers and visitors alike can orient themselves easily in the new city spaces.

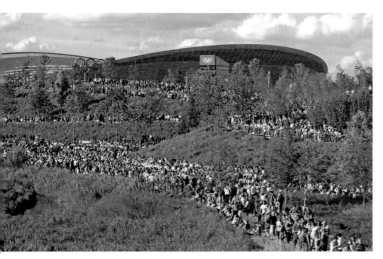

— 11

— 12

—13
New family play park,
South Plaza.

Conclusions

It is rare in an historic city such as London to have a
clear ring-fenced site of the size of the Olympic Park.
The momentum of investment in support of London
2012 provided the catalyst to create a green framework
for a new urban neighbourhood in the Lea Valley using
its waterways and landscape features as a starting
point whilst retaining many of the original land boundaries. The strong environmental agenda that shaped
the Olympic Park landscape and infrastructure has set
a new precedent for investment in sustainable masterplanning, design and delivery in the UK.

The basis of the masterplanning was to create
a new piece of city that knitted together previously
disconnected neighbourhoods as it is built out over
time. The renamed Queen Elizabeth Olympic Park is
more than a park with iconic sporting venues. All of the
Games buildings, footpaths and roads were sited with
a view to their long-term use as hubs of activity and
community landmarks. They were located not only to

function for the Games themselves but also to relate
to the existing and proposed transport links, with full
recognition and design intent for their place in the
fabric of the future city.

London 2012 lives on for many great reasons and
amongst these is the memorable presence of the park
itself: so much more than a green passive reserve, natural-
ising and softening the effects of urban life, it is hugely
significant to the economic, social and environmental
performance of the regenerated city, breathing new life,
energy and pleasure into neighbourhoods old and new.

The Queen Elizabeth Olympic Park is particularly
special in that it is a park that physically connects
previously disjointed communities via a living
green-blue network supporting walkways, cycleways
and waterways. Together these have a transformative
and catalytic effect in the development of a strong
ecologically, socially and economically successful
21st-century community.

1

Sir John Armitt, Chair of the ODA: http://www.guardian.co.uk/
sport/2012/feb/06/olympic-site-stratford-urban-park/print.

2

https://www.rgs.org/NR/rdonlyres/1E506FE2-3179-439C-81F2-
B43D0B97D058/0/CGT_NetRaising_8Olympicpresentation.pdf

3

Through the London Olympic Games and Paralympic Games Act 2006,
the ODA was established to act as both developer of the Olympic Park
and Local Planning Authority (LPA) in relation to the park and adjoining
lands. Prior to this, planning powers were divided between the four
London boroughs. Set up as a non-departmental public body of the
Department for Culture, Media and Sport, the ODA was responsible for
ensuring the delivery of venues, infrastructure and legacy for the 2012
Summer Olympic and Paralympic Games (https://en.wikipedia.org/
wiki/Olympic_Delivery_Authority). Together with the London Organising
Committee of the Olympic and Paralympic Games (LOCOG), the
ODA was one of the two main agencies that organised the London
Olympic Games. In advance of the formal establishment of the ODA,
the London Development Agency (LDA) and Transport for London (TfL)
had undertaken the development work for the Olympic Park and for the
transport infrastructure needed to serve the Games. As part of this early
involvement, the LDA was able to drive the early stage of land acquisition, including instigating the biggest Compulsory Purchase Order in
UK history to assemble the 250-hectare site for the Games development. During the period between 2006 and 2011, the planning delivery
team managed and determined over 2,400 planning applications and
submissions, including the 2007 Olympic Masterplan applications (site
preparation and Games and legacy facilities).

4

The London bid to host the 2012 Games set out a vision and plan
for how the Games could play a major role in the revitalisation of east
London, and for regeneration, in a sustainable way. This sustainable
development vision was encapsulated in the theme 'Towards a One
Planet Olympics', developed in partnership with WWF and BioRegional.
It set out a series of actions for how the Games could help advance the
UK towards 'One Planet Living'. http://webarchive.nationalarchives.gov.
uk/20120403073945/http://www.london2012.com/publications/sus-
tainable-development-strategy-full-version.php

5

http://webarchive.nationalarchives.gov.uk/20120403073945/http:/
www.london2012.com/publications/sustainable-development-
strategy-full-version.php

6

The Building Research Establishment.

7

BREEAM – the Building Research Establishment Environmental
Assessment Method.

8

http://learninglegacy.independent.gov.uk/documents/pdfs/
design-and-engineering-innovation/119-irrigation-sytem-for-the-
park-dei.pdf

9

https://www.newscientist.com/article/mg20827802-000-going-for-
green-at-the-olympics/ *The New Scientist*, retrieved 29 March 2016.

10

http://www.tandfonline.com/doi/full/10.1080/19401493.2013.791343

11

Owen Gibson, (21 January 2009), "Government forced to bail out major
Olympic project", *The Guardian*, retrieved 29 March 2016.

12

The wildflower meadows were designed by James Hitchmough and
Nigel Dunnett of the University of Sheffield and the 2012 Gardens by
Sarah Price Landscape.

15

The Cheonggyecheon river restoration— From highway to greenway

Dr Gyeng Chul Kim

The Cheonggyecheon River Restoration Project came about because of transport issues that required a response to problems with transit and with public space reform.[1] The root of the project dates back to the Korean War, which over three years (1950–53) led to the total destruction of Korea's infrastructure. By 1954, Korea was one of the poorest countries in the world. As refugees from North Korea fled south to Seoul, a shortage of homes led to unregulated development in shanty towns along the banks of the Cheonggyecheon River, with waste discharged directly into the river that became more and more polluted.

The South Korean Government responded to this housing need and, from 1969 on, began to provide high-rise apartments for the population that resulted in an additional two million people moving to Seoul in less than five years. This caused severe infrastructure demands on transport, water supply, education and health. In the early 1960s, buses were the main mode of travel but by the late 1960s and the 1970s, as Seoul's population continued to grow, the public transportation system could no longer cope, with demand leading to increasing car ownership. In response, the government built urban expressways. There are now over 4,000 kilometres of these routes (800% more road than in the 1970s). This has benefits: Koreans from anywhere in the country can access the expressway network within 30 minutes and it is one of the best mobility networks in the world. The network was seen as a major advance in engineering and development.

As the network of expressways developed, so car use increased. In the 1970s, there were 60,000 registered vehicles in Seoul but by 2010 there were nearly 3 million – nearly 50 times the number of cars over a 40-year period. Road construction could not keep pace with traffic growth and by the 1990s, gridlock was common in downtown Seoul from 7am to 11pm. This gradually spread to the wider urban areas and, as a result, everywhere was becoming congested.

Seoul sits in a natural bowl surrounded by mountains. By the 1990s, it was becoming clear that traffic congestion was having a negative impact on the city's environment and the health and wellbeing of its citizens. Air pollution was high, cancers were increasing, energy consumption was increasing and there were more road accidents, culminating in a general loss of liveability. Seoul was no longer a comfortable place to live.

A change in approach by the metropolitan government was needed to deal with traffic congestion and improve the quality of urban living for Seoulites. Change came in the mayoral elections of 2002 and the election of Mr Lee Myung-Bak, who persuaded the Metropolitan Government to think differently about the transport and environmental issues facing the city. This resulted in a change in urban policy from a focus on cars to a focus on people and nature and opened up the possibility of urban space

— 1
Seoul sits in a natural bowl surrounded by mountains: increased traffic
congestion had a negative effect on
the environment and the health and
wellbeing of citizens, with high air
pollution, increasing cancers, energy
consumption and road deaths.

reform alongside transport reform. The policy objectives
were to reduce the number and space available for
private cars; to remove illegal parking; to improve safety
for pedestrians by increasing the number of pedestrian
crossings; and to develop and encourage the use of
public transit facilities.

The first urban space project was completed in
2004 in front of Seoul City Hall. It was designed to
restrain traffic flow by reducing the number of cars
using the junction, thereby winning space to create a
major, new green space that has also greatly improved
pedestrian movement. Further schemes reduced the
space available to cars by converting two-way streets
into one-way streets and expanding the pedestrian
pavement, including the now well-known Gangnam
Street (as in 'Gangnam style'). The reduction in space
for cars has been matched by provision of high-quality
public transport, including transfer terminals from
downtown to suburban areas. This has included install-
ation of well-designed, privately funded street furniture.

This investment in public transport has had
significant benefits. Dedicated bus lanes are effective
and efficient, carrying six times as many people as
car lanes. With fewer private cars on the road, travel
speeds have increased for buses (and for cars) from a
typical average of 10 kilometres/hour to 20 kilometres/
hour. Thus a 5-kilometre journey that used to take two
hours on a Friday afternoon can now be achieved in

less than 15 minutes. This demonstrates that high-
quality public transportation benefits all road users.
These early schemes proved successful and provided
the foundation for a much bolder proposition – the
restoration of the Cheonggyecheon waterway.

The Cheonggyecheon watercourse was developed into a stream with fourteen tributaries by King
Taejong in 1412. This river system lay at the heart of
Seoul and the surrounding district was rapidly urbanised
after the Korean War. The watercourse became the
default sewer and from 1958 was covered over, in
common with urban watercourses in many countries.
Between 1967 and 1976, some 5.84 kilometres of
the Cheonggyecheon was covered by the elevated
Cheonggye highway, allowing 125,000 vehicles per
day to reach the city's downtown area. At the time, the
elevated route was seen as a symbol of modernity and
mobility and a sign of Korea's economic growth as it
emerged from post war blight to economic prosperity.

However, by 1991, concern was mounting about
the costs associated with maintaining the road network.
A study by the Korean Society of Civil Engineering identified serious corrosion of the steel beams in the piers
and plates of the elevated highways. With a three-year
shutdown to carry out repairs and a bill of 100 billion
Korean won (about £60 million), other options had to
be considered. At the same time, safety concerns about
the highway and growing environmental lobbying was

— 2

— 3

— 2
Following the introduction of the Bus
Rapid Transit system to Seoul, average
bus speed increased by 100% and
capacity by 600%.
— 3
Traffic congestion in downtown Seoul
– a 50-fold increase in traffic between
the 1970s and the 2000s.
— 4
The transformation of City Hall Plaza:
the first public space project of Mayor
Lee Myung-Bak.

— 4

building a ground swell for change. The Metropolitan Government provided a new metro system in the Cheong area to help address demand. Meanwhile, research by a local study group was delivered in 2000 to Mayor Lee Myung-Bak arguing for the restoration of the Cheonggyecheon watercourse. Once elected, Mayor Lee set about the task to: "take away the grey concrete and make the new Seoul into a delightful place." This became his catchphrase. He wanted to see "the stream flow into the downtown" instead of a line of traffic. His vision was clear: remove 5.4 kilometres of elevated motorway and replace it with a 'water park' of new urban green/blue space.

Following a period of detailed research and impact studies, dismantling began in July 2003 and continued until December 2004. All the iron and steel from the elevated highway was recycled, along with 95% of the concrete and asphalt (around 872,400 tons).

The old highway was replaced by two-lane streets on either side of the river together with 22 new bridges, of which 7 are for pedestrians. A new combined sewer system was also constructed, designed to accommodate three times the volume of waste water and to cope with 200-year flood volumes.

Work on the water restoration and landscaping began in September 2003 and was completed in September 2005. The river has a flow of nearly 809 cubic metres of water per day through the new water system. Planted terraces and walkways provide access to the water.

This feat of engineering and physical renewal was paralleled by an even bigger social achievement to build consensus for the project, to reconnect Seoulites to the history of the city and to build on its cultural and environmental heritage.

Initially, traffic engineers argued that the project could not work and would result in traffic chaos. The city's high earners, who never used public transport, did not favour the project and preferred the convenience of their cars. Property owners were also resistant as they feared loss of rental income for the period of the works. Some merchants and street vendors also complained,

— 5

— 6

— 5

The culverting of the Cheonggyecheon water course from the 1960s
to the 1990s.

— 6

Reclamation design of the Cheonggyecheon water course.

— 7

The radical improvement to the urban
heat island brought about through the
Cheonggyecheon project.

fearing relocation out of the area. Environmental non-governmental organisations (NGOs) were also concerned that the project would deliver only
a semi-natural river restoration solution. There were public hearings and
several mass demonstrations against the project as late as November 2003.
In all, local government staff held 4,200 meetings with stakeholders to win
over doubters and objectors. Conflict resolution included making available
an old football stadium for the street vendors to move to.

With a focus on building consensus but meeting future needs, the
government engaged with young people. Children in local primary schools
were asked about what their dream was for their future. The ideas and
drawings were collected and made into a wall of images known as the
'hope wall'. This had an impact on their families and older people and was
influential in showing decision-makers the scale of change they desired.

As the demolition got underway the process was documented so that
everyone could see what was happening. More than 10,000 people were
invited to jog along the highway as it was closed to traffic on 1st July 2003.
Then the deconstruction got underway and by June 2005 the water began
to flow again in the Cheonggyecheon.

The river is now a source of delight and pride for Seoul's citizens. It is
very beautiful by day and night and accessible to all age groups. The hopes
of the local primary school children were made permanent in 2005 in a wall
of tiles, the Hope Wall, which records that 'Seoul is alive again': a fitting
legacy of their dreams.

Nature has returned to the city with clean water in the system. Fish
species have increased from 3 to 15 and insect species from 15 to 84.
With these have come increasing numbers of birds. Over 34 species have
been recorded including herons, cranes and kingfishers.

The project has also achieved its transport aims. Traffic flow has
reduced by 18.6% and public transport patronage has increased by nearly
10% on both the buses and the metro. This has led to environmental gains
with reduced air pollution and noise levels. The water corridor has created
a cool air mass, increasing the local ambient wind speed by up to 50%.
That, together with the vegetation, is having a cooling effect, reducing
peak daytime temperatures by as much as 3.6° centigrade compared with
neighbouring city districts. Environmental benefits are valued at 390 billion
Korean won (about £234 million) annually.

— 7

— 8

— 9

—8
The completed scheme showing
some of the paved spaces adjacent
to the water.
— 9
The completed scheme showing
some of the green spaces adjacent
to the water.
— 10
In some areas the landscape along
the watercourse has a semi-natural
character with many habitat qualities.
— 11
Some of the paved spaces at night.
— 12
(Overleaf) A river reborn.

— 10

— 11

Learning from the Cheonggyecheon

Firstly, there needs to be strong leadership, someone with authority to take decisions and champion the programme. In Mayor Lee and the Hannara political party, Seoul had leadership with the track record and the power of persuasion to deliver the project. Known as the 'bulldozer', he was a demanding boss who pushed himself and those working under him to get the job done. The Mayor's staff put in place a team with the expertise to develop strategies to review, develop and 'sell' the project.

Secondly, there needs to be a long-term vision with well-articulated goals supported by a very clear action programme. For Seoul, the vision was about creating the 'World's Best Human City' with a goal to underpin the competitiveness of the country. The action programme was intended to bring about a step change in transport policy and delivery, leading to social and environmental changes and citizen benefits. Progress was measured against annual targets, including the achievement of 75% of all journeys by public transport to underpin long-term aims such as an 'enjoy more time for life' target.

Thirdly, there are always obstacles to overcome. This can take the form of external resistance or internal opposition, which can be very difficult. Resources need to be won; this might include getting more staff resources or winning arguments to reallocate budgets. There needs to be consensus-building so that doubters, especially internal doubters, can be won over if big projects are to be achieved. Both communications and

marketing were key to raising awareness and support. They and need to be adequately resourced and planned from the outset.

Fourthly, this project has demonstrated that building roads to improve the competitiveness of cities is a redundant paradigm. Instead, it has shown that removing major roads and delivering effective public transport measures can revitalise a city, establishing a new paradigm.

Fifthly, and perhaps most importantly, there is a need to focus efforts on delivering the dreams of younger generations. The Cheonggyecheon Restoration Project took two years and three months to deliver on site. It cost 390 billion Korean won (about £234 million) to deliver, three times the repair budget. However, land values have increased by at least 30%, much more in some areas, and commercial rentals have also increased by 5%. Overall, the future direct economic effect on Seoul is valued at up to 22 trillion Korean won. The project has resolved traffic issues and gone a long way to alleviating heat island effects, while the natural environment and ecology of the district has been recovered. The area has become a major tourist attraction, helping to revitalise the Cheonggyecheon Business District so that, once again, it has become the centre of Seoul.[2]

As for the future, there is now a desire for 'sky-opening' initiatives and new green ways and greenspaces are appearing across the city. The city is becoming walkable. The long-cherished desire to make Seoul alive again is being achieved. People want to live by, work near to and visit transformational green spaces.

---

[1]
The project was carried out by the the Seoul Metropolitan Government, theoretically supported by the Korea Transport Institute (KOTI), which is a national think tank funded by the government and reporting to the Office of the Prime Minister. KOTI has a workforce of 300 highly-qualified staff and works with land, infrastructure and transport in support of government policy with three main functions: research and policy around transport (highways, railways and aviation) and logistics; developing transport strategies and future technologies to create growth; and managing a global knowledge exchange programme.

[2]
Further information on the project can be found in: Kee Yeon Hwang, Kyounga Park, 'Cheonggye-cheon Restoration Project – Building a Human-oriented Greenway in Seoul' (Seoul: The Korea Transport Institute (KOTI), 2011), ISBN 978-89-5503-484-4.

Ecological waterscapes—
Celebrating water in cities

Dieter Grau

The need to establish interactive, ecological infrastructure and create an interconnected network of public spaces is critical to enhancing a city's function, safety, health, comfort levels and aesthetic appreciation. Some 38% of the world's population experiences water scarcity[1] and the latest UN statistics indicate that 60% of the world's cities will face water shortages by 2025.[2] At the same time, many cities across the globe are simultaneously experiencing devastation caused by extreme rainfall and flooding events, even as statistics reveal how precious and scarce water is for our world. Now more than ever before, an integrated approach to city design has become a necessity to reconcile the challenges of resource management, environmental protection and the quality of our urban realm.

Whether visible or invisible, water plays an essential role in the vitality of urban life. Multiple urban challenges can be resolved by creating desirable public spaces while simultaneously solving stormwater and flooding problems, improving water quality and, in the process, creating harmonious blue-green solutions. Blue-green solutions are those that establish a more holistic synergy and approach to resources in cities, where the involvement of local people and local authorities are integral to the solution and where urban innovations (whether low-tech or high-tech) connect people with nature.

Working with water in the urban area presents one of the most fundamental and rewarding challenges in our cities today – and is a challenge that the Ramboll Studio Dreiseitl (formerly Atelier Dreiseitl) practice has addressed since its inception in 1980. At that time, a focus on stormwater design as an integrated component of city design was much less common than it has become today. Only 35 years ago, water was seen simply as a challenge and a danger rather than an opportunity for enhancing the urban realm. In natural and urban environments, water systems have always been the driving structural component for ecology – without water, there is no life.

Urban ecological waterscapes, the design of blue-green infrastructure, represents the next generation of water infrastructure considerations where natural, urban and recreational spaces are combined into integrated solutions. In this way, technology becomes transparent and social and economic synergies are realised in order to fulfil indispensable resource management tasks and create beautiful, functional, ecological and safe cities that are fit for the future.

The following three projects demonstrate how blue-green infrastructure can be applied within urban areas to create ecological waterscapes both in the retrofitting of existing cityscapes and in new neighbourhoods: the Cloudburst Masterplan in Copenhagen, Denmark; Bishan Ang-Mo Kio Park, part of the larger ABC Waters Programme in Singapore; and Tianjin Cultural Park in Tianjin, China.

Cloudburst Copenhagen – a climate adaptation story

On 2nd July 2011, over a period of two hours, 150 millimetres of rain poured down, leaving large areas of Copenhagen under up to a metre of water. Manhole covers were blown off and access for emergency services was blocked. This 1-in-1000–year storm was a national disaster in a city where many offices and shops are located below street level. This was not a one-off occurrence as it was sandwiched between 100-year rainfalls in 2010 and again in 2011. Was this climate change? While the scientific debate continues, Copenhagen is already experiencing a new reality.

The Danish word 'Skybrud', used for these increasingly frequent heavy downpours, can be translated as 'Cloudburst'. The term has a humanistic slant and captures the reality that many cities are facing worldwide. Although the standard engineering solution of reductionist hydraulics and infrastructural enhancements (i.e. larger pipe sizes and capacity) has provided the answer in the past, the concern is that this approach may not be sufficient to meet the challenge in the future.

Selected as European Green Capital in 2014, Copenhagen is set to be the first city worldwide to be carbon neutral by 2025. Copenhagen has one great advantage – in recent decades the city has proven to itself that progressive improvements in city life deliver economic regeneration and positive social development.

In response, Copenhagen has, like New York and Rotterdam, set its sights on managing flooding through a city-based approach. Together, with engineering consultants Ramboll, the Studio was invited to create a Cloudburst Masterplan for addressing key issues of flood management and water quality, while seeking to create the greatest possible synergy with the urban environment. Three central city catchments (Nørrebro, Lådegardsåen and Vesterbro), extending to 14 square kilometres, were selected as the test areas for the masterplan.

Two masterplan options were developed in order to compare the relative benefits and constraints offered by an approach based on conventional infrastructure practice (generally technical, underground and non-interactive with the city) and blue-green infrastructure practice (generally low-tech, on the surface and interactive with the city). It was estimated that the blue-green masterplan, once implemented, would result in a net socio-economic benefit 50% greater than the investment required.[3] This cost–benefit estimate can be considered conservative as it did not take into account the potential health benefits of a blue-green city nor the potential loss of GDP caused by extreme flooding.

Since the strategy's completion, blue-green infrastructure has been implemented in various projects in the city, addressing essential city services such as mobility, recreation, safety and biodiversity and creating a strategic and feasible approach to ensure long-term resilience and economic vitality. Ten city 'hotspots' were selected to illustrate the implications and potential of the masterplan at the local street level. These 'hotspots' were selected based on two criteria: a critical flood situation where there was heavy flooding in 2011; and their suitability as exemplars of a 'cloudburst toolbox' that was developed to provide a range of prototypical solutions transferable to other situations – cloudburst squares, cloudburst parks, cloudburst boulevards, cloudburst lakes and so on.

The resulting 'hotspot' visualisations illustrate a beautiful, well-managed and liveable city. They have been welcomed by both the city and stakeholders for their integration of design, function and feasibility within an implementable framework for the future of Copenhagen, as well as acting as a model for other cities combating climate change. The pay back is a vibrant, healthy and flood-resilient city. A cost–benefit analysis carried out after project design was complete reveals how the potential socio-economic rewards are greater than the investment costs.[4] Copenhagen illustrates how cities needing multimodal responses to urban water management can add value to essential socio-economic assets, rather than in effect burying money underground in costly engineering infrastructure.

— 1
Cloudburst Copenhagen design and process
considerations.

Toolbox 01—04

01 Park
Hans Tavsens

02 Plaza
Blågårds Plads

03 Street
Korsgade

04 Green Street
Svend Trøsts Vej

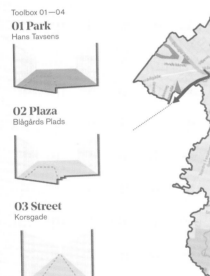

Fredericksberg Municipality
Copenhagen Municipality

Copenhagen Harbour

Toolbox 05—08

05 Urban Canal
Vodrofsvej

06 Urban Creek
Gasværksvej

07 Retention Boul
Istegade

08 Boulevard
Sønderboulevard

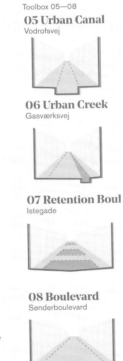

— 2
Cloudburst Copenhagen design and
process considerations.

Bishan Park – a jewel in the heart of Singapore

The Kallang River–Bishan-Ang Mo Kio Park project that opened in 2012 is a prime example of blue-green city infrastructure that addresses the dual needs of water supply and flood protection, while creaing spaces for people and nature in the city. The 65-hectare Bishan Park is Singapore's most popular park receiving more than three million visitors annually, most of them local people. Rather than being treated as separate components, the water features and infrastructure of the park and its surrounding area are thought of as a whole, where recreation and community integration is supported together with the water conveyance system. Instead of a physical boundary like the canal had been, the redesign of the river unifies the park with neighbouring housing estates (which had built on landfill which had settled over time, causing difficulties for drainage management).

The existing concrete canal has been broken open and rejuvenated into a 3-kilometre long natural river park. The overall flood storage capacity of the park has been increased by 300% while creating an attractive and significant new city park where residents can get close to water and to nature.

Conceptualised as part of the Central Watershed Masterplan for Singapore, this project is a key pilot applying the Active, Beautiful, Clean Waters (ABC Waters) Urban Design Guidelines, a long-term Singapore initiative that was begun in 2006 as a collaborative effort between Atelier Dreiseitl and Singapore authorities including the Public Utilities Board (PUB) and the National Parks Board of Singapore (NParks).[5] The ABC Waters Programme was launched to transform the country's water bodies beyond their functions of drainage and water supply into clean and beautiful streams, rivers and lakes with new spaces for recreation and community integration. The programme promotes simultaneously the application

of a new, water-sensitive urban design approach with sustainably managed rainwater. The ultimate goal is to harness innovative technology to improve the overall water quality of the island and to encourage Singaporeans to appreciate water as a precious natural resource. This is a long-term initiative, with over 100 projects identified for implementation in phased developments by 2030. Some 20 projects are already completed.

Today, Bishan Park is one of the most actively used open spaces in Singapore, providing protection from flood events, while creating a multifunctional open space and hubs for community interaction, culture and recreation.

Historically, Singapore is an island city-state with no natural aquifers nor an abundance of land. Although the island is blessed by generous tropical rainfall of approximately 2,400 millimetres per year, as compared say to London's 600 millimetres for example, there is limited land to collect and store rainwater and expansive development and significant population increase in the 1960s has meant that the city has also faced drought, flooding and water pollution in recent years. Many natural rivers, including the Kallang River that runs through Bishan Park, were channelled into concrete canals to alleviate widespread flooding.

Singapore has since turned these apparent weaknesses into strengths. Through integrated water management, Singapore's national water agency, the PUB, has ensured a robust and sustainable supply of water for its people and Singapore has become a model city for water management and an emerging global 'Hydrohub'.[6] The city has also seen the integrated management of its water resources as an opportunity to encourage the people of this small island nation to take joint ownership of Singapore's water resources and create a vibrant 'City of Gardens and Water'.

— 3

— 4

— 5

— 3
Location of Bishan Park within the watersystem of Singapore.
— 4
Masterplan for the park.
— 5
Aerial view of the completed park.
— 6
Bishan Park: design considerations.
— 7
Bishan park before and after the work.

— 6

— 7a

— 7b

On the Kallang River, the unique plan to break the concrete channel and create a naturalised waterway was conceived for the first time in Singapore. With a design based on a floodplain concept, people can enjoy recreational activities along the riverbanks during dry weather but during heavy rain, the parkland doubles up as a conveyance channel, increasing carrying capacity by approximately 40%. This enables multiple land uses to occur within the park, creating more spaces for the community, as well as enhancing ecologically valuable and diverse habitats. To date, the park's biodiversity has increased by 30% with 66 additional species of flora, especially wildflowers, 59 species of birds and 22 species of dragonfly identified, including some quite rare in a city environment. The most recent addition is a family of otters which have migrated inland and are an attraction that testifies to the ability of green spaces in urban environments to stimulate biodiversity.

An outstanding element of the new park is a four-metre high lookout point by the river known as 'The Recycle Hill'. Here, concrete recycled from the old canal was reused to build the hill. This adds a new aesthetic to the place and acts as a reminder of its previous heritage and history. At the same time, the winning entry of 2009's nationwide sculpture competition, 'An Enclosure for A Swing' by local sculptor Kelvin Lim Fun Kit, was commissioned on top of the hill in commemoration.

As well as a city feature, it is also a neighbourhood local park. It is a place for the different cultural groups, young and old to mingle and practice tai chi, play football, garden, jog or just enjoy the park and river. An increasingly recognisable part of Singapore's landscape, its large event lawns also provide the setting for large community festivals and events such as World Water Day, Community Art Celebration, Mid-Autumn Festival and smaller intimate events like weddings and birthday parties.

In the effort towards promoting environmental sustainability and management, numerous green innovative methods were introduced into the making of this pilot project. The use of soil bioengineering is a first for Singapore and involved the use of natural indigenous materials, together with new engineering methods for bank stabilisation and erosion control. A seamless blend between the blue and green environments is achieved and an enhanced habitat is created for wildlife and visitors. These methods are more cost-efficient to install and less costly to maintain than concrete structures in the long-term.

Other green developments include vegetated swales and green roofs, where drought-tolerant plants are especially selected to minimise reliance on irrigation. Another innovative addition is the introduction of a cleansing biotope. The biotope offers effective water cleaning treatment through natural means that uses plants and substrates to filter pollutants and absorb nutrients. The pond water was monitored, tested and found to have improved significantly. The water is then pumped to a new water playground constructed downstream for visitors to learn the importance of clean water through entertaining and engaging methods.

Community engagement is a fairly new element to public realm design in Singapore. During pre-construction, a children's educational workshop was organised where children were brought close to the water and shown the newly established fauna and flora from a test bed. The children made clay imprints that are now integrated into one of the playgrounds. This fosters a sense of ownership between the children and the park.

Essentially a community park lying between two mature estates (Bishan and Ang Mo Kio), it has received much interest and many partnerships with local communities in the area. These range from primary schools, secondary schools and junior colleges to senior citizen groups and communities centres. The different groups bring various dynamics and life to the park. For example, students volunteer regularly to keep the park and river clean and one school, Raffles Institution, has even taken steps to integrate facts about the park's water and ecology into a community learning trail. Stewardship of the park and river starts from education and awareness for young and old. The direct and active involvement of the community has raised awareness and pride in the park which can be passed on. Bishan

Community Centre organises events, like a photography competition, drawing people to appreciate the beauty within the park. Following the completion of the project, enthusiasm about the park has seen the formation of informal groups such as the Friends of Kallang River @ Bishan Park, whose activities encompass park patrols, quarterly clean-ups and educating the public about the park.

The redeveloped park boasts a variety of new amenities that support and promote active lifestyles. These include three new themed playgrounds, fitness areas, toilets with showers and playing fields. The existing dog run, community garden and foot reflexology area were also refurbished and given a new lease of life. These amenities are located strategically at various points around the park to ensure that each neighbouring community would have a convenient yet unique outdoor recreational space within their proximity. At the same time, a new Park Connector Trail links Bishan-Ang Mo Kio Park to a larger nation-wide bicycle and jogging network, creating much enthusiasm for groups like Love Cycling Singapore that organise trips along the river and through the park.

Open grass fields were intentionally designed as additional spaces for physical exercise and self-initiated play like kite flying, ball games and football. This approach of leaving ample space for self-invented activities is something new and experimental in Singapore. In addition, the tai chi grounds were expanded and large groups of tai chi practitioners can be seen every morning.

The boundaries of responsibility needed to be redefined between NParks, which is responsible for the park, and the PUB, which is responsible for the canal. For the first time, the two agencies are working together to manage the river park, allowing them to combine resources and meet their goals of providing outstanding open green spaces for recreation and health, while managing Singapore's water resources effectively. For this collaboration to be fruitful, regular workshops were held throughout the entire design process to foster integrated thinking, stimulate consensus and form joint goals.

The greatest change is the focus of the waterway for community interaction and the bonds people form with each other as they interact with it. Now, with its open banks, it is a common sight to see families wading in the river, catching fish, lending total strangers a hand (or a net) or just enjoying the water flow. Here, families come together to spend quality time outdoors. It is this beauty and asset of the park and river that appeals to people; as they get close to water and appreciate nature's rhythms and wonder, their experience of water and their sense of responsibility to their environment changes towards that of better stewardship today and for the future of generations to come.

— 9

The park in use: interpretation facilities.
— 10

The park in use: informal recreation and
interpretation.

— 9

— 10

— 11
The park in use – a new ecology and a
source of delight.
— 12
The park in use – areas for tai chi and
other organized exercise.

— 11

— 12

Tianjin Cultural Park – urban water management and creating a new centre for the city

The People's Republic of China is addressing the need for flood protection and improvement of its water quality and the public realm in its major cities. Tianjin, a major city east of Beijing and 20 kilometres from the coast, is a bustling and rapidly growing metropolitan area in eastern China. The city is located in the lowest reach of the Hai River Basin that connects to the Huang He (Yellow River) and Chang Jiang (Yangtze River). Generally flat and swampy near the coast, the city is hilly in the far north at Yanshan Mountains with seven of the nine major rivers in the basin flowing through the Grand Canal of China to Bohai Bay. The opening of the Grand Canal in 610 during the Sui Dynasty prompted the development of Tianjin into a trading centre. The city's prosperity is founded on well-established industries connected to a sea harbour providing access to worldwide markets. Sometimes called the Pearl of the Bohai Sea, Tianjin has rich natural resources, a well-developed industrial base and a long cultural history with a valuable heritage of colonial architectural in the city centre. Tianjin is one of the municipalities directly managed by the central government and is identified as the Third Economic Growth Focal Point of China, after Shenzhen in the 1980s and Shanghai Pudong Area in the 1990s.

Only 30 minutes from Beijing with the new high speed train connection, Tianjin is a vast urban region and currently one of China's most booming cities. In 2007, the municipality had a total area of 11,760 square kilometres and a population of 11.6 million. Economic growth in

China's cities has drawn residents from the countryside into major cities like Tianjin, creating an accelerated wave of urbanisation, leading to growing environmental threats and widening social inequality.

Though the country is still in the early stages of economic growth, managing water resources, controlling water pollution and ensuring a safe supply of drinking water are critical challenges for China as it seeks to balance its continued economic growth and sustainable development. Statistics indicate that per capita water resources in China are only about one third of the world's average.[7] Today, of 600 urban areas, the number experiencing water shortage problems exceeds 400, affecting some 160 million people. Between drought and rampant pollution, clean water is becoming increasingly scarce in the country. Tianjin is no exception. Subject to a strong monsoon climate with dry winters and humid summers and affected by climate and topography, the Tianjin region is currently faced with a major problem of seasonal and regional water shortages, frequent drought, flooding and water-logging hazards.

Constrained by inadequate water supplies and recognising the challenges, the Tianjin government is seeking to create a new urban legacy which will reduce pollution, recycle water and promote more aggressive treatment of wastewater, whilst maintaining a high water table to prevent seawater encroaching inland.

Tianjin Cultural Park, the city's most significant urban redevelopment project within the last 10 years, was officially opened to the public in May 2012. This new urban development project manages stormwater for microclimate improvement and flood protection, while creating a high-quality civic stage for Tianjin City's new cultural centre. Tianjin Cultural Park offers innovative solutions that combine urban water management and increased development density. The integration of blue-green infrastructure into the urban space was timely as Beijing was inundated in July 2012, experiencing the most severe flooding for 60 years. In the design of the new cultural district between the new opera house and existing city hall in Tianjin, a main goal was to increase outdoor comfort and create dynamic, social pedestrian routes. The lake waterfront is aesthetically pleasing with dramatic views to the opera house and museum, gallery and library frontage. Avenues of trees and planting shield the waterfront from cold north winds from Mongolian while, at the same time, storing water for irrigation.

The multifunctional lake acts as a balancing pond that can effortlessly handle a 1-in-10–year storm event while buffering a 1-in-100–year storm. Generous areas of tree planting link subsurface, decentralised retention trenches that feed into the lake via a cleansing biotope. The urban lake has its own natural biology and reduces temperature extremes. Its scenic beauty sets the scene for Tianjin's most outstanding new cultural architecture, where crowds are drawn day and night to enjoy the surrounding museum and theatre amenities – or to simply stroll along the water's edge, through the eco-gardens, or connect via the public transit links into the city beyond.

— 13
Tianjin Cultural Park — very popular in the
evening.
— 14
Tianjin Cultural Park — water bodies and
ecological planting.
— 15
Tianjin Cultural Park — showing areas of
planting and walkways.

— 16
Tianjin Cultural Park – by day and night from the air

.

Conclusion

Atelier Dreiseitl, now Ramboll Studio Dreiseitl, has been involved in projects that embrace a renewed approach to planning and design with a water-centric focus. Coping with less-than-optimal environmental conditions, the goal has been to always think beyond the actual task and consider every project as a smaller puzzle piece within a larger, more complex system. The practice believes that every project has to contribute beneficially to the overall ecological network, while retaining local sensibilities for people and the environment. Working on the municipal scale in China, South East Asia and Singapore is comparable to the firm's work in Europe and other western countries – yet, in order to concep-tualise ideas from a masterplan level through to its implementation, a careful embracing of local culture and considerations for active and passive use of open space and waterscapes must be considered.

　　Resilient urban ecological waterscapes are the foundation for establishing vibrant public spaces that are culturally and socially significant, contribute to the economic wellbeing of cities and sustain the longevity of liveable cities in the future. The result of an integration of resources, people, elements and systems is strengthened communities where people are in touch with nature; where the environment is a source of learning, pleasure, health and wellness, even in the city; and where interdisciplinary collaboration, hands-on public participation and cross-agency coordination is understood as the critical first step in arriving at inspirational solutions that generate pride in our civic spaces and places.

1
Frauenhoffer Institute, Stuttgart.
2
Food and Agricultural Organization of the United Nations (FAO).
3
Ramboll Management Consulting Socio-Economic Results.
4
Ramboll Management Consulting Socio-Economic Results.
5
http://www.greendotawards.com/submit/upload/2007/large/3-461-11_Singapore_Central_Watershed.pdf
6
http://www.pub.gov.sg/ewi/Pages/default.aspx
7
Resources Accounting in China, Alessandro Lanza.

Section 4 —
Reflections

Detail from *Agricultural landscape beside the River Tyne, East Lothian, Scotland*, 1988, from *Above Edinburgh* (1989).
Patricia & Angus Macdonald of the Aerographica Partnership.

Greening Central Scotland— Genesis, vision and delivery

Sue Evans MBE

"A national development with a
broad purpose and scope to achieve
multiple benefits as it increasingly
delivers transformational projects
on the ground." [1]

The Central Scotland Green Network (CSGN) is a national development
in the Scottish Government's third National Planning Framework.[2] With a
wide-ranging remit, far beyond a 'green initiative', the CSGN is creating
an environment which supports sustainable economic growth, which
encourages healthy lifestyles and good physical and mental wellbeing and
which will help central Scotland to thrive in a changing climate and enable
nature to flourish.

The CSGN area extends from Ayrshire, Inverclyde and
Dunbartonshire in the west to Fife and the Lothians in the east, covering
19 local authorities across 10,000 square kilometres. It is the largest
greenspace project in Europe with the potential to immediately benefit 3.6
million people, around two thirds of Scotland's population.

The CSGN supports the Scottish Government's economic, social
and environmental objectives through a strategic programme with wide
political and partner support. The overarching vision for the CSGN is
that 'by 2050, the area will have been transformed into a place where the
environment adds value to the economy and where people's lives have
been enriched by its quality'.

The development and delivery of the Green Network is a commitment
to create a better place for our children and grandchildren. The scope
of the ambition – a 'step change' in environmental quality – is such that
the Green Network will take many years to deliver. Whilst early action is
essential, so too is the development of processes of engagement and
consensus around a shared ambition for the CSGN. These will ensure both
visionary and long-lasting outcomes for the people and the place that is
central Scotland.

— 1
The area of the
Central Scotland
Green Network.

© Central Scotland
Green Network Trust.
Contains Ordnance
Survey data © Crown
copyright and database
right (2016) OS Licence
number 100002151.
Source: Esri, Digi-
talGlobe, GeoEye,
Earthstar Geographics,
CNES/Airbus DS,
USDA, USGS, AEX,
Getmapping, Aerogrid,
IGN, IGP, swisstopo,
and the GIS User
Community.

— 2
Aerial view over
Strathclyde Park, land
reclaimed from former
steelworks.

CSGN priorities for action

— Vacant and Derelict Land: transforming places by bringing vacant and derelict land back to life through permanent, interim or temporary greening. In all, 77% of Scotland's vacant and derelict land lies within the CSGN area.

— Disadvantaged Areas: working with disadvantaged communities to address environmental inequalities or deficits where they live: 86% of Scotland's most deprived areas are located within the CSGN area, affecting the lives of 641,000 people.

— Active Travel: delivering strategic green routes for walking and cycling to encourage journeys on foot for work, education and shopping and to reduce future costs to NHS Scotland due to inactivity.

— Employment and Training: supporting economic growth through aligning employment, training and volunteering opportunities with the delivery of the Green Network. Some 36,000 young people living in the CSGN area currently are not in education and have never had a job.

— Urban greening: increasing urban greening to improve the resilience of our cities and towns in a changing climate and to encourage nature where people live and work.

— Green Network and businesses: raising the private sector's awareness of the value of greenspace to business and engaging them in investing in green infrastructure to support commercial activity.

— Greenspace for living, health and wellbeing: ensuring every home in central Scotland has access to attractive, safe and well-maintained greenspace and developing greenspace as a healthcare asset.

— Woodland creation: increasing woodland cover to provide timber, help to mitigate the effect of climate change and pollution and provide employment and opportunities for recreation.

— Carbon sequestration: one third of the CSGN area is covered by carbon rich soils (including peatlands). The safeguarding of these soils is essential in reducing the impact of global warming.

— Landscape: restoring and improving our rural and urban landscapes and connecting the green and blue spaces in towns and cities with the wider countryside and coast.

— Community growing: significantly increasing the area of land being used for allotments, community growing spaces, orchards and gardens. This improves social cohesion, increases the quality of the food we eat and improves food security. In the CSGN area, it is estimated there are more than 5,000 people on waiting lists for an allotment.

— Habitat connectivity: safeguarding and extending habitats to create ecological networks across the CSGN bringing nature into our cities, towns and villages and helping species adapt to climate change.

— Water environment: reducing and managing the risk of flooding, while improving water quality and creating opportunities to improve or establish new habitats. Around 100,000 properties in Scotland are thought to be at risk of flooding but if climate change predictions are realised, a much larger number could be at risk in the future.

— Outdoor learning and play: provide access for all children and young people to high-quality outdoor environments that support play, learning, social relationships and emotional and physical wellbeing. Contact with nature can help children improve concentration levels, support healthy cognitive development and develop an increased sense of wellbeing and mental health.

Genesis and legacy

The second National Planning Framework, the precursor to NPF3, identified the opportunity to "create a Central Scotland Green Network capable of delivering a step change in the quality of the environment for the benefit of people, landscape and nature" that would "build on initiatives such as the Glasgow and Clyde Valley Green Networks, the Central Scotland Forest, the Millennium Canal Link, the Falkirk Helix and the Edinburgh and the Lothians greenspace and forest habitat networks." [3] [4]

The genesis of the CSGN extends back to the 1970s and the land renewal programme of the Scottish Development Agency, the Countryside around Towns programme initiated by the former Countryside Commission for Scotland (CCS) in 1976, the Central Scotland Woodlands Project (CSWP) begun in 1979 and two regional programmes advanced since mid-2000. [5] [6]

The CSWP was set up by the CCS and three former Regional Councils – Strathclyde, Lothian and Central – to improve the landscape by planting trees, making more productive use of marginal land, tackling issues of derelict land and providing new areas for recreation and wildlife. These core purposes, in one form or another, have endured until today. In the first six years, the project planted 1.8 million trees on 500 sites. A significant amount of this work was done through Manpower Services Commission (MSC) teams giving hundreds of men and women work experience and an opportunity to engage with their local environment. In 1989, Sir Malcolm Rifkind, then the Secretary of State for Scotland, committed long-term support to the Central Scotland Countryside Trust (CSCT),

established in 1985 as a successor body to the woodlands project, to further develop the initiative. This commitment provided greater security for the project as it developed.

Whilst delivery on the ground continued, the CSCT and its partners developed and published the first Central Scotland Forest (CSF) Strategy in 1995, which established a consensus with a wide stakeholder base for what a central Scotland forest could achieve. The forest strategy established baseline figures and targets with a central aim to double woodland cover from 11% to 22% through the creation of 17,000 hectares of new woodland. The strategy enabled action and stimulated the formation of new grant mechanisms to realise the newly set targets and to help motivate private landowners and farmers to plant their land. The CSCT worked with its public sector partners on projects such as the Falkirk Greenspace Initiative, which has delivered over 272 hectares of new woodland and access networks around Falkirk. Around Airdrie, another coordinated set of projects delivered 451 hectares of woodland planted within 5 kilometres of Airdrie and treated significant areas of vacant and derelict land.

During this period, it became clear that planting in remoter locations could be delivered in partnership with private landowners, through proper incentives, whereas work in and around towns needed public sector bodies and the CSCT to stimulate it. In 1999, Forest Enterprise (FES) established the Scottish Lowland Forest District (SLFD), signalling a shift in emphasis for this body to one with a specialised focus on multiple-benefit urban and urban fringe woodlands.

— 3
Early CSF planting
project

The Forest Strategy was updated in 2005, introducing an emphasis on the importance of the Forest and the wider environment to the quality of peoples' lives, recognising that whereas great strides had been taken towards the target of doubling of woodland cover, much of the planting had taken place remote from the 750,000 people who lived in the Forest area. Thus the revised strategy set out to maintain the creation of new woodlands and to deliver benefits arising from the management and use of the woodland resource for greater accessibility, recreational opportunities, contributions to public health and education, volunteering and participation.

Along with this shift in emphasis, the CSCT became the Central Scotland Forest Trust (CSFT) in 2002 and increasingly worked with communities on woodland and greenspace schemes on their doorsteps. An example of this approach is the Greenlink project in Motherwell, where an area of dereliction and abandonment has been converted into a well-used community asset. In this period, the CSFT was a mechanism for innovation, including early participation in intermediate labour programmes (a successor regime to the MSC), community engagement, tourism, health, education and heat from wood biomass. The CSFT also worked closely with Scottish Canals and Falkirk Council to develop the Helix concept and help to secure £47 million project funding (including £25 million from the BIG Lottery) that has transformed 300 hectares of underused land between Grangemouth and Falkirk.

Further momentum for greening to the west and east of the CSF area came about through the establishment of the Glasgow & Clyde Valley (GCV) Green Network Partnership in 2006 and the Lothians & Fife Green Network Partnership (originally the Edinburgh & Lothians Forest Habitat Network Partnership) in 2008. To the west, the partnership has focused on strategic planning for green infrastructure; to the east, reflecting the additional capacity of the Edinburgh & Lothians Greenspace Trust, the focus has been on project delivery. Together these initiatives and organisations provided the context in which the CSGN could be taken forward.

Delivery in partnership

Reflecting the government's desire to position Scotland at the forefront of action to build a greener economy, the proposals for the CSGN are amongst the most extensive anywhere in the world. Its delivery requires the ongoing commitment and collaboration of a very wide range of organisations nationally, regionally, locally and at a project level working with local people, community groups and businesses. Since 2010, when the CSGN was launched, partners across the CSGN have been developing strategic approaches to policy development, planning, delivery and management of green networks and green spaces across central Scotland.

There is strong policy support for the CSGN through NPF3, which identifies the CSGN as a National Development. NPF3 indicates that remediation of derelict land, prioritised action in disadvantaged communities and active travel (walking and cycling) should be the priorities for action during the lifetime of the plan. NPF3 also requires that development plans identify green networks in all city-regions to further drive delivery through the development process. Beyond NPF3, Scotland has a strong suite of other national policies on forestry, biodiversity, access and health that all provide a supportive context for the CSGN.

The governance of the CSGN is achieved through the CSGN Programme Committee, the Central Scotland Green Network Trust (CSGNT) and a wide range of partners.

The CSGN Programme Committee

Ownership of the CSGN initiative lies with the Environment & Forestry (EnFor) Directorate in the Scottish Government. Oversight is provided by the CSGN Programme Committee that ensures progress is in line with ministers' ambitions (as expressed through the CSGN Vision, the National Planning Framework and other relevant plans, policies and strategies).[7] It also seeks to establish mutually supportive links with other relevant policies and programmes. The committee is chaired by the Scottish Government Director for EnFor with representation on the committee from different departments including health, housing and planning to develop support across government.

CSGNT

The CSGNT was established in 2014 to provide capacity to help to realise the Vision for the CSGN.[8] Its mission is to drive forward the delivery of the CSGN to bring real change to the environment and the economy and for the people of central Scotland. The CSGNT is a collaborative and enabling organisation whose roles and activities are intended to be complementary to, and supportive of, a wider CSGN organisational and delivery network.

CSGN Partners

The CSGN is being delivered by: national agencies, including Forestry Commission Scotland (FCS), Scottish Natural Heritage (SNH), Transport Scotland and the Scottish Environment Protection Agency; the 19 local authorities; third sector organisations, including greenspace scotland, Sustrans, Paths for All, Buglife and TCV; regional green network partnerships, notably GCV Green Network Partnership and the Lothians & Fife Green Network Partnership; local delivery bodies; and other stakeholders. Collectively, they add substantive value by combining expertise, resources and people to realise ambitious projects. A CSGN Regional Advisory Forum acts as an interface between the regional partners, the CSGN Programme Committee and the CSGNT.[9] In addition, specialist partners meet as the Scottish Green Infrastructure Forum, for whom the CSGNT provides secretariat support. Critical to the success of the CSGN are the many community groups, landowners and land managers, businesses and individuals who enable or help the development and delivery of projects on the ground.

SNH and FCS have played an active role in embedding green infrastructure concepts and policies into the two strategic development plans for the metropolitan areas of Glasgow and Edinburgh (Clyde Plan and SESplan) and the 19 local development plans for the area. SNH, FCS and NHS Health Scotland are also cooperating on a programme to green the NHS estate. FES has for a number of years targeted land acquisition and new woodland planting in central Scotland and FCS through its 'Woods In and Around Towns' (WIAT) programme has supported the regeneration of hundreds of hectares of urban woodlands. SNH has led the development of the £2.3 million John Muir Way, a 216-kilometre (134-mile) route from John Muir's birthplace in Dunbar in the east, through Scotland's first National Park at Loch Lomond to Helensburgh in the west.[10]

Delivery on the ground

Over the five years to 2015, regional, local and grassroots projects have been supported through the CSGN Development Fund and the CSGN Community Projects Fund. Through these funds, over £5 million has been invested in a variety of projects, from new path networks promoting active travel to the reclamation of vacant and derelict land for community growing projects. Larger strategic projects have also benefited from the funding, such as the Central Scotland City to City Canoe Trail.

The Seven Lochs Wetland Park, promoted by the GCV Green Network Partnership, is a wetland park situated across the Glasgow and North Lanarkshire boundaries with an aspiration to become Scotland's largest urban nature park. It demonstrates how the integration of green network principles and practice into regeneration projects can protect and enhance local natural and cultural heritage sites, as well as promoting the general health and wellbeing of residents and visitors.

The Cuningar Loop is a £6 million Legacy 2014 project led by Forestry Commission Scotland located opposite the Commonwealth Games Athletes' Village in the east end of Glasgow. This once vacant and derelict land site has been transformed into an attractive community greenspace that aims to attract over 100,000 visitors by 2021. Local people and visitors can now enjoy newly created recreational spaces and extensive path, bridge and boardwalk networks within the surroundings of 15,000 newly planted trees, all on their doorstep.

The East Ayrshire Coalfield Environment Initiative aims to improve the quality of the natural environment in East Ayrshire, creating a place where people can live, work and visit. By transforming vacant, derelict and contaminated land, enhancing biodiversity and encouraging community engagement and pride, the initiative is helping to tackle the economic decline of the area which has been a contributing factor to high unemployment, poor educational attainment and poor health and wellbeing locally.

Through the Larbert Woods Hospital Grounds greenspace project, located at Forth Valley Royal Hospital, patients, visitors and staff now have access to a high-quality, multifunctional greenspace, which they can use to help to improve their physical health and mental wellbeing. In addition, local schools have a dedicated outdoor learning resource within the woodland, enhancing children and young people's education through learning in natural settings.

— 4
A view of the East Ayrshire
Coalfield Environment Initiative area.
— 5
A view of Forth Valley Royal Hospital.
— 6
Cuningar Loop masterplan.
— 7
Seven Lochs Wetland Park
viewpoint design.

— 6

— 7

Raising Awareness

A key task for CSGNT is to raise awareness of the need for, and the
benefits of, delivery of green infrastructure among decision-makers,
policymakers and practitioners. Over time, once this awareness and
practice is more established, the focus of the communications effort will
move to embrace the general public in a more substantive way.

   Awareness raising is delivered through press communications, a
monthly eNewsletter, events and tours. The most significant event is the
CSGN Annual Forum, which has been taking place since 2011 and whose
work and research form the core content for this volume. Each forum
has included presentations from speakers from across the world along
with workshops, masterclasses and local site visits. The aim is to bring
inspiration from elsewhere and to demonstrate what is already being
achieved in central Scotland by local authorities, public agencies and
third-sector partners. The event is free to delegates thanks to government
funding and private sector sponsors and the content is made more
widely available to anyone who might be interested beyond the forum
itself through the CSGN website as an online resource where keynote
presentations can be accessed.[11] 'Growing Awareness' provides an
opportunity for CSGNT to disseminate even further the learning from
these events. As well as the book, the content will be made accessible
online in due course.

"A more integrated approach and
'greening' of the urban environment
through green infrastructure and
retrofitting can improve quality of life
within our towns and cities, alongside
enhancing their longer-term
environmental performance and
climate resilience."[12]

Realising the benefits

"A more integrated approach and 'greening' of the urban environment through green infrastructure and retrofitting can improve quality of life within our towns and cities, alongside enhancing their longer-term environmental performance and climate resilience."[12]

The long-term delivery of the CSGN is a win-win-win for the economy, for people and for the environment. In 2014–2016, work was carried out to establish the costs and benefits of delivering the CSGN. The capital cost (excluding ongoing management) is estimated at around £2.8 billion, or £80 million a year, and it is estimated that much of this annual sum is already available through local authority and others' budgets and through existing grants. Many of the benefits of the CSGN are difficult to value in monetary terms (e.g. community coherence or biodiversity) but for others there is a strong evidence base and this has been used to inform some recent valuing work. Based only on calculations for crime reduction, improved physical health, improved mental health, forest carbon sequestration, peatland carbon sequestration and water management to reduce flooding, the benefits have been calculated as having a net present value to 2050 of in excess of £6 billion. This means that more than £2.16 of benefits are generated for each pound invested in capital projects. This compares very favourably with 'grey infrastructure' projects.

The cost-benefit work and an exercise looking at resourcing undertaken in 2015–2016 are currently being used to inform the development of a new delivery plan for the CSGN that will set out a series of major initiatives and projects to be delivered by 2020. The aim will be to accelerate and increase delivery and provide greater impact, thus ensuring that the project remains on target to deliver its aims and objectives by 2050.

1
Scottish Government, *The Third National Planning Framework* (Edinburgh: Scottish Government, 2014), http://www.gov.scot/Publications/2014/06/3539/5.

2
http://www.centralscotlandgreennetwork.org/.

3
Scottish Government, *National Planning Framework for Scotland 2* (Edinburgh: Scottish Government, 2009), http://www.gov.scot/Publications/2009/07/02105627/4.

4
The regeneration of the canal network and the Helix project are described in: Richard Millar, "The Lowland Canal Network: creating places and destinations", in the "Learning from Place" section of this volume.

5
The land renewal programme of the Scottish Development Agency was written up using data provided by Professor Alistaire Gilchrist, former SDA director responsible for the Agency's land renewal programme, and published as: B M Evans, "Ripristino ambientale delle aree abbandonate: l'esperienza scozzese (Environmental restoration of abandoned areas: the Scottish experience)" in Giovanni Campeol, *La pianificazione nelle aree ad alto rischio ambientale* (*Planning in areas of high environmental risk*) (Milan: FrancoAngeli/Urbanistica,1994). ISBN 88-204-8876-0. See also: S. Barrett & P. Healy, Land policy: problems and alternatives (Gower, 1985). D. Yuill, *Regional Development Agencies in Europe: An International Comparison of Selected Agencies* (Gower, 1982).

6
CCS M. Dawer et al. *The Countryside Around Town in Scotland* (Battleby: Countryside Commission for Scotland, 1976) and J. Fladmark, *The Countryside Around Towns: a programme for partnership and action* (Battleby: Countryside Commission for Scotland, 1988).

7
http://www.centralscotlandgreennetwork.org/about/programme-committee.

8
http://www.csgnt.org.uk/.

9
http://www.centralscotlandgreennetwork.org/partners/regional-advisory-forum.

10
http://johnmuirway.org.

11
http://www.centralscotlandgreennetwork.org/news-and-events/csgn-forum.

12
Scottish Government, *National Planning Framework 3* (Edinburgh: Scottish Government, 2014), http://www.gov.scot/Publications/2014/06/3539/5.

Towards a new paradigm in landscape and environment

Professor Brian Mark Evans

The work of the Central Scotland Green Network Trust in bringing the CSGN Forum together over the past five years has been an important and noteworthy study of the contemporary landscape and environment in Scotland and internationally. There are few initiatives that underpin their approach with this form of intellectual enquiry and pedagogic learning that the Forum has been able to deliver with support from the Scottish Government. This book is a significant opportunity to document this enquiry in order to make it available for everyone.

This chapter draws together the learning from the Forum's research into a series of conclusions that inform the emerging paradigm of the landscape of city and region today. As humankind becomes ever more urbanised and long-lived, it is important that we resolve what role the natural, semi-natural and formal landscapes and environment play in our cities and regions and how we in turn may act as stewards of them. Hopefully, this book will assist the required discussion and debate.

It has been a fascinating exercise, as editors, to bring these papers together into the three sections of learning. There are many resonances between the authors. The body of work allows us to follow Jonathon Porritt's advice to look back from 2050 and reflect on what, as a society, we need to be doing now to ensure that the landscape and the environment play a central and equal role in establishing what we must do, such that, as Jonathon himself writes, "we legitimately improve our own lives today without imperilling the lives of people tomorrow".

It is clear that for many of the authors in this book, and for many public bodies and agencies, the year 2050 has something of a talismanic significance. It is the mid-point of the twenty-first century and the date by which the United Nations (UN) estimates that world population will have crept towards ten billion.[1]

In this book, there are trends, principles and practice concerning green consciousness that should make us all think and act as we approach this date. The following pages summarise what some of these might be, together with links back into the individual chapters where the reader will find more detail by the authors themselves.[2]

There is a changing context in our cities and their hinterlands: in the coming decades, 80% of the population will experience their daily interaction with ecosystems in city-regions.

There are a number of global and international trends that support this proposition. The first is that, as stated above, the UN now estimates that by 2050 there will be just under ten billion people living in the world. This issue should be of concern to all countries but the consequences vary greatly in different parts of the world. In the developed countries of the northern hemisphere, including North America, Europe and Eurasia, the trends in demography are somewhat different to those in the developing world that are the focus of so much attention. For one thing, the population has levelled out and in some countries it is shrinking. This is due to longevity and reduced fertility, which, in Europe in particular, is leading to an ageing, static and, in some places, declining population. Some agencies, notably the UN and the European Union (EU), estimate that Europe requires an additional 50 million people to sustain itself over the coming years to 2050.[3] Furthermore, as Peter Head and Evert Verhagen point out, climate change, water stress and conflict are driving people to migrate from desert areas near the equator towards more temperate regions – particularly Europe. An ageing population and an in-migration (that many would contend to be necessary) seem set to continue as key trends for the foreseeable future in Europe. These will have important consequences for Europe's cities and regions and the landscapes that support them.

If current trends continue, 75% of the world's population will live in cities by 2030 but most developed countries in the northern hemisphere have already reached or exceeded these levels. In the USA and Canada, more than 80% of people live in cities. In Europe, the figure is 77%.[4] In 2014, the Scottish Government estimated that some 70% of Scotland's people live in towns and cities of 10,000 or more.[5] What is less well known, however, is that in both North America and Europe, there is a further concentration of these figures with very high percentages of the population living in clusters of the most successful cities (for North America, it is 75% and a little less in Europe). These 'super-cities' are agglomerations of a number of the biggest cities in the most advantageous locations and include, for example, the Boston-Washington metropolitan region in the north-eastern USA.[6] In Europe, the urban concentration is not quite so marked given the EU's spatial policy of attempting to retain a degree of dispersal among the city-regions of Europe – the so-called 'bunch of grapes' spatial model, as opposed to a concentration into the 'dynamic banana', curving between London in the north-west and Barcelona in the south-east.

— 1

A nighttime view of the 'super-cities' of northern Europe seen from space. The regional sprawling effect of coalescing cities is evident in the networks of light. The crescent of the 'dynamic banana' is visible extending from London east through the cities of the Low Countries and then south following the cities along the Rhine before crossing the Alps into the northern Italian cities of Turin and Milan. Britain's polycentric cities are also visible: the horseshoe of the 'northern powerhouse' from Liverpool through Manchester to Leeds and then south through Sheffield, Nottingham and Leicester towards Birmingham; 'Glas-burgh' in central Scotland; and the growing agglomeration of Newcastle, Sunderland and Middlesbrough.

Even so, polycentric urban regions with high concentrations of city dwellers
in comparison with the remainder of the population prevail in Europe too –
the Randstad of the Netherlands, the Rhine-Ruhr region of Germany, the
Ørestad region of Denmark/Sweden, the 'northern powerhouse' of England
and 'Glas-burgh' in central Scotland. Cities within these successful clusters
are growing economically, whereas those isolated from the clusters are at
risk of decline caused by an ageing population, low-fertility and out-
migration while being unattractive to the in-migration described previously.

In both types of city, urban sprawl is exerting a pressure on their
regions that is manifest through 'edge city' conditions, as business
campuses, retail parks, transportation infrastructure and suburban housing
abound – all causing pressure on hinterlands and ecosystems.

These matters are very much to the fore for UN Habitat III in Quito
2016, with the development of the 'new urban agenda' intended to
prosecute the 17 Strategic Development Goals (SDGs).[7] Peter Head is
absolutely correct, therefore, to infer that the battle to deliver the SDGs
and, by definition, the 'New Urban Agenda' will be won or lost in cities and
city-regions. In this regard, the sprawling and coalescence of cities and
'super-city' clusters represents a major threat to the natural and semi-natural
systems that these cities – and 80% of the population – depend on.

For these reasons and for the successful prosecution of green
consciousness, it is important to stress the immense importance of the
initiatives that provide hope and opportunity to address these challenges.
One of the principal opportunities to counteract the threat of sprawl and to
help sustain the urban ecosystem is the compact city concept documented
by the EU and the Organisation for Economic Cooperation and Development
(OECD) – often referred to as the 'city of short distances'.[8] The OECD
work in particular illustrates how a movement towards the compact city
model may provide outcomes in support of green growth and indicates
where governance can become a valuable tool for national, regional and
municipal governments to address economic and environmental challenges
through the development and implementation of spatial strategies.

These are high-level considerations but it is clear that the issues
raised in this book will, over the coming decades, concern most of
humankind and will take place in city-regions.

The principal challenges are climate change and health – and they are interrelated. Community interaction and engagement offers a mechanism to address this; however, the way we have built cities in the recent past has exacerbated health problems, increased heat effects and magnified the likely impacts of climate change.

A number of the authors highlight current threats and challenges for the environment and landscape in cities and regions. Tom Armour provides a very crisp summary of the negative effects of climate change through flooding: extreme weather events; urban heat and drought; scarcity of resources; environmental degradation; loss of biodiversity; and pollution of air, soil and water. It may be taken that with the governments of 185 countries signing a protocol to address climate change, the need to address the threats from climate change is settled.

A further area of accord among authors in the context of climate change is to be found in the negative effects of city heat – the urban heat island effect. Armour discusses the evidence from London and Kim in Seoul through the remarkable benefits derived from the restoration of the Cheonggyecheon River. Trees and water have a huge effect in reducing the effects of urban heat islands; one of the most effective means to address climate change in developed countries is through the proper design and management of water systems and this is returned to below.

But first, Armour also stresses that these threats provide clear dangers to human health and wellbeing since they are making urban conditions uncomfortable and, in places, intolerable for people and communities and they are concentrated in urban areas with significant risks for people, assets, economies and ecosystems. In their response to the UN Habitat regional report on the United Nations Economic Commission for Europe (UNECE), the World Health Organisation put this simply "environmental threats (and economic threats) are also health threats".[9]

The health issue runs deeper than climate change, however. As Sir Harry Burns, Scotland's former Chief Medical Officer, makes very clear: as a society, we spend too much time on illness and not enough on wellness; too much time on treating sickness and not enough on promoting health. In his essay, Burns shows that beyond reasonable doubt and that, by extension, this stress has been endured by the less well-off parts of the population that created the wealth of the industrial society. As he puts it himself: "we now know that the reconstruction of the 1960s and 1970s had biological consequences". This has left Burns as a powerful advocate of good urbanism because "planning and designing environments that bring people together are critical for what should be happening to support

wellness – to promote social connectedness".
There is compelling evidence and unanimity between
Burns, Porritt, Head and Armour that there are significant benefits for health from access to the natural
world. Evidence points to significant uplifts in mental
and physical health from enabling people to spend
more time in the natural environment. There is, therefore, a clear need to place the same emphasis on
creating an environment that supports wellbeing as
there is in creating physical infrastructure for economic
health or mitigating climate change. There is a lingering
concern for Burns, however, that the promotion and
creation of wellbeing is still seen as 'someone else's
responsibility'. Here then is a health argument for Jan
Gehl's proposition that all cities should have a
'department of public space planning'.[10]

    Many of the authors stress that the engagement
of communities in their environment is one of the
foremost means to accelerate beneficial change. These
ideas are well known and well understood but not yet
universally accepted and as Burns advocates, "we need
to change the way we do things in order to define what
we do, agree methods for achieving change and involve
people in testing and implementing change in order
to engage the community in its widest form in shaping
action to be undertaken on their behalf."

    The example Burns cites is from Colorado in the
USA but it could be from the Yorkshire Renaissance
programme or the Scottish Sustainable Communities
programme: "look at the law to establish what changes
are possible, consider the policy context of what you
are trying to achieve, develop the brief and get involved
in the design of places" (Burns). This is a recipe for the
charrette process and for community engagement as
a consultative design process – more than community
planning, it implies leadership through a process that is
well documented and established in practice if not yet
universally applied.[11] These processes provide a significant dividend in wellness and happiness – the societies
that maximise these benefits and minimise inequality are
also those that are the happiest and the healthiest.[12]

Water systems are key.

As much as 'green consciousness', this book is about 'blue consciousness'. Whether implicitly or explicitly, water it is at the heart of over half of the chapters of the book and runs through the sections on 'learning from place' and 'learning from action'. The River Emscher is at the heart of the Emscher Landscape Park and the River Lea is an essential feature of the Olympic Park landscape in London. The canals of Scotland are the unifying link for all the projects described by Richard Millar and water has shaped and is signified by the watershed landscape of the Pennines. Howard Neukrug and Tom Leahy describe the leadership of two great cities in water planning and management, Dieter Grau provides an exposition of water as the basis of contemporary landscape design and Gyeng Chul Kim illustrates vividly the recovery of a water course in the Cheonggyecheon River Restoration Project in Seoul. The transformation of landscape and environment is to a greater or lesser extent about the stewardship of water and water systems. The two are inseparable and fundamental to understanding and addressing climate change. They are also irrevocably bound into wider urban processes just as they are with health.

Part of the importance of water is its attraction for people and its life-giving and -affirming qualities. But the lessons to be learned from the work recorded in this book relate to practicality as much as to spirituality and aesthetics – although, in truth, these are all bound together. One of the important lessons from Philadelphia concerns science and regulation. The city took aspiration, turned it into science from a clear understanding of how much water falls where and when (and to the nearest millimetre) and, in turn, developed regulations to deal with it. Not simply rhetoric but compelling science, engineering and regulation backed up with education to enable people to meet the regulations. Philadelphia is an exemplar of encouraging

and enabling businesses and individuals to comply with rules rather than policing transgressions.

Howard Neukrug writes that there has been a sea change in how US cities consider water pollution and waste water. Understanding that too much stormwater runoff can have an effect on water scarcity, flooding, pollution, erosion and fish habitat, he makes it clear that today there can be no choice between grand engineering schemes with large underground storage and tunnel systems and a softer, greener approach managing water where it falls rather than washing it down the drain. Neukrug's mission has been to encourage the US to value rain and capture it, use it and filter it into the groundwater system. Rain has become part of 'one water' where all sources, reservoirs and discharges of water are part of one system to be managed in a coordinated and integrated fashion. He records a beneficial coincidence of this coming about at a time when city leaders are making greater efforts to achieve greener, more liveable cities. Philadelphia, as with Dublin, is actively seeking to use water management techniques to balance nature, development and people in the urban setting. It is quite clear that, in the face of climate change, this is a necessity – as expressly documented by Dieter Grau in Copenhagen. Increasing sewer capacity, through the construction of ever-bigger pipes, tunnels and pumping stations, can no longer be considered affordable, justifiable or sustainable.

Both Philadelphia and Dublin have made many steps forward in terms of retrofitting the water system to address quality, runoff and management but it remains a challenge of education where costs for plumbing, potable water and wastewater systems are understood as a cost to the individual but the costs of managing stormwater are not and are paid for collectively by the city and, therefore, considered 'free'.

Economic trends and technological developments are a cause for optimism.

Whereas it is clear that there are threats posed by climate change, insufficient awareness of and commitment to wellness and an imperative to make a step change in the way that water systems and ecology are managed, there are also a number of reasons for believing that economic and technological trends can be made to work in favour of the environment and landscape. As well as the imperatives described elsewhere in this book and chapter, there is strong evidence to suggest that in the developed countries of the northern hemisphere, the transition from the industrial economy to the knowledge economy is accompanied with a significant urge to achieve a more well-balanced place.[13]

The knowledge economy has altered the dynamics of urban economics, encouraged the growth of agglomerations and increased the importance of spaces for encounter and their role in innovation. These are new forms of economic clusters and they are formed by public policy or by individuals and firms and include universities, science and technology parks and centres of the 'creative economy' with studios and home-working. The clustering of knowledge enterprises around centres of education and research has reinforced urban concentration as described by the UN earlier in these conclusions.[14] Many, however, are located at the edge of city centres and around airports: they have fragmented urban space further and contributed to the effects of sprawl internationally and in Scotland.[15]

The spatial expression of the knowledge economy is likely to be the model for cities and urban areas for the foreseeable future. Knowledge as both a productive capacity and an output has no particular spatial requirements other than the proximity of those engaged in its pursuit. The new spaces of production, therefore, are the spaces of knowledge: universities, science parks and cultural quarters, which are created side by side with new spaces of consumption and new patterns of social inequality.[16]

In the emergent years of the knowledge economy, an early proposition was that 'place' was no longer of importance: all that people required was a good internet connection to bring the entire globe within easy reach. The consequence of this 'death of distance' was said to be that the city of streets, squares, stations, parks, shops and restaurants would be replaced by a 'city of bits', a virtual city with a street pattern consisting of digital information highways.[17] In fact, the converse has proven to be the case. New ideas and innovative solutions come into being through intensive communication and exchange of knowledge with others. The proximity of people is very important. It makes more sense for knowledge workers to pop into a colleague's office than to work via email on a new project with an unknown person on the other side of the world.[18] People still need physical contact with others, not only in their work but also in their free time. And cities, with an 'Experience Economy' of cafes, restaurants, parks, squares, cinemas, galleries, venues and shopping centres, offer all these services on demand. This is the underlying reason why innovative cities such as Stockholm, Barcelona, Munich, Toulouse, Dublin and Louvain have blossomed in the knowledge economy.[19] It is Verhagen's talented individuals who seek to live in these places. These forces are equally driving Scotland's principal cities and towns — notably Edinburgh, Glasgow, Dundee and Aberdeen.

The digital revolution now drives many and various aspects of the world economy, including banking, retail, energy, transportation, education, publishing, media and health. Information, Communications and Technology systems (ICTs) are transforming the ways social interactions and personal relationships are conducted, with fixed, mobile and broadcast networks converging. Devices and objects are becoming increasingly connected through the 'Internet of Things', leading to convergence between ICTs and the economy on a grand scale. Cities and city-regions are well-placed to maximise the opportunities of the digital economy. These economies of scale also reinforce the trend towards urban concentration described by the UN and others.[20]

Many cities are adopting digital strategies. In terms of the ecosystem supporting cities, Peter Head describes the forms of technology platforms that can support the mainstreaming of ecosystem services described by Tom Armour and Jonathan Hughes, such as digital resource flow modelling for human and ecological systems that are operable at national and regional scales. Such systems will help more efficient management of oxygen, water, energy, food and raw materials in a world that will need 30% more water, 40% more energy and 50% more food by 2030 (Peter Head). The ideas of the Carbon Sequestration Trust, described by Peter Head, providing open-source tools to manipulate metadata to help city-regions make the transition from an industrial to a knowledge economy means that the aims and aspirations called for by a number of the authors in this book are in line with emerging market demand and therefore stand a greater chance of success in the economy of the twenty-first century. There remains, however, the need for further research and development to achieve the interconnected system that will allow people to interact better with the systems and services that serve them (Peter Head).

There is widespread recognition and embracing of the need for new ways to view the natural world and Jonathon Porritt advocates embracing in part the monetised view of natural resources as green or natural capital. This he sees as key to winning over the business community since relying on the public sector and non-governmental organisations will be insufficient to deliver the ideas described by the authors in this book. Wealth creators need to be part of the movement. Porritt maintains that business people know when to embrace a good idea and how to make it work.

These propositions and ideas, central to the knowledge economy and accelerated by the technological innovations of the digital revolution, help reinforce the use of resources in a resilient way in a 'circular economy' rather than the prevalence of the 'take-make-dispose' model described by Peter Head. Transition strategies to move from a consumption economy to a resilience economy are essential for society to embrace what Head and others have described as the 'ecological civilisation'.

There are very clear lessons on how to do things with considerable best practice to rely on.

There is a very significant body of best practice in this book for people to learn from. The story of the Emscher Landscape Park (ELP) described by Michael Schwarze-Rodrian is internationally recognised as an exemplar of long-term sound environmental practice. The ELP is much more than a park — it is an approach to urban greening driven by a long-term vision of attractive city landscapes within a regional park system. This long-term commitment by the cities of the Ruhr is one of the most significant lessons that can be learned for current practice today. Strategic and voluntary cooperation at regional and local level, politically and technically, has been essential to realising the Ruhr and Emscher vision and to deliver the new regional park system.

The Emscher programme has been delivered through public investment in a cluster of cities in the Ruhr agglomeration that has been consistently supported by the State of North-Rhine Westphalia and the German Federal Government to enhance the budgets of the cities thought to be otherwise inadequate for the scale of the task. Political consensus and moderation have ensured the programme has continued unimpeded through an approach that has been cooperative, pragmatic and based on 'learning by doing'. ELP is a central and integrated element of a sustainable economic regeneration strategy — including cultural renewal — through processes of transformation rather than demolition and through the delivery of nature-based landscape solutions in and around the cities of the Ruhr. These processes have helped to replace an economy founded on coal and steel with a diverse service and knowledge economy with investment in cultural, educational and technological institutions where existing buildings and infrastructure have been reused wherever possible. The five iterations of ELP have served it well.

ELP also innovated by reconfiguring a linear and hierarchical process of feasibility through strategy to delivery by establishing two simultaneous planning processes with different skill sets for developing strategies on one hand with the operational and technical knowledge for delivering projects on the other, while at the same time also working at three scales: the regional, inter-urban and local. It is one matter to develop such a process for a quick burn intensive project like delivering a major event such as the Olympic or Commonwealth Games, it is quite another to sustain this momentum over decades to repurpose the programme and deal with changing political priorities and language whilst keeping the core mission intact — the comprehensive regeneration and transformation of the Ruhr region. This requires long-term revenue investment in core teams, not just in capital projects, to build a reputation for quality in strategies, programmes and projects which deliver economic, cultural and environmental benefits.

In the context of Jonathon Porritt's plea for the involvement of business, it is interesting to note that in the Ruhr-Emscher programme significant public intervention was needed in the first twenty or so years to deliver the manifest change necessary for the private sector to come on board and make significant investments. Although they are of a different scale, other programmes such as the lowland canals of Scotland and the Pennines watershed landscape, between Leeds and Manchester, underline the precepts of good practice developed in the Ruhr-Emscher. The Pennines has worked with the cultural landscapes of the Brontës and Ted Hughes and the lowland canals have delivered exemplar iconic projects including the Falkirk Wheel, the Kelpies and the Helix Park. These smaller place-based programmes nonetheless demonstrate that whatever the scale, it is possible to deliver the highest quality of outcomes through approaches rooted in place, maintaining commitment to vision, retaining a clarity of mission and a determination in delivery over time and which are led by dedicated personnel who champion the corporate memory of the organisations and the landscapes they serve.

These initiatives have common elements including: the ability of partnerships to deliver landscape change that underpins social and economic benefits; the time needed for partnerships to build political support and organisational capacity and to put in place the resources to achieve results on the ground; the need for strong and robust project planning to ensure continuity to meet the challenges of changing circumstances; the importance of maintaining a coherent initiative with a strong narrative to engage communities and the media; and the celebration of success, which is important for wider recognition and should not be underestimated.

The New Normal: There are new standards emerging that have changed the perception of what is possible – they are game changers in what is done and how it is done.

Although everything in this book stands out in some way, four of the projects have achieved international recognition: the High Line, the Queen Elizabeth Olympic Park, the Cheonggyecheon River Restoration Project and the canal projects around Falkirk; together, they mean that things in practice will never be quite the same ever again.

At a time when meaningful open space in urban areas is becoming a more precious commodity and with awareness of resource depletion and recycling gaining ground, society is turning to the innovative repair and restoration of land with new uses now being sought for decommissioned waterfronts, landfill sites, abandoned infrastructure and other post-industrial structures. These places can provide a new form of urban nature when transformed into open and green spaces that provide environmental, aesthetic and recreational benefits, serve as locations for civic interaction and urban life and support economic development. What is remarkable about the High Line, the Olympic Park and the Cheonggyecheon River and the Kelpies/Helix Park is the degree of innovation and creativity that Verhagen ascribes to successful transformation and changing perceptions.

Consider the challenge of presentation and communication faced by the High Line team to turn public and official perception from a starting point of 'why would you want to go up there' to embracing a 'park in the sky'. Part of this was achieved through revealing the intrinsic beauty and regenerative opportunity in transforming rather than demolishing the old heritage structures much like ELP. Here the artist, a photographer, changed people's perceptions of a space seen from below by revealing the beauty and character of the line from above – to move people from a perspective of a redundant structure to 'a green roof extending to three hectares in the middle of the city'. As Switkin states: "much of the appeal of the finished project lies in the plurality of meaning for disparate people and groups – politically, ecologically, historically, socially and economically". Politically, it is a testament to community activism. Ecologically, it has delivered a range of linked habitats valuable in this dense city area. Historically, as a conservation project, it has enabled the retrofitting and transformation of an abandoned rail line as a new public space. Socially, it is at the heart of a revitalised neighbourhood and is a world-class park, where families, tourists and the community come together. Economically, the entrepreneurial effort involved has demonstrated that public spaces can generate revenue, attract businesses and stimulate local economic growth.

With the Olympic Park in London, the challenges were complexity, pace, budget and deadline, as well as coping with the consequences of the financial crash in order to move attitudes away from a picturesque view of landscape to the emerging aesthetic of the 'new nature'. Environmental sustainability was at the core of this vision, including waste minimisation and reducing the consumption of energy, materials and potable water. The aim of 'one planet living' was used as a mantra to drive the London Games and their legacy to be as sustainable as possible. A Sustainable Development Strategy became an essential and practical tool to assist in the measurement of progress with objectives and the delivery of impacts, thereby ensuring that aspirations became targets with a carbon footprint study commissioned to assess embodied and created carbon. The five overarching policy themes established by London's Olympic Delivery Authority have become watchwords for a 'new normal' in environmental design: climate change; waste; biodiversity; inclusion; and healthy living developed into the 12 principles described by Neil Mattinson in his essay.

In Scotland, the innovative design of the Falkirk Wheel together with the Kelpie sculptures and the Helix Park have become internationally recognised and have helped to turn Falkirk into one of Scotland's premier visitor destinations (Richard Millar).

In a further synergy between contributions in the book, the projects in 'learning from action' stress the principle described by Jonathan Hughes that it is no longer sufficient to maintain 'islands of nature'. No matter how elegant, well-executed and intrinsically sustainable, all projects need to help link up networks of green and blue infrastructure in order to ensure that the ecological system can continue to benefit natural habitats, drive down the carbon footprint and enhance the liveability of the city and the wellness of its inhabitants – in short, to increase what was once described as the carrying capacity of the city. The biodiverse nature of the design of these and other leading projects maximises the opportunities for a rich ecology whilst contributing to atmospheric cooling through the introduction of extensive green spaces with tree planting and water bodies which help reduce the effects of the 'urban heat island'.

The conclusions from the authors of these chapters echo those from best practice: the need for strong leadership to take decisions, champion the programme, put in place a team with the expertise to develop strategies to review, develop and promote the values of the project; the need for a long-term vision with clear goals and action plan to bring about a step change in delivery, leading to social and environmental changes and citizen benefits; the ability to overcome the inevitable obstacles, whether external resistance, internal opposition or the attrition of resources or budgets; the ability to build consensus such that doubters can be brought on board through communications and marketing to raise awareness and support; the recognition that building roads, pipes and concrete is a redundant paradigm to improve the competitiveness of cities, whereas removing major roads and delivering effective public transport measures can revitalise a city, establishing a new paradigm; and finally, and in an echo of Porritt's opening call to arms, there is a need to focus efforts on delivering the dreams of younger generations.

The New Aesthetics of Landscape – new environmental imperatives are changing the way places look.

In the eighteenth century, when (western) man was exploring the world, society was transfixed by the wonder of nature and the smallness of people – nature was held in awe and the environment was described as 'sublime', invoking wonder and a desire to explore understand and conquer. Wildness and wilderness were feared, or at least respected, for their power.

Later in the nineteenth century following the industrial revolution, no longer were nature, the land-scape and the environment to be feared, for they could be tamed and made into a pleasure garden for our enjoyment and, as a result, the aesthetic changed and the 'picturesque' was born. For many decades, those concerned with landscape planning and design could answer many if not all of the challenges they faced by balancing their thought and their aesthetic somewhere between these two schools – from the great houses of the late eighteenth century to the municipal parks and gardens of Victorian cities through to the new landscapes around Loch Faskally in Perthshire, where picturesque areas of deciduous almost decorative planting rather than indigenous woodland was laid out to soften the edges of the new lochs required for the hydro system on the rivers. If not formal, all of these landscapes were at the very least neat, manicured and maintained.[21]

But by the end of the twentieth century, the desecration of the industrial revolution had left society with a truly epic mess to clear up; a desire for greener more natural places emerged with recognition that these green places were important for health then and would be for the health of future generations. At the beginning of the twenty-first century, we have passed from the sublime appreciation of landscape through the romantic picturesque to a time where a new aesthetic is emerging – a new-natural, a re-wilding – when areas once thought to have unkempt characteristics have been rediscovered for what they are – richly biodiverse and of great importance to human beings. This sense of wildness is becoming loved once again for its intrinsic and indigenous qualities of distinctiveness. In a world where most daily objects (smart phones and cars) and experiences (food and retail – walk down most high streets) are universal and increasingly anonymous, the possibilities for landscape to bring distinctiveness to our places is very clear. Furthermore, Sir Harry Burns has invited us to consider the salutogenic landscape – a landscape for wellness and one that encourages social contact. So we are changing what we do – the landscape is no longer municipal, nor picturesque, nor sublime – it is neo-natural – a biophilic approach to design and to management – one that embraces the meaning and science of ecology and salutogenesis – and a good thing too.[22]

— 2a
The sublime landscape – a view of
nature untamed, mysterious and awe-
inspiring. A place of wildness, wild
habitats and wild creatures.
(Scottish lake landscape in front of
mountains, oil on canvas, Frank E
Jamieson, 1834-1839)

— 2b
The picturesque landscape – nature
is tamed, shaped, fitted to man's
needs and occupation. A classical and
pastoral rather than a natural aesthetic.
(Easby Hall and Easby Abbey with
Richmond, Yorkshire in the Background,
oil on canvas, George Cuitt, 1743-1818)

— 2c
The biophilic landscape – unthreatening
nature is welcomed back into the city.
Order is replaced with a natural and
informal aesthetic. The natural and
semi-natural is recognised to possess
salutogenic and ecological properties
necessary for its own sake and for the
future of humankind.
(digital visualisation for the Garden
Bridge, London)

Into the mainstream and an integrated process of design, management, governance and funding places and environments.

In the essay by Jonathan Hughes and in the introduction, we have seen that there has been a transition in green thinking from the romantic views of nature of the eighteenth and nineteenth centuries through the scientific analysis and taxonomy of the nineteenth and twentieth centuries to the political mainstream in the late twentieth and early twenty-first centuries
– a journey increasingly seen as essential if we are to address the threats of global population growth and climate change. It is clear from the essays in this anthology that from the start of the millennium, huge strides have been made with this transition. With this comes the need for further work to ensure that greater awareness is accompanied by equal weight in the future design and management of places and the integration of disciplines. The need for integrated thinking, integrated design and integrated management occurs again and again in the essays but we are in the beginnings of being able to define how this might come about.

For example, Howard Neukrug has explained how Philadelphia is seeking opportunities to use urban redevelopment as a means to coordinate and integrate key systems and services to create a more sustainable, attractive and liveable city. One of the key lessons from Philadelphia is recognising the degree to which urban land management and land use decisions impact on water quality and quantity and that water management becomes harder and harder if the complexity of the urban systems of land management are not addressed. This is precisely the issue that the resilience systems under development by the Carbon Sequestration Trust described by Peter Head are intended to address.

Neukrug contends that as we rethink and rebuild our urban centres as sustainable, attractive and productive places to live and work, we also need to engineer them to be more resilient to natural and man-made disturbances. It will take vision and leadership to overcome the multiple barriers that confront us

in finding local solutions for our global water problems and to do so in a way that supports a liveable, growing and sustainable city. Given the level of future investment that will be necessary to renew Victorian urban water systems, it is an ideal time to integrate environmental protection strategies and responsible land use and zoning with infrastructure improvements through the use of integrated urban systems thinking.

Equally, the notion of urban liveability, as both Lisa Switkin and Evert Verhagen have pointed out, is becoming more and more relevant as cities position themselves for growth and to compete to attract residents, workers, entrepreneurs and tourists. In this respect, a thriving economy, affordable housing and access to public transportation all contribute to urban liveability. Above all, however, many people who describe their cities as 'liveable' attribute this in no small part to the 'public realm', which includes greenspace and nature, of a 'human scale' with walkable streets and a strong sense of community fostered by public spaces. This is key to the understanding of public space design through sensitivity to natural and social systems and knowledge of global challenges including water quality management, deforestation, urbanisation and land reclamation (Switkin).

The vision for the Olympic Park was rooted in social and economic sustainability, including the provision of high-quality affordable housing, improved education facilities and improved health facilities. Environmental sustainability was at the core of this vision, minimising waste and the consumption of energy, materials and potable water.

To date, huge amounts of data have been, and are being, assembled without any clear purpose and proper means to use the data. Peter Head's work directed at linking ecology, resources, human wellbeing and the economics of the market is another way to achieve the integration that Porritt, Burns and Hughes are all calling for.

But whereas we all recognise that this is needed, we do not yet have the tools or understanding to make it happen. Both Jonathon Porritt and Peter Head refer to the importance of these technological breakthroughs to the natural world in respect of water technologies, energy technologies, waste technologies and an innovation process established to drive these forward all the time. Evert Verhagen has added creativity to these. As Jonathon Porritt has put it: "society has the technology platforms to build a sustainable world for 2050".

Knowledge development, globalisation and 'authentic' towns and cities are mutually supportive. As the knowledge economy takes hold, the cities that are able to adapt early to the new economic requirements will also be able to capitalise on their local distinctiveness, as localisation (the increasing importance of city distinctiveness, authenticity and identity) becomes as important as processes of globalisation.[23] The emergence of the knowledge economy has revealed an apparent contradiction between cities and globalisation as a 'global-local paradox': in a world that is becoming increasingly more integrated, cities must rely more on their specific local characteristics — expressed by some as 'authenticity'. These unique characteristics help to determine what a city or major town excels in and the ways in which it can distinguish itself in the competition with other cities. The knowledge economy and the related global-local paradox mean that cities, as in the past, compete for the favours of inhabitants, companies and visitors. Every city derives benefits by drawing in knowledge workers and knowledge-intensive activities and, as a result, gains a competitive advantage. In order to maintain and increase their attractiveness to knowledge workers and

other target groups, cities must reflect on what sort of profile they should have and many have developed a competitiveness strategy as a consequence. Thus, inter-city competition for knowledge and innovation requires cities to become 'creative'. These topics and trends are well-described by Evert Verhagen in his essay on creativity.

The job of city development is never concluded: it is a process, just as community development is never complete since communities — residential, business or visitor — are dynamic and constantly changing. The spaces that serve their needs must change with them. The economic case has never been stronger for a reinvigoration of, and investment in, public space, whether that is public squares or parks and gardens. But there is a fundamental mismatch between the beneficiaries of these places and those who pay for them that causes a logjam in the delivery of this proposition.

Integrated planning and decision-making in city-regions — supported by modelling of urban-rural resource flows — meet the 'measuring' called for by Hughes in his chapter. Basically, Head is suggesting that right now we have the technology to embed integrated planning and decision-making into city-regions that are supported by modelling of urban-rural resource flows from human and ecological activity for food, water, energy and materials including pollution. Modelling should cover the water, carbon, nitrogen and phosphorus cycles that are critical for all life not just human life. For this to be useful for decision-making, this modelling needs to include economic, social and environmental aspects, with a common and credible economic and risk management methodology.

Overall conclusions

The evidence of this book is that a new paradigm is emerging for the
environment and landscape: it is integrated and it has new standards.
The paradigm change is characterised through ten clear constructs:

1. Urban Growth

In the coming decades, 80% of the population will experience their daily
interaction with ecosystems in city-regions. Many of these will be in the
successful 'super-city' clusters of North America and Europe. In all of these
cities, urban sprawl is threatening urban coalescence and causing attrition
of the ecosystem. The 'compact city' concept is one of the opportunities
to address this issue.

2. Climate Change

Climate Change has negative effects on human life through extreme
weather events such as flooding, urban heat and drought; scarcity of
resources; environmental degradation; loss of biodiversity; and pollution
of air, soil and water with significant risks for people, assets, economies
and ecosystems. Intergovernmental action to address climate change is
accelerating. Trees, vegetation and water have a beneficial effect on all of
these challenges.

3. Health

Society has concentrated on illness and not on wellness. Many health
problems in the developed world are a consequence of de-industrialisation.
There are significant benefits for health to be gained from access to the
natural world. Planning and designing environments that bring people and
nature together are critical to supporting wellness and promoting social
connectedness. Continued and enhanced attention on involving people in
testing and implementing the changes that affect them is very important.

4. Water

The transformation of landscape and environment is to a greater or lesser
extent about the stewardship of water and water systems. The two are
inseparable and fundamental to understanding and addressing climate
change. They are also irrevocably bound into wider urban processes just as
they are with health. Increasing sewer capacity to carry rainwater, through
the construction of ever-bigger pipes, tunnels and pumping stations, can
no longer be considered affordable, justifiable or sustainable.

Reflections
Towards a new paradigm
in landscape and environment
275

5. Economy and Technology

The knowledge economy has no particular spatial requirements other than the proximity of those engaged in its pursuit. The proximity of people is very important. The knowledge economy thrives in cities with concentrations of higher education and an 'experience economy' of cafes, restaurants, parks, squares, cinemas and galleries. Concepts of 'green' or 'natural' capital are key to winning over the business community. Open data platforms growing out of the digital revolution offer significant opportunities to monitor the urban ecosystem and build resilience – for the natural system, for the city-region and for the health of its population.

6. Best practice

There is significant evidence to demonstrate that partnerships can deliver landscape change that underpins social and economic benefits. These need to use resources wisely and build capacity to achieve results on the ground. There is a need for strong and robust project planning to ensure continuity and to meet the challenges of changing circumstances. It is important to maintain a coherent initiative with a strong narrative to engage communities and the media over what can sometimes be a sustained period of time. The celebration of success is important for wider recognition and should not be underestimated.

7. An emerging 'new normal'

There is new practice emerging that has changed the perception of what is possible – a game changer in what is done and how it is done. Characteristics include: the need for strong leadership to take decisions, champion the programme and put in place a team with the expertise to develop strategies to review, develop and promote the values of the project; a long-term vision with clear goals and action plan in order to bring about a step change in delivery, leading to social and environmental changes and citizen benefits; the ability to overcome the inevitable obstacles and build consensus such that doubters can be brought on board; and recognition that building roads, pipes and concrete is a redundant paradigm to improve the competitiveness of cities whereas reducing major roads and delivering effective public transport measures can revitalise a city, provide space for greening and help to establish a new paradigm.

8. The new landscape aesthetic

New environmental imperatives are changing the way places look. In the twenty-first century, our aesthetic has become a new-natural, a re-wilding, when areas once thought to have unkempt characteristics have been rediscovered for what they are – richly biodiverse and of great importance to human beings and highly regarded for their intrinsic and indigenous qualities. These are landscapes for wellness and for social contact. They are neo-natural and biophilic.

9. Into the mainstream

Landscape and environment have made a journey from romantic and scientific appreciation into mainstream thinking. This is essential in order to address the threats of global population growth and climate change but this greater awareness needs to be accompanied by equal weight in the consideration of future design and management of places. It is increasingly recognised that all the disciplines, activities and services in the city-region are inter-connected and now require integrated thinking, integrated design and integrated management.

10. Green infrastructure

Cities and regions require a network of natural and semi-natural land scape and water (green infrastructure) that is the equal of their networks of transport and utilities (engineering infrastructure). This will ensure that the benefits of natural and semi-natural environments work well for natural and human habitats (ecosystem services) through a process of designing and regenerating (retrofitting) cities, towns and neighbourhoods to create elegant, economically viable and resilient places (biophilic and ecological urbanism) that are socially balanced for the benefit of their populations (wellness).

1

United Nations Department of Economic and Social Affairs, 2015.
http://www.un.org/en/development/desa/news/population/
2015-report.html.

2

By its nature, this chapter is synoptic and is based to a substantive
degree on the content and evidence assembled by the individual authors
in the book. Where conclusions are based on the findings of the authors,
the reader is directed by author name, chapter number or title to the
original context and, through their footnotes, to the sources for the work.
Where new points have been raised in the text, footnotes are provided
here for these sources.

3

HABITAT III Regional Report on Housing and Urban Development
for The UNECE Region, Brian Evans et al, *Towards a City-focused,
People-centred and Integrated Approach to the New Urban Agenda*
(Geneva: 2016), http:// www.unece.org/housing-and-land-management/
projects/habitat-iii-regional-report.html.

4

Brian Evans, Pietro Elisei, Orna Rosenfeld, Gulnara Roll, Amie
Figueiredo & Marco Keiner (2016) HABITAT III – Toward a New
Urban Agenda, *disP - The Planning Review*, 52:1, 86–91,
DOI: 10.1080/02513625.2016.1171053. To link to this article:
http://dx.doi.org/10.1080/02513625.2016.1171053.

5

Mid-2014 Small Area Population Estimates Scotland, National Records
of Scotland, December 2015, http://www.nrscotland.gov.uk/files//
statistics/population-estimates/sape2014/sape-2001dz-2014mye.pdf.

6

Evans et al, ibid.

7

UN General Assembly, *Transforming our world: the 2030 Agenda for
Sustainable Development*, September 2015, A/RES/70/1, https://
sustainabledevelopment.un.org/post2015/transformingourworld; Draft of
the New Urban Agenda, HABITAT III, May 2016.

8

OECD, *Compact City Policies: A Comparative Assessment*, *OECD
Green Growth Studies*, (OECD Publishing, 2012) ISBN 978-92-64-
16784-1.

9

HABITAT III Regional Report on Housing and Urban Development
for The UNECE Region, Brian Evans et al, *Towards a City-focused,
People-centred and Integrated Approach to the New Urban Agenda*
(Geneva: 2016), http:// www.unece.org/housing-and-land-management/
projects/habitat-iii-regional-report.html.

10

Jan Gehl, *Cities for People, Island Press*, (2010) ISBN-13 978-
1597265737 and Jan Gehl and Birgitte Svarre, *How to study public
life: Methods in Urban Design* (Island Press, 2013) ISBN-13 978-
1610914239.

11

Nick Wates, *The Community Planning Handbook: how people can
shape their cities, towns and villages in any part of the world*, (Earthscan tools for Community Planning), (Routledge, 1999), ISBN-13
978-1853836540 and Nick Wates, T*he Community Planning Events
Manual: How to use collaborative planning and urban design events to
improve your environment* (Earthscan Tools for Community Planning)
(Routledge, 2008), ISBN-13 978-1844074921.

12

Richard Wilkinson and Kate Pickett, *The Spirit Level: Why more equal
societies almost always do better* (Allen Lane, 2009).

13

HABITAT III Regional Report on Housing and Urban Development for
The UNECE Region, op. cit.

14

Evans et al, UN, op cit.

15

J.D. Kasarda and G. Lindsay, *Aerotropolis – The Way We'll Live Next.*

16

Ali Madanipour, *Knowledge economy and the city: spaces of knowledge*
(regions and cities) (Routledge, 2013).

17

W.J. Mitchell, *City of Bits: Space, Place and the Infobahn* (Cambridge,
MA: MIT Press, 1995). Frances Cairncross, *The Death of Distance,
How the communications revolution will change our lives*, (Harvard
Business School Press, 1997).

18

A.L. Saxenian. *Regional Advantage: Culture and Competition in Silicon
Valley and Route 128* (Cambridge, MA: Harvard University Press, 1994).

19

Madanipour, op cit.

20

Evans et al, op cit.

21

The sublime and the picturesque in the contemporary context, Beauty,
function and sustainability in the age of austerity, Landscape Institute
National Conference, Sheffield, March 2016.

22

In 'a Sense of Place, a sense of time' by John Brikerhoff Jackson and later
in 'Grasping the Thistle', the essay by Frank Arneil Walker, these authors
explore the proposition that concepts of identity in aesthetics are to some
considerable extent governed by the interaction of the genius loci – the
spirit of the place – with the zeitgeist – the spirit of the times.

23

P. Cooke and K. Morgan, *The Associational Economy: Firms, Regions,
and Innovation* (Oxford: Oxford University Press, 1998).

List of Contributors

Tom Armour

Tom Armour is a Director at Arup (www.arup.
com) where he leads the award-winning landscape
architecture business, which he founded in 1990,
with offices in the UK and internationally. He works
with clients on projects around the world on regional
strategies, masterplanning and the design and delivery
of major infrastructure projects, new parks, public realm
and public spaces. Tom played key leadership roles
in the detailed design and delivery of the landscape
design for two of the biggest and most successful UK
projects in recent years: the London Olympic Park
(South) and the £8 billion High Speed 1 railway link
between London and the Channel Tunnel. Tom is also
widely involved in research initiatives, presentations
and academic work. His approach encompasses the
vital role that landscape design plays in contributing
to today's urgent challenges in the built environment,
including the creation of healthy, liveable cities, places
for people, designed-in resilience to climate change
and the promotion of green and blue infrastructure,
biodiversity and wellbeing. This approach is set out
in Arup's 'Best Use of Thought Leadership Award'–
winning 'Cities Alive' document, for which he was the
lead author (www.arup.com/Homepage_Cities_Alive.
aspx). A selection of recent projects include a major
international Botanic Garden, work on the Garden
Bridge and green infrastructure strategies for the
London Infrastructure Plan 2050, the City of Madrid
(Madrid + Natural), the Crown Estates (the Wild West
End), Fitzrovia and the West End in London.

Professor Sir Harry Burns

Sir Harry Burns graduated in medicine from Glasgow
University in 1974. He trained in surgery in Glasgow
and he was appointed Consultant Surgeon in the
University Department of Surgery at the Royal Infirmary
in Glasgow in 1984. Working with patients in the east
end of Glasgow gave him an insight into the complex
interrelationships between social and economic
status and illness. He completed a Master's degree
in Public Health in 1990 and, shortly afterwards, was
appointed Medical Director of The Royal Infirmary. In
1994, he became Director of Public Health for Greater
Glasgow Health Board, a position he occupied until
2005. During his time with Greater Glasgow Health
Board, he continued research into the problems of
social determinants of health and, in 2005, he became
Chief Medical Officer for Scotland. In this role, his
responsibilities included aspects of public health policy,
health protection and, for a time, sport. He was knighted
in 2011 and, in April 2014, he became Professor
of Global Public Health at Strathclyde University
where he continues his interest in understanding how
societies create wellness. In 2014, the First Minister,
Nicola Sturgeon, presented him a lifetime achievement
award from the Scottish Government and the Scottish
Parliament for Public Service.

Professor Brian Mark Evans

Brian Mark Evans is Professor of Urbanism and
Landscape at the Mackintosh School of Architecture,
the Glasgow School of Art and director of the Glasgow
Urban Laboratory. He was previously Artistic Professor
of Urban Design & Planning at Chalmers School of
Architecture in Gothenburg and, from 1990 to 2015,
was a partner with Gillespies LLP where he developed
the disciplines of landscape planning and urban design
and pioneered ecological urbanism. From 2005 to
2010, he was Deputy Chair and Chair of Design Review
with Architecture & Design Scotland and, before that,
Enabler with the Commission for Architecture and the
Built Environment (CABE) London. He is a founding
Director and Academician of the Academy of Urbanism,
London. He has led award-winning projects in some 20
countries on 3 continents, leading to over 50 national
and international awards for professional and design
excellence. He is currently advising the United Nations,
Geneva on cities in preparation for Habitat III, Quito
2016. Brian is author of over 100 publications on
design, landscape planning and urbanism published in

English, German, Swedish, Russian, Dutch, Spanish and French. He has participated in and chaired over 100 national and international conferences in Scotland and further afield, both in the UK and other parts of, Europe, including Scandinavia and Russia. He is a Chartered Town Planner and Chartered Designer. Brian practises, researches, teaches and speaks widely on urbanism, urban design and landscape planning.

Sue Evans MBE

Sue Evans is Head of Development at the Central Scotland Green Network Trust (CSGNT). Since 2009, she has been supporting the development and delivery of the Central Scotland Green Network initiative. Previously Sue was Head of Development for Central Scotland Forest Trust (CSFT) – which became CSGNT in 2014 – where she was responsible for development, community and thematic work. This included major roles in the development of the award-winning Helix project and the Falkirk Greenspace initiative. Sue joined the Board of Architecture + Design Scotland in April 2014. In 2008, she was awarded an MBE for services to forestry. She is a Fellow of the Landscape Institute, a member of the Institute's Policy and Communications Committee and, over recent years, has been acting as a judge for various landscape and architectural awards. Sue has also been a Local Adviser for Strathclyde and Ayrshire for Scottish Natural Heritage. Before joining CSFT in 1993, Sue was in private practice where she worked on a number of regeneration projects, including the masterplanning and delivery of the Glasgow Garden Festival 1988.

Dieter Grau

Dieter Grau is Executive Partner and Managing Director at Ramboll Studio Dreiseitl (formerly Atelier Dreiseitl) with offices in Europe, Asia, the Middle East and America. He has more than 20 years of experience as an acknowledged designer and expert specialising in the interplay between urban water and the impact of infrastructural challenges on the liveability quality of cities and nature. He has extensive international experience in complex urban projects, which achieve resilience, distinctive design and maximum investment benefits through a new generation of blue-green infrastructure solutions. His focus on interdisciplinary collaboration to drive the agenda of open spaces is highly integrated with the often unseen, functional, infrastructural elements set within a diverse range of cultures and regions. Guiding teams and leading the offices' commitment to deliver world-class design, it has been Dieter's privilege to take many innovative projects from concept through to full implementation. A frequent guest lecturer and architectural jury member, he has authored numerous books, including the latest edition of 'Waterscape Innovations'.

Robin Gray

Robin Gray is Development Manager for the South Pennines Local Nature Partnership where he is responsible for managing natural environment projects and programmes across the South Pennines. He managed the Watershed Landscape Project as Development Manager for Pennine Prospects (the Southern Pennines Rural Regeneration Company) from 2009 to 2013. The project was awarded the 2012 UK Landscape Award and the Landscape Institute Award for communications and presentation. A Chartered Member of the Landscape Institute, Robin has over twenty-five years of experience working on regional-scale landscape projects, including woodland creation, waterside regeneration and restoration of derelict sites to community use. Robin has a passion for the landscape of the South Pennines where he lives and works.

Professor Peter Head CBE

Peter Head is a champion of sustainable development. He established the Ecological Sequestration Trust in 2011. He advocates that changing the way we invest public and private money in the built environment could be made very much more effective if the public and private sectors adopt sustainable development principles. Peter is a civil and structural engineer who has become a recognised world leader in major

bridges – he received an OBE for successfully
delivering the Second Severn Crossing as Government
Agent – in advanced composite technology and now in
sustainable development in cities and regions. He has
won many awards for his work, including the Award of
Merit of the International Association for Bridge and
Structural Engineering (IABSE), the Royal Academy of
Engineering's Silver Medal and the Prince Philip Award
for polymers in the service of mankind. He joined
Arup in 2004 to create and lead their planning and
integrated urbanism team, which by 2011 had doubled
in size. He directed work on the Dongtan Eco City
Planning project, which in 2005 was voted by Chinese
developers as the most influential development project
in China. In July 2008, he was awarded an Honorary
Doctorate in engineering at Bristol University, where
he is Visiting Professor in Sustainable Systems
Engineering. In May 2011, he was appointed Visiting
Professor in Ecocities at Westminster University. In
2009, he was awarded the Sir Frank Whittle Medal
of the Royal Academy of Engineering for a lifetime
contribution to the wellbeing of the nation through
environmental innovation. In 2008, he was named by
the Guardian newspaper as one of 50 people that
could 'save the planet'. He was cited by Time magazine
in 2008 as one of 30 global eco heroes and has been
one of CNN's Principle Voices.

Jonathan Hughes
Jonathan Hughes is Chief Executive Officer (CEO)
of the Scottish Wildlife Trust, Scotland's leading
environmental charity. Before being appointed CEO,
Jonathan was the Trust's Director of Conservation
and Deputy CEO. Jonathan is an elected Regional
Councillor of the International Union for the
Conservation of Nature (IUCN), the world's oldest
and largest conservation organisation. In 2013,
Jonathan co-founded the World Forum on Natural
Capital, a global initiative led by the Scottish Wildlife
Trust in partnership with United Nations Environment
Programme, IUCN, the World Business Council for
Sustainable Development and the Natural Capital

Coalition. In his spare time, he enjoys playing tennis,
football and, most of all, table football. He is a
knowledgeable field naturalist.

Dr Gyeng Chul Kim
Dr Gyeng Chul Kim is Special Advisor on the
improvement of public transport to the Secretary for
the Department of Transport and Communication
(DOTC) of the Government of the Philippines. Dr
Kim provides advice on public transport policy and
implementation of the Bus Rapid Transit programmes
in Cebu and Manila. He is Transport Consultant to
the World Bank and the Asian Development Bank,
where he is a mission member of the transport
programmes for Kolkata, India and Jakarta, Indonesia.
Dr Kim was previously President of the Korea
Transport Institute (KOTI – www.koti.re.kr), acting as
a Vice Minister of the Korean National Government.
His career in transport policies and management
spans nearly two decades with specific interest in
various modes of public transport. During his four-year
period as Director General of the Seoul Metropolitan
Government, he conducted the reform of the Seoul
bus network. The reform demonstrated how a large
and rapidly growing city could increase ridership and
significantly relieve congestion in a short period of
time through transit reform. The experience in Seoul
acts as a world-leading, best practice exemplar.
He received his Ph.D. in Transport Planning and
Administration at Seoul National University in 1993.
Upon completing his Ph.D., he taught graduate
research courses at the University of Leeds, UK and
Kyoto University, Japan.

Tom Leahy
Tom Leahy is a Chartered Engineer, a Fellow of
Engineers Ireland, a Fellow of the Irish Academy of
Engineering and an Alumnus of the Kennedy School
of Government at Harvard. He was awarded one
of the first Taoiseach (Irish Prime Minister) awards
for Excellence in Local Government. He has had a
distinguished career serving as Executive Manager

with Dublin City Council and, before that, with portfolio responsibility for traffic management in the city when he acted as EU National Representative on the Dedicated Road Infrastructure for Vehicle Safety in Europe (DRIVE) project, which paved the way for the introduction of autonomous-drive vehicles now appearing on our streets. In recent years, he had responsibility for managing a €600 million capital investment programme for water services and flood risk investment and was responsible for managing daily water services to the city and region, was co-ordinator of non-fire emergency management for the city, CPD Director for Engineering Services and responsible for strategic planning of water, wastewater and flood risk management. He was director responsible for managing the planning and implementation of the EU Water Framework Directive for the East Region, covering Dublin and eight other local authorities and secured an EU Innovation award for his river basin management system. He led the water theme on the 'SMART Dublin Initiative', developing Dublin as a global hub for SMART technology and he is Irish national representative on EUREAU Commission 1 – Drinking Water where he worked closely with EU partners in developing a unique approach to flood management through the INTERREG FloodResilienCity (FRC) project. As director, he was responsible for the delivery of the Greater Dublin Strategic Drainage Study and Strategy (GDSDS) and he pioneered the use of Sustainable Drainage Systems (SuDS). In 2013, Tom joined Irish Water, the new national water utility to reform water services, which took over responsibility for all water services, infrastructure and investment from 31 local authorities. As the Irish Water Regional Operations Manager for the East Region, he now manages a budget of €220 million and daily water service delivery to 50% of Ireland's population.

Neil Mattinson

Neil Mattinson has over 37 years' experience in the landscape profession, spanning local government, government agency and the private sector. Neil's early career was spent in the north-east of England, with positions at Washington Development Corporation and Durham County Council, before entering the private sector to work on the first International Garden Festival to be held in the UK in 1984. Neil is now Senior Board Director of LDA Design, responsible for the leadership and management of the London office with 40 staff, as well as leading LDA's international portfolio and the marketing and branding of LDA Design. Neil has substantial experience of leading complex and large-scale design projects. He led the LDA Design team for the detailed masterplan, design and deliverables for the parklands and public realm for the London 2012 Olympic Park on former brownfield land in the Lower Lea Valley, creating 112 hectares of world-class parkland with sports venues, urban recreation and ecological landscapes, which formed the centrepiece of the Olympic Games. Following the games, Neil led a team to develop the stadium public realm for its long-term legacy. Neil leads the landscape and public realm design of the Battersea Power Station site redevelopment in London where LDA has worked closely with architect Rafael Vinoly to develop the design of a sequence of spaces including a riverside park, streets, squares, podium level courtyards and roof and winter gardens.

Richard Millar

Richard Millar is Director of Heritage, Enterprise, Operations and Sustainability at Scottish Canals where he is responsible caring for the heritage and environment of the nation's 250-year-old inland waterways, as well as project development, fundraising and the promotion of marine and canal-led tourism. Since joining the organisation in 1999, Richard has worked on a number of high-profile projects, including the Millennium Link, an £83.5 million scheme that saw Scotland's canals returned to a navigable state for the first time since the 1960s; the regeneration of the Lowland Canals as a visitor destination; the development and operation of The Falkirk Wheel, the world's only rotating boat lift; and the creation of Pinkston Watersports, Scotland's first urban watersports centre, situated in the heart of North Glasgow. More recently, he played a pivotal role in the creation of The Helix, the £43 million project that has transformed 350 hectares of underused land between Grangemouth and Falkirk into a new visitor attraction, parkland and marine hub with the Forth & Clyde Canal at its heart. The Helix is also home to The Kelpies, the world's largest pair of equine sculptures. Almost two million people have visited the attraction since its launch in April 2014.

Howard Neukrug

Howard Neukrug is Senior Fellow at the US Water Alliance (USWA), an Advisor to the US Environmental Protection Agency and the US Forest Service and Adjunct Professor at the University of Pennsylvania where he teaches classes on 'water, science and politics', 'sustainable cities' and 'future trends in the water industry'. He most recently retired as CEO of Philadelphia Water, a $1 billion integrated drinking water, wastewater, stormwater and water resource public utility serving over two million people in a city located between New York City and Washington, DC. The defining initiative in Howard's tenure as CEO was his 'Green Cities, Clean Waters' programme that placed an unprecedented reliance on innovative green infrastructure to manage urban runoff – in other words, 'plants instead of pipes'. Howard is a Professional Engineer, a Board Certified Environmental Engineer and an Honorary Diplomat of the American Academy of Water Resources Engineers.

Jonathon Porritt CBE

Jonathon Porritt, Co-Founder of Forum for the Future, is an eminent writer, broadcaster and commentator on sustainable development. Established in 1996, the Forum for the Future is now the UK's leading sustainable development charity. The Forum has a growing presence in the United States, India, Hong Kong, Singapore and Malaysia. In addition, he is President of The Conservation Volunteers, a

Non-Executive Director of Willmott Dixon Holdings, a Trustee of Ashden and a Director of Collectively, an online platform celebrating sustainable innovation. He was formerly Director of Friends of the Earth and Co-Chair of the Green Party. As Chairman of the UK Sustainable Development Commission until 2009, he spent nine years providing high-level advice to government ministers. Jonathon was installed as Chancellor of Keele University in February 2012. He is Visiting Professor at Loughborough University and UCL. Recent books are 'Capitalism as if the World Matters' (2005) and 'The World We Made' (2013) – which seeks to inspire people about the prospects of a sustainable world in 2050. Jonathon received a CBE in January 2000 for services to environmental protection.

Michael Schwarze-Rodrian

Michael Schwarze-Rodrian is Head of the Department of European and Regional Networks and the EU Representative of the Regional Association Ruhr (RVR) in Germany. In the 1990s, he moderated the Emscher Landscape Park (ELP) in cooperation with the International Building Exhibition (IBA) Emscher Park. From 1997 to 2000, he was Head of the Regional Development Department of the Kommunalverband Ruhr (KVR). From 2001 to 2006, Michael worked for the state-run Projekt Ruhr GmbH and was responsible for the Masterplan Emscher Landscape Park 2010 on behalf of 20 cities and several regional agencies. From 2007 to 2011, he worked for the regional business development agency Metropoleruhr GmbH, encouraging sustainable development throughout the cities of the Ruhr. With the inter-local working groups of 'Concept Ruhr', 'Chance of Change' and the 'Knowledge Report Ruhr', Michael supported the upcoming Metropolis Ruhr. Michael studied Landscape Planning at the Technical University (TU) Berlin in the 1970s. He was Scientific Assistant at the Institute of Landscape Economy at TU Berlin from 1980 to 1985, where his research topic was 'Protection of soil as a new field of Federal Environmental Politics in Germany'. Michael has great experience with integrated strategies, project management, regional, inter-local and local moderation and speaks internationally on sustainable urban and regional development.

Lisa Tziona Switkin

Lisa Tziona Switkin is a Principal at James Corner Field Operations, a leading international firm practising landscape architecture, urban design and public realm based in New York City. As the Principal-in-Charge of many of the practice's complex public realm projects, Lisa led the design of the High Line in New York, Tongva Park in Santa Monica and the Race Street Pier in Philadelphia. She is currently overseeing the South Street Seaport, Domino Sugar Waterfront and Greenpoint Landing in New York, Nicollet Mall in Minneapolis and the masterplans for the Lincoln Road District and The Underline in Miami. She oversaw work on the Navy Yards Central Green in Philadelphia, Shelby Farms Park in Memphis and the masterplans for Freshkills Park and Seattle's Central Waterfront. Lisa was a Rome Prize Fellow from 2007 to 2008. She has a Bachelor's degree in Urban Planning from the University of Illinois and a Master's degree in Landscape Architecture from the University of Pennsylvania. She has taught graduate-level design studios and has lectured at universities, symposiums, foundations and institutions around the world.

Evert Verhagen

Evert Verhagen is Senior Project Manager for Creative Cities and REUSE. Following the successful development of the Westergasfabriek project, he set up Creative Cities in 2006 and REUSE in 2007. He now works in different regeneration projects throughout the world, among them the Street Art Museum, St Petersburg in Russia and Nova Friburgo in Brazil. Evert's main interest today is migration and the causes and the effects for the migrants, as well as for the city. Evert started working for the district of Westerpark in 1990 as the manager for public works and for 15 years he was the project manager responsible for the Westergasfabriek project. The site of a derelict gas factory in the centre of Amsterdam was decontaminated and the grounds were turned into an urban park designed by the award-winning American landscape architect, Kathryn Gustafson. Fifteen listed historical buildings were retained and are now the home of the Dutch cultural avant-garde. Reflecting the success of this project, Evert was awarded the state prize for best manager in an urban project in 2004. Earlier in his career, he worked as an assistant to the manager in Amsterdam's notorious high-rise area, Bijlmermeer. In 1986, his book on Bijlmermeer was published.

Acknowledgements from the CSGNT Board

The thanks of the CSGNT board go to Sue and Brian Evans for pulling this publication together. Sue has been central to the success of the CSGN Forum over the past five years and has been instrumental in getting such a distinguished group of speakers, and now authors, together. Without their knowledge and insight, this publication would not have been possible and for that the board is immensely grateful.

Acknowledgements from the editors

It was during the day of the fifth CSGN Forum, held in 2015, that the idea occurred to prepare this book. It seemed that the evidence that had been assembled for the first five of these events warranted collection, documentation and dissemination. This has taken a great deal of work that could only be achieved with the encouragement and assistance of many people.

First and foremost, we would like to express huge thanks to all of the authors in this book. We also thank all those who have assisted them, particularly Jeremy Anterola for his help with Dieter Grau's chapter; Chris McDonald for helping with Richard Millar's chapter; and Joanna Layton, Andre Head, Alison McCormack and Joanne Wanjohi for their assistance with the chapters for Jonathan Porritt, Peter Head, Sir Harry Burns and Neil Mattinson respectively. Thanks also go to Nicky Langridge-Smith and Corinne Thompson of Scottish Wildlife Trust; Maggie Dunn at Philadelphia Water; Joe Pundek of Gustafson Porter; and Margaret Jankowsky of James Corner Field Operations for sourcing illustrations.

We are indebted to the Scottish Government and GreenBlue Urban Limited for their funding support, without which we would not have been able to print such a high-quality publication. We thank the Central Scotland Green Network Trust and, in particular, the Chairman, Keith Geddes CBE, and the Chief Executive, Simon Rennie MBE, for their ready agreement and encouragement to pursue the task. We also thank the Research Office and the Mackintosh School of Architecture, The Glasgow School of Art for support for the venture.

Thanks go to everyone who provided the images that enhance the text throughout – they are all listed separately. Particular thanks go to Patricia and Angus Macdonald for the use of their images, which have introduced an additional aesthetic quality to the publication.

For design we are indebted to Stewart Drummond, David Whyte and the team at Tangent Graphic Ltd, including Jack Shaw, Graeme McQuarrie and Kristoffer Wilson; to Philip Allen of PJA Editorial Ltd for proofreading; and to our printers The Printing House Ltd.

We were delighted that the Royal Incorporation of Architects in Scotland agreed to publish the work and our thanks go to Neil Baxter, Secretary and Treasurer, who made the publication process so straightforward, and to his colleagues Jon Jardine and Carol-Ann Hildersley.

And then there are those who do the hard and often unsung tasks in the process. A very, very big thank you goes to Christine Kelly, Elaine Duffy, David Wilson, Stephen Hughes and Ewan McGill, who do so much to make each year's Forum such a success. In addition, Elaine Duffy transcribed several of the presentations and Christine Kelly assisted with proofreading. Ewan McGill, David Wilson, Johanna van der Velden and Stephen Hughes all helped with IT, images, maps and logos.

It is customary in books like this to thank one's spouse for their forbearance. On this occasion, thanks are due to one another: the forbearance was, however, as those who know us realise, as usual a one-way street – so thank you Sue.

Brian and Sue Evans (editors)

Image Credits

The Central Scotland Green Network Trust, The Glasgow School of
Art and the Royal Incorporation of Architects in Scotland gratefully
acknowledge copyright permission granted from the following sources
for the right to reproduce photographs and images in 'Growing
Awareness':

2. Greening the paradigm
— 1 Brian Mark Evans.

3. Green infrastructure –
Responding to climate change and adapting cities
— 1 Boeri Studio Milan.
— 2 Arup.
— 3 IndustryAndTravel, Shutterstock.
— 4 Jeroen Musch, West 8.
— 5 Arup/LLDC.
— 6a Arup/UK Space Agency.
— 6b Greater London Authority.
— 7 Aleksandra Kazmierczak and Jeremy Carter,
University of Manchester.
— 8 Green Roof Consultancy/The Rubens at the Palace Hotel.
— 9 Victoria BID/Land Use Consultants/Green Roof Consultancy.
— 10 Arup/Heatherwick Studio/Dan Pearson Studio/Garden
Bridge Trust.

4. Wellness not illness – why 'place' matters for health
— 1a — 1d Images of Colfax Avenue, Denver, Colorado courtesy of Dr
M Gordon Brown, Space Analytics, LLC, Wauconda, IL 60084, (www.
spaceanalytics.com), Colfax on the Hill, Inc., the Denver Foundation.
— 2 based on information from AH Leyland, R Dundas, P McLoone,
FA Boddy "Cause-specific inequalities in mortality in Scotland: two
decades of change. A population-based study." BMC *Public Health*.
2007 Jul 24; 7:172.
— 3 based on information from WHOSIS, 2012 and Whyte B, &
Ajetunmobi T, "*Still the sick man of Europe*"? (Glasgow Centre for
Population Health, 2012).
— 4 Gillespies.

5. The 'nature' of green networks
— 5 iStock.com/gehringj.
— 8a Jonathan Hughes/Scottish Wildlife Trust
— 8b Laurie Campbell/Scottish Wildlife Trust
Other images Patricia & Angus Macdonald of the
Aerographica Partnership.

6. Ecological sequestration
— 1, 2 Based on information supplied by The Ecological
Sequestration Trust.
— 4 iStock.com/maldesowhat.
— Other images The Ecological Sequestration Trust.

7. The Emscher Landscape Park – A journey of renewal
— 1 Regional Association Ruhr (RVR)
— 2 bottom left page 84, top left and right page 85 Brian Mark Evans.
— 7 Top page 94, Projekt Ruhr GmbH.
— 7 Bottom page 94, Emschergenossenschaft.
— 7 Top left page 95, Brian Mark Evans.
— Other images Michael Schwarze-Rodrian.

8. The South Pennines Watershed –
Conservation of a cultural landscape
— 1 Richard Stroud/Pennine Prospects.
— 2 CSGNT.
— 3 Natural England: Landscape Beyond the View
(http://publications.naturalengland.org.uk/publication/2705143).
— 4.1 Andy Spencer/Pennine Prospects.
— 4.2 KidzArch/Pennine Prospects.
— 4.3 JheapCAD/Pennine Prospects.
— 4.4 Peter Maris/Steve Morgan/ Pennine Prospects.
— 4.5 Steve Morgan/Pennine Prospects.
— 4.6 Janina Holubecki/Pennine Prospects.

9. Philadelphia – The 'Green City, Clean Waters' programme
— 1 Philadelphia Water Department/Philadelphia Parks & Recreation.
— 2 Andrew Dobshinky/WRT.
— 3a, 3b The Trust for Public Land Archives.
— 4 Andrew Dobshinky/WRT.
— 5a blog.arborday.ork/Paul Fugazzotto.
— 5b Louis Cook/Philadelphia Water Department.
— 7 Cloud Gehshan/Philadelphia Water Department.
— 9 iStock.com/Davel5957.
— Other images Philadelphia Water Department.

10. The Lowland Canal Network – Creating places and destinations
— 1 Scottish Canals.
— 6, 8 Ironside Farrar Ltd.
— Other images Peter Sandground/Scottish Canals.

11. Dublin – A blue system for a green city
— 1 Peter Barrow Photography/Dublin City Council.
— 2 Dublin City Council.

— 3 CIRIA – The SUDS Manual C697.
— 4, 5 Tom Leahy.
— 6 https://www.flickr.com/photos/flynn_nrg/8512727556

12. Creative projects and talented people –
The power of transformation
— 1 Gustafson Porter.
— 2 Thomas Schijper/Gustafson Porter.
— 3, 4, 5 Google images/Knowlton School, The Ohio State University.
— Other images Evert Verhagen.

13. The New York High Line
— 2b, 3b, 4, 6 Brian Mark Evans.
— 5a James Corner Field Operations/Switkin.
— 5b iStock.com/sx70
— 7 Top left James Corner Field Operations/Switkin,
others Brian M Evans.
— 8 Iwan Baan.
— Other images James Corner Field Operations.

14. London – Designing the Olympic green legacy
— All images LDA Design.

15. The Cheonggyecheon River Restoration –
From highway to greenway
— 1 www.flickr.com/photos/malink_ks/8504562955/.
— 4 www.flickr.com/photos/grego1402.
— 8, 9, 11 iStock.com/TwilightShow.
— 10 iStock.com/coleong.
— 12 iStock.com/ksbank.
— Other images The Korea Transport Institute.

16. Ecological waterscapes – Celebrating water in cities
— 1 Based on information supplied by Ramboll Studio Dreiseitl.
— Other images Ramboll Studio Dreiseitl.

17. Greening Central Scotland – Genesis, vision and delivery
— 1 CSGNT.
— 2 Patricia & Angus Macdonald of the Aerographica Partnership.
— 3 Douglas Worrall/CSGNT.
— 4 East Ayrshire Coalfield Environment Initiative.
— 5 AB Images.
— 6 Gillespies.
— 7 Collective Architecture.

18. Towards a new paradigm in landscape and environment
— 1 VIIRS, Nasa Goddard Space Flight Center, commons.wikimedia.org.
— 2a public domain work of art, Hargesheimer & Günther.
Kunstauktionen Düsseldorf, commons.wikimedia.org.
— 2b public domain work of art, Google Art Project, Google.
Cultural Institute, commons.wikimedia.org.
— 2c Arup/Heatherwick Studio/Dan Pearson Studio/Garden
Bridge Trust.

Particular thanks go to the photographers in Creative Commons
who allow royalty-free use of their images.

Every effort has been made to source all the images used in
this publication.